PORTRAIT OF THE BROADS

Portrait of
THE BROADS

J. WENTWORTH DAY

ILLUSTRATED
AND WITH MAP

ROBERT HALE · LONDON

Robert Hale Limited
63 Old Brompton Road
London S.W.7

PRINTED IN GREAT BRITAIN
BY EBENEZER BAYLIS AND SON, LTD.
THE TRINITY PRESS, WORCESTER, AND LONDON

CONTENTS

Appendix

ILLUSTRATIONS

ACKNOWLEDGEMENTS

The above photographs were supplied by the following: Alan Savory (Nos. 1, 4, 7, 8, 9, 14, 22, 23, 25); Ford
Jenkins (2, 12, 15, 16, 18, 26); A. Sinclair (3, 10);
Sport and General (5, 6); G. R. Temple (11, 13, 19,
21, 27, 28); A. E. Coe and Sons (17, 20, 24).

ACKNOWLEDGEMENTS

I desire to express my sincere thanks to the Nature Conservancy, whose *Report on Broadland* has provided me with invaluable facts, statistics and proposals for the salvation and expansion of Broadland. I also thank most sincerely my old friend Mr. H. F. Brooker, Managing Director of Blake's Broadland Tours Ltd., who has given me most valuable help and assistance in the past, and finally, but by no means least, that great Broadsman—sportsman—naturalist, Mr. Alan Savory of Brundall who combines the knowledge of a Richard Jefferies with the pen of a poet. He knows every inch of the Broads, many of which we have explored together. If I have, by chance, omitted to mention any old friend or acquaintance who has helped me better to understand the Broads and their problems, they will, I trust, forgive the oversight.

James Wentworth Day

Ingatestone
Essex

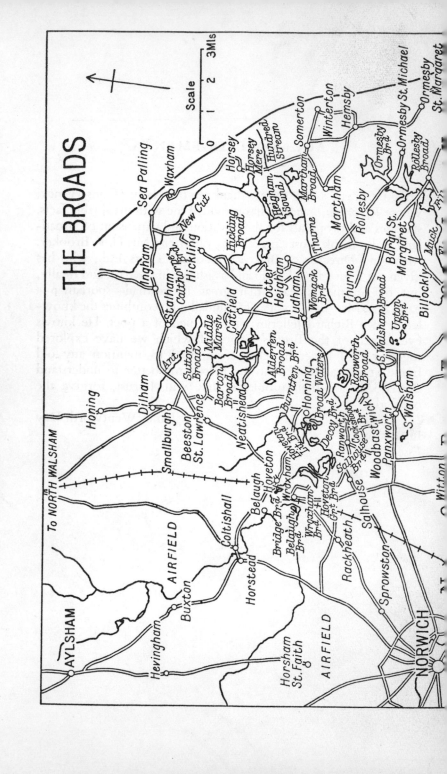

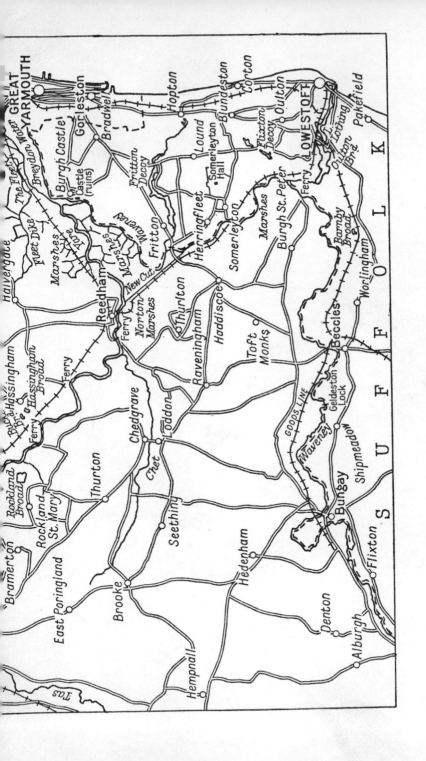

I

A BROADLAND PARADISE—AND THE SEQUEL

Too Little Water For Too Many Boats and People

THE decoy is a memory. The cottage is a shadow in the sand. Yet I like to think of the last of the decoy-men who dwelt, as secret as his art, alone with the sea-winds on these lonely levels.

He lived in a one-storey cottage of Norfolk cobblestones. Rounded by the grind of endless seas, blue from the blue of pre-Palaeolithic clay, the round stones were built into walls a foot and a half thick—fortress walls that would stand the buffet of winter gales, the drive of spinning sandstorms, perhaps even, on an evil night, the lap and suck of the sea, trampling in through a sudden breach in the hairy sandhills at the cottage back-door. For this cottage stood in the warren where rabbits played, and sea-eagles swung in airy circles. It was hard under 'the hills', its back to the sea-wind out of the east, its front door of oak. Its tiny windows winked to the western sun.

West lay the woods, old and tall and scrawny, of oak and ash and thorn, with here and there a tamarisk in the sand. Under their branches grew great luxuriant ferns such as you will see in few English woods. And from the wood's foot, far to the east, where Winterton church tower stood like a fortress, a sea-mark for sailors, ran marshes, tussocky and rough. Rabbits scuttled, and the hares lay snug. The peregrine stooped like a quarrel from a cross-bow, and ruffs and reeves fought on the hillocks by the black pools of water.

There were snipe springing, and avocets, dainty as Dresden china, and now and then, of a rare chance, a Great White Stork or a 'black curlew', as they called that long-legged bird of delicate gait, the glossy ibis.

To north and south lay farther, dimmer, marshes. A wild, far-gleaming prairie of water and reeds and swamp where pool ran into pool, rond into quaking hover, and bulrush melted into reed-mace, and all the wild marsh grasses turned brown and yellow, purple and red, and chrome and umber and bleached white, and then died in a riot of rust and flame when autumn marched over the levels, coloured as an army with banners.

It was a place of the night-candles, the Wills-o'-the-Wisp, with their summons to the drowned dead. A place of the croaking, booming bittern and the chorus of frogs. A place of unearthly water-mists that rose sudden as ghosts from the wet marsh. They swirled upward in whorls of grey-white like elementals at Walpurgisnacht and closed, choking, on the marshman lost in the night—the 'eynds', or water-ghosts, of the old, far days, the mist-wraiths that are not yet dead even in these days of electric draining-pumps and hard roads that run like swords through the ancient heart of the Broadland.

Those levels to the east, which ran on, wet and wild and gleaming, to the lonely, stranded isle of Horsey, were white with feathers of wild geese, their silences lit by the sudden thunder of clouds of wildfowl on wing. The greylag geese nested there, and the black tern dipped in slow and lovely majesty over pool and pulk.

Low in their sliding punts went the old, forgotten gunners—Thains and Nudds, Hewitts and Turners, Applegates and Hales, Kettles and Kings—village sportsmen of Winterton and Somerton, Hickling and Horsey, in whose veins ran the wild blood of Danish sea-rovers, and in whose bright yellow hair and sea-blue eyes gleamed the stamp of the Norsemen.

Beyond Horsey the marshes ran on, mile after mile of wild swamp and glittering pool, behind the old grey hall at Waxham of the Wodehouses, who were Lords of these levels for centuries—beyond that flint-faced, grey old house with its tall, encircling wall, its pepper-pot turrets above the seaward gate, its curious carvings and mighty barn and noble church. Beyond this, to the high heath-lands of Palling, the lonely sea-hamlet, and Happisburgh, the cold village on the northward shore whose little bluff, a mountain in this flat land, is first of English land to catch the Arctic wind and the Arctic tide-flow.

A bitter land of bitter spaces. A land of ghostly mists and sea-fogs stealing like grey armies. A land of shouting gales and thunderous surges. A land, too, of wide, quiet meres and secret waterways, of sighing reed-beds and the whimper of endless wings, of old, small woods of oak and monstrous fern, and of blown, stinging sand and the whipping feet of sleet before the strong sea-gales.

That was the land and the scene in which the old decoy-men of the early Wodehouses lived alone between sandhills and wood, with marshes to north and south, when James I was on the throne. It had not changed a tittle when Colonel Hawker came up here to shoot wildfowl in 1816, and although he laments that, by 1824, drainage and decoys had reduced the number of fowl, I do not think he would find it so very different in appearance today.

That is the imagined picture which I wrote in 1949 of the wild marsh country of the Brograve Level, and the Fens surrounding Horsey Mere, Hickling Broad and Martham Broad as they were nearly a century and a half ago when 'Old George Skelton', known to wildfowling history as 'The Father of English Decoy-men', lived in the vanished cottage under the sandhills east of Martham Broad. He made and worked the Winterton Decoy between 1807 and 1840 and is buried in Winterton churchyard.

For a few enchanted years in the 1940s I rented the shooting on the Burnley Hall estate near Winterton, which includes Martham Broad, remotest and most easterly of the broads; the Winterton Decoy pond; several miles of wild sandhills by the sea-shore without a house to break their lonely skyline; a ridge of windswept farmland; gaunt woods of great oaks, bleached and shriven by salt floods and salt winds and a wide sweep of marshes, cut up by dykes, cattle-dotted and lonely.

It was a land of wild geese, clanging under the stars, and of bitterns, booming their haunting love song on quiet nights of spring. There were wild swans, like white Valkyries in snowy dawns, the threnody of their wing-music like mighty harp notes across the lonely levels.

In the woods grew great Osmunda ferns, high enough to hide a man. There pheasants strutted, like splendid rajahs, and woodcock dropped in, wing-weary under the golden Woodcock Moon of October, from their flight across the North Sea. They had last seen land under a Baltic moon where great pine forests step down to the salt tides and elk move like prehistoric shadows.

So you will see that, all in all, that Broadland estate, with its mere and rustling reed-beds, its cattle marshes and lonely sandhills; its little Georgian hall, snug amid walled gardens, with a ruined church in the wood to give it holy peace, was something of an earthly paradise. It was out of this world.

In its way, it was typical of much of the rest of Broadland as the Victorians knew it when they first discovered it as a place for peaceful holidays, aboard slow-moving boats, a hundred years ago.

One could perhaps sum up the haunting charm, the aura, of Broadland, in a phrase—a land of peace and space, of lonely beauty and quiet waters, of infinite colour and the charm of birds, a little world much as God and nature made it.

And so it was, before it was 'discovered', exploited, capitalized, vulgarized, transistorized and turned into a holiday water-playground for a quarter of a million visitors each year. It has become smirched. If we are not careful, soon it will be utterly ruined. It will become, not the place of peace, but a mess. It is too small and limited an area to take the impact of a quarter of a million visitors who may soon, within a few years, be multiplied to half a million. That can easily happen since Broadland is within swift reach of populations which total eighteen millions.

Consider these facts; in 1965 The Nature Conservancy produced a *Report on Broadland*. It is balanced, objective, full of facts and full of warnings.

When I wrote *Marshland Adventure* in 1949, and followed it with *Broadland Adventure* in 1951 and later with *Norwich and the Broads* in 1953, one could say with reasonable accuracy that there were 200 miles of navigable waterways in Broadland and about 5,000 acres of open water on the Broads and rivers themselves. The scene has changed remarkably since those three books were written and the area of open water has shrunk alarmingly.

The *Report on Broadland*, detailed though it is, admits that "it is not altogether easy to decide what should be included under the term 'Broad' because several areas so-named have been almost completely overgrown by vegetation during the last century. However, forty-two Broads are recognized in this Report. . . .

"Tithe Redemption Commission maps show that in the 1880s the acreage of these Broads was 3,011, but this had decreased to 2,535 acres by the time of the twenty-five-inch Ordnance Survey. Acreages obtained from the most recent air photographs obtainable show that there are now about 1,692 acres of open water in these forty-two Broads.

"Fourteen Broads are now less than three feet deep and although some of these could possibly be used by rowing boats, canoes and other small craft, they are not regarded in this Report as being navigable. These fourteen Broads have a total of fifty four acres. The remaining twenty-eight Broads, having a total water surface of some 1,638 acres, are three or more feet deep. Nine of these Broads, having a total acreage of 567, cannot be reached by boat from the main river system; three more, having a water surface of 124 acres, are closed to the general public because they form part of the Bure Marshes National Nature Reserve. The remaining sixteen navigable Broads, with a total water surface of 948 acres, are available for general recreation and holiday making."

You will note that less than a thousand acres of navigable Broadland waters reachable from the rivers but excluding river surfaces, "are available for general recreation and holiday making". How many boats would one imagine populated these restricted waters including the land-locked Broads and the rivers? The answer is that no less than 9,247 licensed craft were on Broadland waters in 1964. That is roughly five and a half boats to every acre of water. One shudders to think what would happen if all these 9,247 boats were anchored, bows to stern, in a continuous line over the 200 miles of navigable riverways. This does not include unlicensed boats or those which are brought on trailers for a day or so—and there are plenty.

Now consider the types of craft involved, both hired and privately owned. In 1964 there were 2,395 motor cabin cruisers; 618 yachts, propelled by sail and motor; 396 sailing yachts; 2,071 open motor-boats, including auxiliary sailing dinghies; 1,225 rowing boats; 368 paddle canoes; 82 static house-boats; 11 motor house-boats, including curious craft called Flat-a-floats; 6 passenger launches carrying up to 40 passengers each; 12 ditto carrying up to 100 passengers each and 3 river steamers, each with a capacity of 250 passengers.

The cabin craft vary from two-berth to twelve-berth capacity, but if we take the average boat as a four-berth craft, it means that about 10,000 visitors can live and sleep aboard their hired boats at any one time. That is quite a lot of people to have living on 200 miles of rivers plus about a thousand acres of open Broad. Where is the peace and where is the space?

In Victorian days holiday-makers went to the Broads because they loved sailing on quiet waters and the quietude which goes with sail. Today 93 per cent of the 2,200 cabin craft for hire are

2

power-driven. Add to that 750 motor-boats—and peace takes wing.

Hats off, therefore, to the small boat sailor. There are about 10,000 of them who annually use the Broadlands winds and no other form of power. The Norfolk and Suffolk Yachting Association has about 6,000 members and fifteen member clubs. About a third of the clubs race on the larger Broads such as Hickling, Barton, Wroxham and Oulton. The others sail on the rivers. The Norfolk Schools Sailing Association, the Hertfordshire Education Committee Sailing School, the National Association of Youth Clubs, the Central Council of Physical Recreation and other bodies organize sailing courses in the area. In short, Broadland is probably the greatest single inland nursery of small-boat sailors in the country.

The canoeists naturally avoid the over-populated rivers and Broads where the wash from large motor-cruisers is a hazard to them. They stick to the quiet backwaters and headwaters of the rivers, where locks can be easily by-passed by carrying the canoe, but the larger boats are held at bay. Rowing is understandably not very popular although there are two rowing clubs on the Yare near Norwich. The average rowing boat is kept either for fishing on the quieter Broads or as a tender for the larger boats.

Speed boating and water-skiing have become a nuisance. They upset fishermen, wash away the banks, endanger small boats and should be prohibited on most Broads.

The limited area of water has been stressed. Now let us consider the make-up and acreage of the actual area which is known as Broadland. It embraces pretty well every sort of countryside from open water and quaking reed-bed to farmland, woodland, sand dunes, rich grass marshes, inferior 'litter' fens, carrs or marshland thicket growths and even tidal waters, e.g. Oulton Broad with its shining mud-flats and quick tides, Rockland Broad, and Surlingham Broad.

The area as a whole is bounded on the east by the coast, on the south by the farms and rivers, towns and villages of the Lowestoft and Bungay area, to the north by Stalham and westward by Coltishall and Norwich. Most of it lies in East Norfolk and a part, the Waveney Valley area, in East Suffolk. The main rivers are the Waveney, the Yare, the Bure, the Ant, Thurne and Chet. Most of the Broads are connected with the rivers, but some of them such as Fritton Lake, about a mile long and ten to twelve feet deep, and

Ormesby, Rollesby and Filby Broads lie by themselves and cannot be approached by boat. This applies also to smaller Broads such as Alderfen, Burntfen, Upton Broad and Blackfleet.

The whole area of Broadland covers the rural districts of Loddon, Blofield and Flegg, and Smallburgh, with a few parishes in the rural districts of Forehoe and Henstead, and St. Faiths and Aylsham.

Within this area lie not only open broads, slow rivers and rich farmland, but no less than 7,769 acres of undrained fenland, most of it reed-beds and shaking swamps and about 50,000 acres of grazing marshes. The latter represent reclaimed marshland and include some of the finest fattening marshes in Britain. Beef cattle, sent there for the summer grazing, improve out of all recognition. The result is that some of the best marshes are let on short summer tenancies at £7 to £8 per acre or more, or on long tenancies at £3 to £4 an acre upwards. Short-term grazing tenants do not pay the occupier's or owner's drainage rates, which can be high, or the cost of fertilizing the marshes, ditching, known locally as 'dydling' or cultivating the land and re-seeding it. Many of the poorer marshes are let at much lower rents, but usually the tenant has to pay the rates and the cost of ditching, cultivation and the like.

It is a sad fact that bullocks, which were once the peaceful familiars of the Broadland scene, are declining in numbers so far as marsh grazing is concerned. That is partly because artificial fertilizers have largely taken the place of bullock manure and also that more and more livestock are reared indoors. The result is that many marshes have either been put down to corn, roots or other crops, or they are gradually deteriorating. Some of them are becoming increasingly flooded, owing to the increase of flood water coming down from the uplands. It will be all to the good in the long run if some of the very poor quality, low-lying marshes could be flooded and turned into new broads. They would contribute, in that fashion, more to the national and local economy than they do by failing to grow any very productive yields of food.

There is no doubt that, since Broadland is a unique holiday area, which inevitably will be more and more in demand by the town populations of Britain, the area of available water *must* be increased. This can be done partly by opening up broads which have grown up completely, such as Sutton Broad, or by clearing floating 'hovers' from broads such as Barton, which have shrunk noticeably even in the last twenty years. If some of the low-lying useless marshes are flooded the water-borne holiday-makers whose waterways are now bursting at their banks will have more space in which to enjoy themselves and, incidentally, spend their money.

It has to be remembered that apart from the vast numbers of holiday-makers who come for a short stay of a week or more, the Broads have an all-year-round appeal to various types of sportsmen and others who find there unique opportunities for what one may call 'recreational activity'. That includes angling, with its many thousands of devotees, small-boat sailing, canoeing, bird-watching, botany, wildlife photography, marine biology, painting, sketching and shooting.

From a natural history point of view the area is practically unique, but that will be dealt with in a later chapter.

Meanwhile the local permanent population, as distinct from the quarter of a million annual holiday-makers is mounting rapidly. In 1921 there were 32,833 local inhabitants in sixty-five parishes between Loddon and Palling. Forty years later in 1961 the population had risen by 61 per cent to 53,000. This was partly accounted for by the expanding holiday industry which offered more work in boat building and boat servicing yards, to a lesser extent in inns, hotels, cafés and guest houses, and also by the fact that many more people like to live in Broadland and commute to their work in Norwich, Yarmouth, Lowestoft and other towns. Furthermore, an increasing number of people, particularly from the Midlands, retire to Broadland to spend the rest of their years.

The Nature Conservancy has worked out a highly interesting analysis of what they call "land-based accommodation" in the Norfolk part of Broadland, e.g. licensed hotels, unlicensed hotels, holiday chalets, caravan sites, camping tents, private holiday accommodation with friends and relatives and bed and breakfast guest-houses or farm-houses. Under this heading they estimate that 78,600 visitors can be catered for over a twenty-four-week period, whilst in one month only, August 1964, 1,850 people slept out in tents. And so it will go on, up and up.

It is an odd fact that extensive hotel accommodation is not common in Broadland. I discovered this when I organized moderate-sized shooting parties in winter-time twenty years ago. It took all one's time to find enough bedrooms for eight or ten people in the village of Potter Heigham in the months of

November or December. Today, Potter Heigham has chalet accommodation for 900 people!

Caravan sites have fortunately been restricted to a minimum. Otherwise they could very easily have got out of hand and ruined much of the peaceful, flat landscape, just as they have ruined hundreds of miles of coastline. There are, however, several small holiday caravan sites, for example at Ludham, Reedham, Ashby with Oby, Loddon, Haddiscoe, Claxton and Surlingham, and rather larger concentrations at Potter Heigham, Oulton Broad and Beccles.

II

HOW THE BROADS BEGAN

Medieval Turf-Diggings and the Marshman's World

How did the Broads begin? The question has occupied historians, geologists and others for centuries. It was thought for a long time that they were, in many cases, natural broadenings of the river system—hence the word 'broad'. Another theory was that some, notably Breydon Water and Oulton Broad, were the last remnants of the great estuary of Gariensis, of which I wrote in *Norwich and the Broads*:

"When Aulus Plautius subdued those early Icenic builders of the stockaded wooden village (where Great Yarmouth now stands), the sea ebbed and flowed through four great estuarine mouths which fed the salt and shallow waters of Gariensis. There was one opening at Horsey to the north-east, another at Kirkley near Lowestoft, a third at Lake Lothing and a four-mile-wide bay between Caister and Burgh Castle, of which Breydon is the last wild relic today.

"The Romans christened Norwich 'Venta Icenorum', and there they built a new and thriving settlement with a fort and garrison at Ad Tavum, which is now Tasburgh, to protect it with greater forts and larger garrisons at Caister and Burgh Castle.

"The triremes and galleys with banked oars ploughed the waters and patrolled the estuary mouth to ward off the sea-raiders and pirates who swept down in the kind months of summer from their Danish and Baltic roosts."

There is no doubt that the salt waters of Gariensis flowed right up to Norwich. Breydon is, therefore, the last relic on the Yare with Lake Lothing and Oulton Broad as lesser survivors behind Lowestoft.

As for the rest of the Broads, the patient researches of Lambert, James, Smith, Green and Hutchinson have shown in recent years that practically all the Broads are the result of deep excavations for peat, many of them up to sixteen feet in depth which were dug out during medieval times, when peat or 'turf', as the Broadsmen and Fenmen still call it, was the main fuel. These researchers suggest that the 'turf diggings', to use the phrase still used by older marshmen, went even deeper than sixteen feet, at Filby Broad and Fritton Lake. I personally cherish the belief that Fritton is the landlocked remnant of a one-time salt-water estuary.

Be that as it may, we do know that peat digging was a major industry in the area from the twelfth century onwards and possibly earlier. They were digging turf at Hoveton until the end of the fourteenth century and although the workings were flooded at Barton in the fifteenth century, peat was still being brought up to the surface. Shallow turf diggings, similar to those which I remember as a boy in the fens of Wicken and Burwell in Cambridgeshire, were being worked well up to 1900 or a little later. The result of these extensive diggings, practised with the most primitive tools for at least four or five centuries, was the creation of a network of great inland lakes, most of which, it will be noted, are by-passed by the rivers although they are connected thereto in many cases by artificial cuts or dykes. Isolated turf-ponds account for the small, shallow little broads which one finds often in a remote valley or in the middle of a marsh, half a mile or more from a river. Most of them have grown up and been choked by vegetation in the last fifty or sixty years.

It is a sardonic twist of the wheel of history that a Government Enquiry should now solemnly, and rightly, recommend that many of the grown-up broads and low-lying marshes which were shallow turf-diggings, should once again be excavated and flooded to make new or larger broads. That should not be difficult with modern tools and dredgers.

The original turf-diggers, of whom I have vivid memories, were a race apart. They were born and bred in fen and marsh. They lived in wattle-and-daub cottages with clay lump chimneys and thatched roofs. You can still see some of the old marsh cottages of that type on Catfield Common. These cottages were built by the men themselves at night by the light of the full moon.

I remember Arthur Leath, a farmer friend, who farmed White-house Farm at West Somerton for years giving me a first-hand picture of one of these old marshman's homes.

Arthur began life in an old clay-built, thatched house, built of wattle and daub on a framework of oak and alder poles, on Catfield Common, where the old green lane melts into the reed-beds and lily-starred waters of Hickling Broad.

Such houses were built by their owners at night after they had finished their work on the farms. They dug the clay from a great hole on the Common, pounded it, and moulded it into walls, working by moonlight and lantern-light; they cut the oaks and the alders from the marsh carrs, and sometimes took not a wink of sleep from dawn to dawn. These houses have lasted for a hundred years or more, and are still snug in winter and cool in summer. In cheapness and downright comfort they beat a hundred of the expensive, jerry-built tin and concrete Government-sponsored shacks which today deface the face of England in thousands and breed rheumatism, mortgages and discontent.

One must remember that the medieval turf-diggers of East Norfolk, ancestors of the sturdy marshmen of today, dug their turf with a primitive spade, probably wooden, with, if they were lucky, a metal edge and they stacked them to dry along the edges of the turf-digging trenches. When the water had dried out, the turf, originally dark brown and sodden, became greyish in colour as though crusted with a fine lichen. Small white shells, many of them dating from prehistoric ages when the sea flowed over the land, starred the turves. When the turves were dry the diggers carried them over the quaking swamps on long stretchers, half as big again as the stretcher used for carrying a sick man. Where the ground was firm enough, broad-wheeled wooden barrows, without sides, but with tall slatted backs were used.

The turves were then loaded on to flat-bottomed, double-ended barges, rather larger than the present reed-cutters' barges which are still a familiar craft on the Broads. Usually a donkey, grey and wicked, towed the leading barge with a tail of other barges swishing through the peaty water behind him.

The late Dr. Charles Lucas of Burwell in the Cambridgeshire fens who, incidentally brought me into this world in 1899, wrote a very good little book called *The Fenman's World*.[1] What he had to say about the Cambridgeshire turf-diggers may well be quoted here since the general conditions apply to the Norfolk turf-diggers. Harken to the wisdom of our old fen doctor, who, in his own

[1] Published by Jarrold and Sons, Ltd., of Norwich, 1930.

right, was an erudite naturalist, a painstaking local historian and a great sportsman. This is what he wrote:

"Turf-digging was also a prosperous industry and carried on up to quite recent times. In the earlier time sods or hassocks were dug with a moorland spade, heart-shaped, but about 1856 a tool eighteen inches long and four inches wide, with an iron flange, called a becket, was used, which enabled the work to be done more systematically and laid up in rows to dry properly. The becket was first used in Isleham Fen, and was of smaller dimensions than that used in Burwell Fen, being fourteen inches long and two and a half inches wide. It cut a thousand turf blocks to the ton, whilst the Burwell becket, eighteen inches long and four inches wide, cut only sixty to the hundred. Therefore if a hundred of Burwell turf were asked for only sixty would be supplied. This was the rule observed by the trade, though somewhat confusing to strangers. Nearly all the village people burned turf in their houses.

"The turf in our fens differs from the peat of the moorland in the manner of cutting and also in the smell of the smoke. That of the Fen is formed from the decaying hypnum moss, and the smoke is acrid and makes the eyes water. The peat or turf of the moorland is formed from the moss sphagnum, and it has more or less a whisky smell and does not affect the eyes at all. Therefore the Scotch crofters, who have nothing else to burn, are not particular about their chimneys; they live in the smoke and look and smell like kippers.

"In many parts of the Fen two or three turfs deep have been taken, which is one cause of the low level of the Fen country. As the drainage has taken away the water, of course the moss has ceased to grow and is disappearing; but in some places when the turf has been taken out three times, as in the case in the land round Pout Hall,[1] the surface has become lower than the drainage level, and in wet seasons or floods is under water for many months in the year. So the conditions for turf formation still exist, and it has been found that it grows about four inches in twelve years."

To sum up, it is incredible to think that the medieval marshmen with the crudest of hand-made tools and with little or no wheeled transport were able to excavate peat diggings up to sixteen feet or more in depth and covering, more than a square mile in places. Hickling Broad and Heigham Sound between them, with their

[1] Formerly part of my property. J.W.D.

surrounding reed-beds, extend to more than a square mile. It was all dug out by hand! It should be no great task, therefore, with modern machinery, to extend the existing broads and create others.

Peat, incidentally, is an accumulation of plant remains, most of which only grew with their roots and stems under water. When such plants had grown so densely that they provided a platform, the more usual damp-loving land plants began to grow on top of them. Thus one had a plant strata. Dr. J. E. Marr, a Cambridge University scientist, who, with the late Sir Arthur Shipley, Master of Christ's, whom I revered almost as a god when young, said in *The Natural History of Cambridgeshire* (which the pair of them wrote) this about peat: " . . . the lower peat consisting of Juncus and water plants is generally under water, but the higher layers of damp-loving plants are very well exposed and are exceptionally free from silt. Experience has shown that if peat is only removed down to water level it at once begins to grow again and grows at the rate of a foot in twenty years."

Shallow peat-cutting went on throughout the nineteenth century, between Barton Broad and Catfield and peat was still being dug up to about the First World War not far from Horning Ferry. Soon after the First World War peat-digging died out in the Cambridgeshire Fens also. I regret its passing, for there is no more haunting, delicate scent than that of a peat fire in an old house. It is a blend of all enchantment and leaves a white creamy ash which is a joy to behold. In many old farm-houses a peat fire never went out. It smouldered in a vast mound of white ash, year in, year out, giving out a comfortable warmth and a scent unforgettable. Today one has to go to the North of England, to Somerset, to Ireland or to Scotland to recapture the magic of peat.

The reed harvest, however, is still a Broadland industry. Norfolk reeds are the best in Britain for thatching. And Norfolk thatchers have no peer. Some of them can command very high prices for their labour and materials and one at least drives an impressive old Rolls. Even the reed harvest, however, is declining and reeds have to be imported from Holland, where incidentally, many Dutch meres owe their genesis to peat cutting. The *Report on Broadland* says: "Although successional changes in the vegetation of the unreclaimed marshes surrounding the Broads would normally have given rise to fen carr, or possibly fen woodland, such changes were held in check for a prolonged period by management for the production of reed, sedge, marsh litter, alder poles and other crops. An extensive system of dykes was dug, so that these products could be extracted conveniently. The table which refers to about 500 acres of marshland near Woodbastwick, in the middle of the Bure valley, demonstrates the changes in land-use management which have occurred since 1845.

	1845 Estate map	1880–84 O.S. Survey	1958 Aerial photograph
Open water (mainly 'turf ponds' which quickly became overgrown)	114 acres	15 acres	15 acres
Grazing and mowing marshes, reed and sedge beds	345 acres	409 acres	190 acres
Woodland and carr	51 acres	86 acres	305 acres

"Most of these marshes were exploited until about forty years ago, but then the demand declined and large areas of marshland ceased to be used for producing traditional Broadland crops. As a result, large areas of open water and marshland have reverted to carr and woodland during the last hundred years. From the scientific point of view, this increasing uniformity of the vegetation is unfortunate, because the ecological interest of the Broadland marshes depends largely on the mosaic of the different vegetation types resulting from the varying forms of land-use in the area. Many of the interesting Broadland plants and animals are associated with these man-made habitats, particularly with the areas of open fen, and the status of the Marsh Pea, the Bearded Tit, Bittern, Marsh Harrier, Swallowtail butterfly and many other rarities would decline still further if the traditional forms of management on these Broadland marshes were to cease altogether."

Precisely the same 'growing-up' process whereby open fenland is being transformed into marshland carr, e.g. thickets of willows, birch, buckthorn, alder and even oaks, is going on at Wicken Fen, where the National Trust has started a long-term policy of bush clearance; at Woodwalton Fen in Huntingdonshire where the process of afforestation is quite alarming and at Chippenham Fen on the Chippenham Estate near Newmarket.

Fortunately, Broadland, in spite of death duties and repressive taxation, still has a number of landowners who administer their estates according to local conditions and practice with the result that carr growth is kept reasonably in check. This particularly applies on the Woodbastwick Estate which includes Ranworth Broad, Decoy Broad, Cockshoot Broad and the extensive Ranworth and Woodbastwick Marshes, in all somewhere about 9,000 acres: the Beeston Estate, which has been in the Preston family since Stuart times and includes much of the Barton Broad area; the Hoveton Estate belonging to Captain T. C. R. Blofeld; the Hickling Estate which was saved from exploitation by the late Lord Lucas and the late Lord Desborough and is administered by the Norfolk Naturalists' Trust and the Horsey Estate which Major Anthony Buxton has handed over to the National Trust although he continues to live at the Hall and administer the place, are cases in point. Private estates and National Nature Reserves such as the Bure Marshes and Hickling Broad and the proposed National Nature Reserves at Surlingham and Rockland Broad and at the remote little Calthorpe Broad in the extreme north of Broadland, are some guarantee that the essential characteristics of this unique district will be preserved.

It is odd to reflect that Broadland which today attracts, as we have said, more than a quarter of a million visitors annually, was unknown as a holiday centre less than a hundred years ago. It first began to attract attention as an out-of-the-way place of unique beauty and character somewhere about 1880. The first advertisement for cruising boats for hire appeared at that time when Loynes of Wroxham, who were founded as boat-builders in 1878, decided to go into the hire craft business. Christopher Davies put the Broads on the map when he wrote his *Norfolk Broads and Rivers* in 1883. When that charming writer on the East Anglian scene, the late William A. Dutt, produced his beguiling volume, *The Norfolk Broads*, in 1903 illustrated in colour by Frank Southgate, the first of the great Norfolk School of bird artists and marshland landscape painters, the district was still pretty well unknown. Consider this picture which he gives of the reed harvest in the early days of this century:

"In winter, one of the most familiar sights in Broadland is a reed-cutter at work on a broad or by the riverside. For the reed-cutter's harvest is a winter one, beginning about Christmas, when the blade is off the reeds, and lasting until March or April, when the appearance of the 'colts' or young reeds puts a stop to the cutting. Eel-catchers, marshmen, millmen, and the men who sail the cruising yachts, take part in this belated harvest, which comes at a time when there is little else for them to do in the daytime, and only wildfowl to be watched for at dusk and dawn. Scythe and meag are used in cutting the reeds, and the cutter works either in a wide, flat-bottomed marsh boat, or on a plank projecting from a boat or laid flat in a cleared space among the reeds. If, however, the reeds grow in shallow water, the men put on wading-boots and work in the water. The cut reeds are laid in the boat or on a large reed-raft, and rowed, quanted, or towed to the place where they are to be stacked. There they are tied in bundles or 'shooves', five of which are supposed to have an aggregate circumference of six feet and they are sold by the fathom, a fathom of reeds being five 'shooves'. They are used for various purposes, such as supporting builders' plasterwork, thatching cottages, park lodges, and ornamental boat-houses, and screening young shrubs and fruit trees; but the demand for them has decreased considerably since the days when there were 'scythe rights' on the reed fens and the reeds were carefully cultivated. But there are still many hundred acres of reeds in Broadland, and the cutting of them means a welcome addition to many scanty incomes. So, too, does the cutting and selling of 'gladden' and a species of rush locally known as 'bolder'; but turf or peat cutting, which formerly found employment for many of the marshmen, can hardly now be called a profitable business. Still, there are a few men who cut and dry the riverside hovers and the boggy surface soil of some of the swampy lands; for peat is a good and cheap substitute for coal in the hearths of the marshmen's cottage homes.

"If one wishes to know the kind of life that is led by the natives of Broadland, one cannot do better than leave the rivers and broads for a while, go and live on one of the isolated marsh-farms, and make the acquaintance of its occupier and any men whom he may have in his employ. I have in mind a typical marsh farmer, a tall, fair-haired, blue-eyed, ruddy-cheeked giant, who might have stepped out of the pages of the *Saga of Burnt Njal*. He passes his time very differently to the upland farmer, whose success or failure to make farming pay depend chiefly upon market prices and the weather. To the marsh-farmer the price and progress of roots and cereals is a matter of comparative indifference; so long as he gets his hay carted and stacked without its being damaged by rain or flood, markets and weather do not trouble him. In fact, to call him a farmer is almost a misnomer. His occupations are almost as numerous as those of the Rev. R. Lubbock's typical Broadsman. True, he is a dairy-farmer—in a small way; and he keeps pigs and fowls; but he is also a fisherman and wild-fowler, reed-harvester and osier-grower.

"The presence of fowl on his marshes is, during the shooting season, always a sufficient excuse for his taking down his gun from its resting-place above the hearth, and leaving the farmstead to his wife's care for hours together. When the eels are 'running', he sleeps during the day, and is to be found by the riverside or at some dyke-mouth at night, busy with a sluice-net or sett. In winter, when he drives his cart to the nearest market-town, it is as likely to contain mallard as to be laden with pigs and poultry. To the larger towns, where the upland farmer sends his milk, the marsh-farmer sends his catches of eels. When he goes down on to his rush-marshes, it is more often in the hope of flushing snipe or finding plovers' eggs than to see if those marshes are ready to be mown; when he reaps his mid-winter reed-harvest, his breechloader always lies handy in his boat.

"Holding his nose between his thumb and finger, he can imitate the call of a drake so accurately as to bring wild duck to the flighting-ground where he is awaiting them. He knows the cries and call-notes of the wildfowl of the marshes as well as the upland farmer knows the cock's shrill clarion at dawn. The frosty weather, which holds the ploughshare fast in the furrow, brings him out of his bed long before daybreak, grey dawn finding him crouched in a reed-bed or on some river wall, waiting for the flighting fowl.

"His lonely life on the open, level marshlands teaches him self-reliance; the necessity for constant effort in order to 'make both ends meet' compels him to make the most of opportunities. He seldom spends an idle day. Shooting, fishing, eel-netting, marsh-mowing, cattle-tending, reed-cutting and reed-stacking, rush-cutting, dyke-drawing and wall-mending—these and other occupations leave him little time for listless lounging. As a rule, he performs nearly all these tasks unaided, but occasionally, as in the case of my Viking friend, he engages the services of a marshman.

"He is learned in the strange lore of the lonesome lowlands, where curious old customs and superstitions linger, and men live near to Nature, reading her secrets and understanding and fore-casting her many moods. His speech is flavoured with quaint colloquialisms, learnt from his father and mother, who lived and died among the marshes, or from the heavy-gaited, drowsy-eyed marshmen whom, in his youthful days, he fraternized with while they worked with crome and dydle. He calls a marsh-fog a 'roke'— a word which has come down to him from his Norse ancestors; he talks of fish 'roudding', meaning spawning; a sudden wind-squall he describes as a 'rodger's blast'; and when he takes his dinner with him to the dykeside, he carries it in a 'frail' slung on a 'crome stick'. Strange old saws and rockstaffs suggest themselves to him as naturally as they did to the marshlanders of a century ago. If a wart appears on his hand, he lets a 'dodman' (snail) crawl over it—an infallible cure; and he never receives a piece of gold without spitting on it—for luck."

That enchanting old-world picture can still be repeated here and there. I have known more than one old Broadsman who might have stepped straight out of the golden days of Edward VII's reign. The Broadsman's harvest of reed, sedge, marsh litter and alder has however shrunken. There is still a brisk demand for reed, but not enough of it. Sedge is still used for thatching and has a long life if you keep the sparrows out. Reed thatch has an even longer life, but fine meshed wire-netting stretched tightly over the roof not only keeps out the birds but it avoids gale damage and it seems to break up the affect of frost. Marsh litter is still used for potato clamps by market gardeners and farmers, but it no longer goes to London as it did in my youth to feed the wretched cab-horses.

The Norfolk Rural Industries Committee which, incidentally, has to deal with more rural crafts than any other English county can show, takes a very live interest in thatching and encourages young men to train as apprentices. This is all to the good. A thatched roof is warm in winter, cool in summer and if the reed is tight packed and sprayed with a fire-proof spray, it is most unlikely to catch fire. It can last up to seventy years. No-one, however, seems to know precisely how many men are employed in cutting reed, sedge and litter and therefore one can only esti-mate the annual harvest. Probably the most up-to-date estimate is that given by the Nature Conservancy. They say:

"Although reed and sedge cutting occurs over a wide area of Broadland, there are few main centres of production. The largest quantity of reed probably comes from the Woodbastwick Estate, although other important areas are Hickling Broad, Horsey Mere, How Hill (Ludham), Surlingham and Rockland Broads, Burgh

Castle and Martham Broad. Reed cutting cannot take place until the leaves have fallen and must cease in early spring when the new shoots (colts) begin to appear. The season is usually from December to the end of March, depending on the weather and particularly on the depth of standing water; sedge is cut from July to September, and marsh litter in July and August. The annual production of sedge at Hickling Broad from 1945 to 1961 shows a considerable fluctuation, but a peak was reached in 1953 of 26,500 bunches, followed by a decline which has been particularly sharp in recent years because of the damage done to the beds by Coypu. Reed production also fell from about 20,000 bunches in 1958 to less than 7,000 in 1961, but has since increased to 18,000 in 1964. At Horsey Mere the annual production since 1950 has not exceeded 17,000 bunches of sedge, and there were much lower figures in 1960 and 1961; reed production fell from 33,000 bunches in 1952 to 5,500 in 1961 with a recent recovery to 15,000 bunches in 1964. Figures of reed, sedge and litter cut on the Ranworth Marshes are available for 1932–61. These show that since 1954, the quantity of reed cut annually has increased fairly steadily, whilst the amount of sedge and litter has fluctuated considerably."

The author and his daughter with the decoyman
at one of the last decoy ponds in East Anglia

BROADLAND IN THE GOLDEN DAYS

A World of Fish, Fowl, Smugglers and Eccentrics

"I WONDER what the Broads were like in the old days before they were overrun by trippers." Often one has heard that wistful remark. The short answer is that up to 1883 when Christopher Davies published his *Norfolk Broads and Rivers* which with his other book *The Swan and her Crew* first brought the charm of Broadland to public notice, the district was practically unknown to anyone except those who dwelt in it and a few naturalists and East Anglian sportsmen who visited the area. It was wild, largely undrained, sparsely inhabited and utterly lovely. If you want to recapture what is left of that atmosphere of Broadland in the Golden Days you can only do so today in late autumn, in winter and in spring when the holiday-makers are not there.

Just on twenty years ago I took my wife, small daughter and my private secretary on a winter cruise throughout the whole of Broadland with a wonderful skipper, the late Donald Applegate of Repps, to keep us in order and teach us wisdom. I wrote of that never-to-be-forgotten trip thus:

"The last of the summer yachting fleet lay huddled, white-painted and gay, like hibernating butterflies in the yacht basin. The last of the sunshine yachtsmen had gone home to the cinema and the lending library. No bright Cockney motor-cars moved on the Broadland roads. The river was empty of motor-boats and skiffs. The nautical gentlemen had put away their white-topped yachting-caps until Easter, and the girls in their bright head-scarves had folded their raiment and stolen, like the Arab, to the tents of the south.

"Now is the time when Broadland comes into its ancient own again. The old men set their eel nets across the rivers. Young men get out their pike tackle, take down their long duck guns which

Broadland peace . . .

hung all summer on leather thongs from farmhouse kitchen beams.

"Soon there will be wild geese flighting in from sea at dusk. Wild duck will come on sibilant wings in green-washed dawns, and hares will crouch in rusty reeds on the flat, far marshes. There will be snipe by the dyke-sides, and coots in black flotillas. The woodcock are already here, for they came in from Denmark and Scandinavia in the gold of the harvest moon, and lie crouched in little woods of oak and willow where the uplands meet the marshes. The eels are running to the sea, and great pike 'as big as dawgs and strong as hosses' cruise, dark, piratical shadows, in reedy bays.

"The great reed-beds have turned to flame-gold and rusty red, colours that catch the sun and gleam like wet swords after rain. The bulrushes stand up like black pokers. The lilies have faded and died. The river runs bank-full. Cattle stand hunched on the marshes, tails blowing in the flying wind. Great Suffolk Punches gallop with clumsy exultation, and, under a high and windy sky, dappled with wheeling gulls, East Norfolk comes into its wintry own again.

"And this, mark you, is the time to see the Broads in all their ancient silences. For when the summer visitors have gone the ancient arts of fish-net and fowling-piece, of eel trap and pike rod, come into their own.

"I have often wondered why so few people sail these enchanted waterways in the golden days of autumn and the brisk dawns of winter. For, though East Norfolk winds may be sharp and cold, it is the driest corner of all England. It smells of the sea. And the air is champagne.

"It is a marriage of the tamed and the untamed, the old and the new, the drained and the undrained, this flat, lonely land of shining rivers and reedy dykes, of great gleaming lakes and secret hidden pools; a land where the quaking marsh and the foggy fens run from windy uplands crowned by great woods of flaming oaks to a far white line of tossed and hairy sandhills, that march endlessly by manless beaches where the North Sea groans in the night and thunders in the gales.

"Which, perhaps, is why East Norfolk men commonly die young at ninety, and women remain gay and good-looking long after their grandchildren have been splashed at the font. An individual land of bold and individual people. Theirs is a mixed blood of the best that the North Sea could send. For here are descendants of Viking and Dane, of dark-haired Jute and solid Huguenot, of far-off Saxon and Carolean Dutchman. Their names linger even as the blue eyes and fair hair of the sea-raiders persist."

Here is another word picture of a typical, out-of-the-way marsh farm at the end of a dyke within smell of the sea: "The boat dyke runs straight into the farmyard. There in the glow of a winter sunset we tied up the boat. A ship's lifeboat lay moored alongside. A wherry's dinghy belonging to that famous old wherry the '*I'll Try*', which was sunk by a twenty-pound shell in the Dungeon during the War, bobbed on the waves at the lawn foot. A wherry's rudder lay in the yard, cheek by jowl with a rusty buoy from the North Sea. Three eel-trunks swirled, half submerged off our bows, full of squirming eels—last night's catch from Harry Thain's sett.

"They held a mass of squirming eels, representing about £8 in cash, but they would fetch nearly double that price by the time they reached the London market. The biggest, a blue-grey monster of four and a half pounds, I promptly collared for lunch. It was the biggest eel I have ever seen. In my native fens they do not normally run much larger than three pounds to three and a half pounds, although the record at home was a mighty serpent weighing eight pounds four ounces, taken many years ago when I was a boy from a gault pit on Guinea Hall Farm, in Burwell Fen.

" 'I had a six-pounder last week,' said Harry, with a grin. 'He was the biggest this season, but they do run up to eight or nine pounds on some of these broads. Been takin' a lot of tench lately in the net. Had one of five and a half pounds last week, but I chucked 'em all back. They're nice fish if you've got the butter to fry 'em in. Perch, too. I've had several up to one and a half pounds in the nets, but I get 'em out as quick as possible cos they hang in the nets with their fins all spikey, and the eels won't come near the net when they're in it. See you dinner-time. I might have a pike on one of my liggers then, if so you shall have him for your supper.'

"Away he went, short, merry-faced, black-eyebrowed, with a skin tanned like leather by North Sea gales, rowing his boat with a couple of eel-trunks in the stern. Harry, who is a nephew of that fine old Broadland stalwart, old Dionysius Thain—for Dionysius is a family name—who died round about ninety, wears a black skull-cap, which, with his leather jacket and high white mudstained water-boots, makes him an engagingly piratical figure.

"I poked about the yard among the turkeys, the game chickens, the gabbling geese, and waddling ducks, for you never know what curiosity you will find in that uniquely individual farmyard. A ship's anchor; two bottle-shaped eel grigs, made of willows on the same immemorial pattern to which the ancient Briton wove them 2,000 years ago; a bunch of wooden decoy-ducks on a shelf in a shed; the keelson of a wherry; leaning against the flint wall of the barn was a curious contraption of four scythe-blades set in a double V on a wooden frame, locally called a 'mage', and used for cutting reeds and weeds from the river bottoms. A couple of Dutch nets hung from a beam, and in the corner of the granary was a leather-bound flail with which they beat out the corn on the barn floor before threshing machines were invented. I remember them being used in the barn at home, when a boy, to beat out the beans."

A pleasanter picture I suggest than that of a boatyard yacht-basin littered with ice-cream cartons, candy floss sticks, empty potato crisp bags, cigarette ends and thin grey scum of contraceptives on the water.

Now see the picture as it was in the early '80s when Christopher Davies was writing:

"On either side of the river, and around the Broads, is a dense wall of emerald-green reeds, from seven to ten feet in height. Then come the yellow iris flowers, tall and bending rushes and bulrushes, the sweet-sedge, with its curious catkins; tangled feathery grasses, in such variety that, as you stand up to your waist in them, you may pluck a dozen kinds without moving; blue clusters of forget-me-nots, foxgloves, spikes of purple loose-strife, and broad tufts of valerian; bushes of woody night-shade; and, sweeter than all, masses upon masses, all the way along, of the cream-white and strong-scented meadow-sweet—these are what make the immediate banks changing panoramas of kaleidoscopic beauty. Then on the water, beneath the reeds and across shallow bays, and in the little 'pulks' or miniature Broads, which every-where open off the river, are lilies, yellow and white, in dazzling abundance. Here and there are tropical tangles of wood; a pic-turesque house in a cluster of trees, or a reed-stack floating on the river with a supporting wherry hidden somewhere beneath it.

"The far-reaching marsh has a beauty of its own, that of chang-ing colour as the wind bows the many-tinted grasses and flowers, and the wind-waves and cloud-shadows sweep along; while everywhere are the snowy sails of yachts and the red-brown canvas of the wherries. The atmospheric effects, too, are unusually beautiful, and sunrises and sunsets glow with a warmth of colour that gives the placid lagoons an almost unearthly loveliness; while, when the sun is set, the mists often show lakes and ships and islands that vanish with the dawn. Colour is seen far away; a group of red and white cattle, or the scarlet berries of the guelder rose entwined around some fallen willow, with a gleam of sunshine upon them, will lighten up miles of marsh. Then the flight of hawk and heron, snipe and wild-duck, the splash of fish, and the scattering rush of the small fry as a pike makes his raid upon them, are incidents of every hour.

"The marshes often present a curious sight. If the spectator is on the same level, scarcely any water may be visible, and the expanse of marsh may seem continuous; yet here and there and everywhere are the sails of yachts and wherries gliding through it, their hulls invisible."

So much for a purely descriptive word picture of the Broadland scene. It has not altered a lot today apart from the fact that the water is dirtier in most broads, the wherries have practically vanished and the 'sails of yachts' are largely replaced by the varnished hulls and gleaming brasswork of rather tubby looking motor-cruisers.

Many of the old Broadland characters have vanished and their type is not likely to be seen again. The Reverend Richard Lubbock, author of that masterly work *Observations on the Fauna of Norfolk* could paint a far earlier picture of their way of life as he saw it when he first began to shoot and fish in Broadland, from about 1816 onwards.

Writing in 1847 he said: "Since I first began to sport, about 1816, a marvellous alteration has taken place in Norfolk, particularly in the marshy parts. When first I remember our fens they were full of Terns, Ruffs, and Redlegs, and yet the old fen-men declared there was not a tenth part of what they remembered when boys. Now, these very parts which were the best, have yielded to the steam engine, and are totally drained—the marshes below Buckenham, which being taken care of were a stronghold for species when other resorts failed, are now as dry as a bowling green, and oats are grown where seven or eight years back 123 snipes were killed in one day by the same gun. The Claxton marshes, which formerly were almost too wet, are now as dry as Arabia."

He goes on to say: "When I first visited the Broads, I found here and there an occupant 'squatted down', as the Americans would call it, on the verge of a pool, who relied almost entirely on shooting and fishing for the support of his family, and lived in a truly primitive manner. I particularly remember one hero of this description. 'Our Broad' as he always called the extensive pool by which his cottage stood, was his microcosm, his world—the islands in it were his gardens of the Hesperides, its opposite extremity his Ultima Thule. Wherever his thoughts wandered, they could not get beyond the circle of his beloved lake; indeed I never knew them aberrant but once, when he informed me, with a doubting air, that he had sent his wife and his two eldest children to a fair, at a country village two miles off, that their ideas might expand by travel; as he sagely observed, they had never been away from 'Our Broad'. I went into his house at the dinner-hour, and found the whole party going to fall to, most thankfully, upon a roasted herring-gull—killed, of course, on 'Our Broad'. His life presented no vicissitudes but an alteration of marsh employment. In winter, after his day's reed-cutting, he might be found posted at nightfall waiting for the flight of fowl, or paddling after them on the open water. With the first warm days of February he launched his fleet of trimmers; pike finding a ready sale at his own door to those who bought them to sell again in the Norwich market. As soon as the pike had spawned and were out of season, the eels began to occupy his attention, and lapwings' eggs to be diligently sought for.

"In the end of April the island in his watery domain was frequently visited, for the sake of shooting the ruffs which resorted thither on their first arrival. As the days grew longer and hotter, he might be found searching in some smaller pools near his house for the shoals of tench as they commenced spawning. Yet a little longer he began marsh-mowing—his gun always laid ready upon his coat, in case flappers should be met with. By the middle of August teal came to a wet corner near his cottage, snipes began to arrive, and he was often called up to exercise his vocal powers on the curlews that passed to and fro. By the end of September good snipe-shooting was generally to be met with in his neighbourhood; and his accurate knowledge of the marshes, his unassuming good-humour, and zeal in providing sport for those who employed him, made him very much sought after as a sporting guide by snipe-shots and fishermen; and his knowledge of the habits of different birds enabled him to give useful information to those who collected them."

Broadland villages in the old days were ruled, like most English villages, by the squire and the parson. This did not destroy, but rather enhanced the sturdy individuality of the villagers. It is nonsense to pretend, as class agitators and Left Wing sociologists do, that the system of squirearchy was bad. It was overwhelmingly good. The squire and his family had, in most cases, dwelt for centuries in their own villages. This meant that they had a long, continuous tradition of service, responsibility friendship and mutual understanding with their tenants. Each respected the other. The squire gave leadership in local affairs and was usually the pioneer in agricultural drainage and housing improvements. Cottage rents were a shilling a week or so and estate pensioners were the rule rather than the exception. Almshouses were built and endowed for the old. The real rural tyrant was not usually the squire, but all too frequently the farmer, particularly the man who had risen from nothing to become an employer of labour. Hence the rural saying 'Jack makes a bad master'.

The influence of the parson, if he was a warm, human personality and not a dry-as-dust academic, was infinitely good. Let us therefore look at two typical Broadland parsons of the last century. The first is described in that enchanting book *Life and Sport on the Norfolk Broads in the Golden Days* by Oliver G. Ready. Here is an artless, down to earth, highly amusing, day by day picture of the life of a parson's family in the remote village of Waxham-cum-Palling, which lies between the coast and the Broads. It had forty inhabitants, no inn and no shop. Oliver Ready describes how on Sundays, his father often packed his brothers and himself off to the church of a nearby clergyman about a mile from Waxham. He describes the church thus: "It was a grand old pile, built of flint stones from the sea-shore, with leaden roof and massive square tower wherein hung a peal of enormous bells, while the interior showed a beautiful carved screen, noble oaken roofing, and a high gallery at the west end, from where the choir of respectable, elderly men and a few hobbledehoys howled down doxologies, glory-bes, and old-time hymns of unvarying tune, to the accompaniment of concertinas, fiddles, and clarionettes.

"In the very centre of the church was a towering edifice commencing with the parish clerk's desk, above which was the clergyman's reading desk, above which, reached by way of a winding stair, was the pulpit, and above which again was an enormous sounding-board. The pews were of the loose-box type, having door and sides about four and a half feet high, so that when sitting down one was perfectly screened from view. Each pew was privately owned, and so could be fitted up and made comfortable with cushions, carpets and hassocks according to taste.

"There was a grandeur, a venerableness, an atmosphere of restfulness and peace about the ancient edifice which raised it above all ordinary buildings and proclaimed God's House. An era of church restoration, however, was abroad, and the parish elders declared that the beautiful old temple must be 'restored'. The magnificent lead roof was stripped off, sold, and replaced by slates; the screen was torn down and cast out; the old three-decker pulpit was expelled; the comfortable and seclusive pews were supplanted by rows of varnished seats; the old stone pavement was replaced by bright and slippery tiles; the gallery was demolished; the frescoed walls scraped and plastered; in fact, the noble edifice, sanctified by centuries of worship, by generations of marriages, baptisms, and burials, was destroyed, giving place to a modern building with pretty windows, gaudy floor, and rows of brightly varnished seats: of a truth, it was 'swept and garnished'.

"This 'neighbouring clergyman' who was also the squire, and known far and near as simply 'The Rarverand', was one of the now extinct sporting parsons, who, after spending the week in generous living, would preach to full congregations on Sunday. A man of kingly presence and mellow, stentorian voice, of most magnetic and dominating personality, a born swell, he was forgiven everything and literally worshipped by everyone who came in contact with him. Shooting, sailing, fishing and coursing were his favourite amusements. Of greyhounds he kept about a dozen, and as the kennels were close to the church, the dogs would hear the well-known voice booming sonorously through the service, and set up in sympathy an answering chorus of yapping and baying, when the preacher would wheel majestically round and glare at his factotum, who, a little, bandy-legged, rotund person living solely in the reflected glory of his master and called by him 'Activity', would steal down the aisle on tiptoe, but with increasing pace, till he went out of the church door at a run, struggling, meanwhile, to get the dog whip out of the tail pocket of his tweed coat. In another minute a sudden silence, followed by yelps and howls of pain, would tell of his arrival at the kennels; and then, having restored order, he would very slowly return up the aisle, quivering at every step with the dignity of Justice invincible.

"This occurrence took place twice every Sunday, being quite a recognized part of each service, and its omission would have given rise to general comment."

Another enchanting picture of a Broadland parson was given by the late Nicholas Everitt, a sporting lawyer of Yarmouth, who was one of the heroes of my youth. He described going to spend a wintry weekend with a sporting parson, whose parish lay between the sandhills of the coast and the Broads. When he arrived at the marshland railway station, the parson was waiting for him in a small pony cart. The wind was arctic and the road across the marsh levels to the parsonage was flat, treeless and bordered by deep dykes. The night was dark. Sleet and hail cut them to the bone. A gale off the sea blew out both the gig lamps. That meant driving in pitch darkness with the imminent prospect of ending up in a deep muddy dyke at any moment. Finally they reached the parsonage where Everitt dined well by the light of oil lamps and a blazing wood fire.

Next morning his troubles began. The parson and he were going pike fishing in the afternoon and Everitt had promised to bring the live bait. He forgot it, so the Sexton, who was also Clerk of the Parish Council, groom, gardener, keeper of the rabbit warren and general man of all work, went off to catch some live bait. Who was to light the fire in the church and ring the one and only church bell to summon the congregation? Everitt volunteered. His description, written in the slightly pedantic third person fashion of the Victorian, is unforgettable.

"The flue would not draw, the wood would not burn, and when at last, with much persuasion, a small flame was fanned into being, the smoke leaked out in many places and half filled the building. During these operations a starling and two sparrows entered through a hole in the roof to watch operations, but as soon as we had obtained a fair grasp of the solitary bell-rope they departed without staying for service.

"It will be a long time before that call-to-prayer will be forgotten. What the majority of the inhabitants of the parish thought we know not and absolutely dare not inquire.

"The first intimation that the bell was moving was one tremendous smack of the tongue, which sounded as though it had cracked the metal; this was followed by spasmodic clangs and funeral tolling by way of variety; the harder we tried to get anything like a regular ring the more widly afflicted the music (?) seemed to be, until in despair we let go the rope to rest a while. But this was not to be, for a few minutes after we had desisted from the effort our friend arrived coughing violently through the smoke and directed that the bell must be kept going somehow, for ten minutes at least.

"This was no joke. It was cold and a trifle damp in the vestry. The place was full of smoke and we were no hands at all at the art of bell-ringing; besides, our host's remarks were not complimentary to our efforts.

"Soon after this the congregation began to arrive and the opportunity was taken of slipping back to the rectory for an overcoat, the wisdom of which forethought was afterwards appreciated.

"There were eleven of us all told to hear the opening words concerning the wicked man and his wrath, and this number was not increased as time went on.

"Five over-groomed children, the aforesaid Sunday-school class, sat in the front benches. The gardener and a maidservant from the Hall, who, alas! were apparently more interested in each other than in the service, occupied a pew below the rood-screen; a very rosy-cheeked farmer's daughter presided at a small harmonium which at times wandered a trifle by reason of weak notes and want of air; whilst the two children of our host composed the choir.

"The service progressed in the usual manner until a hymn was announced, when an incident occurred. The rector had taken a severe chill in driving over the marsh dam the night previously, and one side of his face was now puffed out to an alarming size. It impeded his speech considerably, but that seemed a matter of small import, for he rattled off the service, and all would have gone well had he not attempted to sing. But when the harmonium had played several bars of music without any response from the congregation, although the opening lines had been passed, he essayed to lead his flock in the way they should go by singing himself:

'Hark! a thrilling voice is sounding'

"The result was ludicrous. Without wishing to appear irreverent one cannot but admit that it was impossible to maintain a serious face. The gardener dug his companion in the ribs with his elbow, whilst she stuffed her pocket-handkerchief into her mouth, and soon afterwards they hurriedly left the church.

"All unheedingly our good-natured rector sang on, alone and out of tune, with an absolute indifference to the large dimunition of his audience. Then he mounted the pulpit to deliver his sermon. It was short and sweet, lasting but ten minutes. It was directed at the children who sat in a row in a pew exactly beneath the pulpit, and when the benediction had been pronounced he solemnly walked to the vestry and the congregation filed out."

The lives of the poorer inhabitants of Broadland, including sea fishermen, marshmen, reed cutters, wildfowlers and farm labourers, most of whom lived on an average income of from ten shillings to a pound a week, was on the whole, not too bad. One must remember that a shilling bought a hen who laid dozens of eggs; every cottage had a pig in its pig sty; butcher's meat was a few pennies a pound; vegetables and fruit were grown in the garden; turf for fuel was cut free from the various Poors' Fens, which were a part of the immemorial economy of each parish; fish was to be had for the catching and wildfowl for the shooting. Rabbits could be ferreted, snared and netted on the sand dunes in myriads. Cottage rents were a shilling a week or in many cases non-existent, since many cottage families had built their own, of the wattle and daub type which you see on Catfield Common to this day.

Thus the marshmen, fishermen and farm labourers lived a life close to the earth, near to the water and half of it in the reed beds. They were hunters and fishermen of a timeless sort. There was little squalor and usually infinite cleanliness in their cottages. They were deeply religious but ready for a fight with anyone. Smugglers went to church and the parson never said no to a keg of French brandy or Dutch gin if it was left on his doorstep after his cob had been borrowed from the pony stable overnight to help run a cargo at Winterton Gap or Somerton Gap where the old 'smugglers' road' still exists, or higher up the coast at Horsey Gap or in the high sandhills of Waxham and Palling.

Oliver Ready as a boy used to go and stay with an old servant from the family rectory who had married a fisherman named Tom

Ropey of Sea Palling. He describes their cottage as being: "just on the landward side of the sandhills and within a hundred yards of the sea, so that sleeping in a tiny but spotlessly clean bedroom with slanting ceiling, the last thing I remembered at night and the first thing I heard in the morning was the dull roar of breakers.

"It was almost like being on shipboard, for Old Salts, nets, tar, boats, and fish were everywhere; while astir at daylight, I would first, as though going on deck, scramble to the top of the sandhills and watch the dull, orange coloured sun slowly rise out of the North Sea, and then returning below, would join Betsy and her husband at breakfast in the little brick-paved kitchen or 'backus' where they practically lived, the front room or parlour, severely beautiful with its polished chairs and china dog ornaments, being kept entirely for show, or used only on the very greatest occasions.

"Mr. Ropey would cook red herrings by just laying them on the live coals, then taking hold of their tails, would lift them all smoking hot on to our plates, whereon, using fingers instead of forks, we would devour them together with new home-made bread and fresh butter, washed down with hot, strong tea; and whatever the verdict of civilized manners may be, never since have I tasted red herrings that were one half as good.

"Thoroughly entrenched at Betsy's, I was thus able to take part in any kind of fishing going forward at Palling-on-Sea.

"At each ebb-tide the sea receded about a hundred yards, leaving bare a line of outer banks of firm, white sand, between which and the beach would remain shallow lagoons or 'lows' of salt water.

"Shrimping in these lows was very pleasant in warm weather, when, dispensing with our nether garments, we boys, and girls too, for a matter of that, would wade to and fro in a depth of about two feet, pushing before us one of the ordinary hand nets, and frequently catching as many as five or six pints before the tide began to make again.

"And what shrimps they were too!—great, big, brown beauties, more like prawns than the ordinary little pink shrimp!

"Boiling them was something of a fine art, for if not properly carried out, besides making the shrimps soft and insipid, their skins could not be removed by one tug at the tail, as should be the case, but would have to be picked off piece by piece, in very messy fashion.

"First of all the shrimps should be well washed in two or three relays of clean, fresh water, to get rid of all sand and seaweed. Then they should be put into an iron saucepan, with just enough cold water to cover them, while one or two handfuls of salt must always be added to give them a flavour. As soon as the water begins to boil, stir up contents of saucepan with a red-hot poker, and there you are!"

What a picture this is of unspoiled Norfolk. Now imagine what Sea Palling will look like if the present plan to build a chalet town for several thousand summer visitors becomes a horrid fact. Bingo and transistor din, ice-cream 'orchestras', candy floss and broken bottles, will mark the March of Progress.

Hickling Broad today, thanks to the fact that it is a Nature Reserve, remains unspoiled. The Pleasure Boat Inn has been enlarged and the houses near it which were once a little settlement of fishermen and marshmen are now the highly expensive modernized houses of a retired general and others. Nonetheless, Hickling retains much of its ancient character. Even so it must have had a very different atmosphere toward the end of last century, when the half dozen cottages on the edge of the Broads all belonged to old Tom Rudd, marshman and gamekeeper. Most of his tenants were members of his own family. Old Tom was a rough, belligerent old man with a heart of gold and a voice like a fog horn. He ruled the roost at Hickling in no uncertain fashion, and only acknowledged the 'Ravarend' who was the squire and parson combined as his master. One of old Tom's sources of income was collecting plovers' eggs on the marshes in the days when it was legal to market them. He also owned a gun punt and a punt gun with which he stalked winter wildfowl and shot them by the score. It was a converted flintlock but had been transformed by the local blacksmith into a percussion cap gun. The trigger was as thick as a man's little finger and the hammer looked like a bed key. It was seven feet long, fired twenty drachms of black powder and half a pound of shot.

Oliver Ready draws a picture of this weapon which he described as the Woolwich Infant and its owner:

"In bitter winter weather with stock-ice forming below water and hanging on to the oars and quant like liquid glass, and with sleet and snow driving before a howling nor'-easter, old Tom, muffled up in seal-skin cap, thick blue guernsey, heavy woollen scarf, crotch boots and oilies, would put out and creep along the windward shore until he spotted a flock of mallard, 'pokers', or wild geese on the water to leeward, when, lying face downwards along the bottom of the punt with eyes just above the gunnel, one hand working a single scull over the side, and the other hand on the trigger, he would bear down before the wind on his prey, until the moment when they began to rise he would loosen into them the eight ounces of swan-shot.

"At times he made splendid bags, the best I have heard him state being thirty-three mallard and pokers at one shot; though in mild, open winters, when the wildfowl were not frozen out of their haunts in the salt swamps along the coasts of Denmark and Holland, he sometimes never even fired a shot, so that the duck-punt, with the big gun mounted and loaded in readiness, would lie majestically in the boat-house for weeks, while Old Tom would sit at home in his armchair, and through the open door continually scan the surface of the broad with field-glasses in hopes of detecting the longed-for fowl."

Punt gunning is not practised on the Broads today and very rightly so. A few punt gunners still go out each winter after fowl on Breydon Water but they are local men, jealous of their 'rights' and I do not advise any newcomer to poke his nose in. A charge of shot can easily go in the wrong direction in the dark!

The half-pound guns commonly used on the Broads by Tom Rudd and others were pop guns compared with the heavy artillery still used on the coast. My larger punt gun for example is nine feet ten inches long, two and a half inch bore, weighs about 300 pounds and fires two pounds of shot. One can hear it go off two miles away across salt water. Such fowling pieces are only possible on broad estuaries and on wide areas of flooded marshes.

Old Tom Rudd like many others in the district came of a smuggling family. His father was a smuggler of the old sort and Old Tom kept his pair of flintlock pistols hanging proudly above the kitchen mantelpiece. When Parson Ready took the living of Waxham, he was warned by his predecessor that he should get downstairs early and open the front door at daylight. If a keg of brandy was on the doorstep, it was a warning not to allow any strangers to go into the rectory barn for several days as the smugglers had stored their stuff there. When they had removed the last cargo another keg would be left on the doorstep. The parson's barn was of course sacrosanct and not likely to be searched.

I remember some years ago being shown a fine old dark-blue glass wine bottle stamped "J. Poynter 1782" which had been dredged up off the mouth of Ranworth Dyke. Mr. Starling, who then kept The Malsters Inn at Ranworth Staithe, showed me the bottle and added;

"Might have been dropped overboard by the smugglers. A lot of that trade went on in these marshes.

"Why they found a smugglers' cave in the school-yard some years ago. Barrels in it too, but nothing in the barrels. That's all blocked up now. So is the tunnel that runs from the church to St. Benet's Abbey. Leastways, some of the old chaps say there's a tunnel, but I can't see how those old monks ever dug one that far."

"I've heard about that tunnel," said I. "Wherever there's an old castle or an abbey, there's always a rumour of a tunnel going for miles. They were usually drains! They dug sewers even in the Middle Ages."

"Ah, I daresay," said Starling. "Sounds more like the truth. But how about the smugglers' cave?"

"Much more likely to be true. A lot of smuggling went on on the Broads up to a hundred years ago," I said. "Sidney Grapes' father always used to say that their old family mill, Grape's Mill, between Potter and Dungeon, was stacked full of tobacco some nights in his father's time. They used to run the cargoes ashore at Horsey Gap and at Winterton and, then again, at the end of the old Holmes road on the Somerton Marshes. Plenty of those old mills were used for hiding stuff. In fact, if the Preventive men left Yarmouth to search a mill at Horsey, the Horsey men knew within a quarter of an hour of the Preventive men leaving the town."

"How was that?"

"Because they set the sails of the mills dead upright—in a cross. One millman used to signal another across miles of country—and I daresay your Ranworth chaps were as deep in it as anyone else."

"Ah! I dessay. Good old times them."

The highlight of Old Tom Rudd's youth was the classic occasion when his father, after a long free-trading career at sea, decided to chuck it up and live a Godly life. But there was to be one last voyage, one last cargo run. He took young Tom, then a mere boy, on the trip with him. They ran into a fearful gale which, as Tom said, "blew we right up the Thames till them there Custom House orficers cam aboard an' took the hull lot on us t' jail, arter strippin' orf the silk laace I had wound all round me under my clo'es."

One highlight of those peaceful days in Hickling, eighty years or more ago, were the occasions when Old Tom came home 'market merry'. Oliver Ready describes how he and his small brother and Old Tom's grandson, Albert, were swarming all over the boatshed roof, in and out of the boats, and enjoying themselves enormously, when "suddenly Grandson Albert took a flying leap from the top of the boathouse on to a pile of litter, exclaiming in a terrified voice: 'Here come my gran'fa, drunk as muck. Be yow a-stirrin' tegither.'

"Stir we did, and in ten seconds everyone was effectually concealed, while Albert had vaulted, cart-wheel fashion, over the stable-yard gate and was chopping turnips for his life between furtive peeps over the fence at, and excited warnings as to, the approaching tornado: 'Massy upon us! he's a-comin' like bells. Lay yow right squat tegither. Th'ole warmin!'

"The sudden stillness about the premises, together with the sound of approaching wheels, instantly brought out Mrs. Rudd, who, pale of face and trembling with fright, kept on exclaiming helplessly: 'Massy upon us! God Know! Boy Ollbut, be yow a stirrin'. Massy upon us!' till her lord and master could be seen coming up the bank, 'hallerin' an' yawlin' and rolling from side to side in his square cart as the small cob tore along at full gallop, till, pulling up at the gate with a jerk, Old Tom was first thrown on to the pony's back, and then slipped down between the animal and the shaft, where he hung with his feet just off the ground, glaring like a tiger and saying all kinds of things while Mrs. Rudd and Albert worked frantically to undo the harness and set him free.

"It could only have been a few seconds, though it seemed an age to me watching from behind an empty tar-barrel, before the cob walked forward and Albert dropped the shaft as though it were red-hot and fled to the hay-house closely followed by Old Tom striking at him with his left hand as he ran, while Mrs. Rudd brought up the rear.

"The hay-house was separated from the turnip shed by a partition some seven feet high, which Albert scaled like a cat, but which Old Tom was unable to get over, and before he could retrace his steps, Mrs. Rudd had banged too the hay-house door and securely fastened it outside, making her husband a prisoner.

"The din inside for a few minutes was awful, but it soon subsided, and in a short time stertorian snores proclaimed that the

. . . and Broadland congestion—at Wroxham

master of the house had found a comfortable bed upon the soft hay.

"It was like having caught and caged a lion, so that after hastily collecting at the gate and briefly talking the event over in excited whispers, we all stealthily dispersed; while Old Tom, having had a comfortable and refreshing sleep, would find the hay-house door open when he awoke, so that things would resume their natural course, every one being most careful not to allude in any way to the 'regrettable incident'."

4

Breydon Water and the River Yare at Berney Arms

IV

THE YARE AND ITS BROADS

Surlingham and Rockland—Old Charms and New Filth

THE Yare is long, broad, deep and, in its little sea-faring way, important. Broadsmen call it 'The Norwich River'. A fine, bold sea-whispering name, like 'London River'. A name which carries the smell of the sea, the busy news of great ports, the urgent message of ships and goods from foreign lands. And such it still is, this fine broad river of Yare, deepest and swiftest of all the Broadland rivers.

Once upon a time it was a great river of ships and shipmen in the coloured medieval days when Norwich was an embattled city, busy with the tramp of soldiers, the pomp of prelates, the hum and clatter of wharves, the coming and going of ships under many flags.

Then Yarmouth stole the pride of being the chief port of Norfolk. Norwich still kept the lowering majesty of its great Norman castle-keep, high on that huge mound of pre-Norman days. It had, and has still, its bishop and its canons, the airy soaring beauty of its great cathedral, the tramping feet of soldiery, and the clatter and bustle of a great mart. But the ships vanished. The mart is a mart of cattle, greatest in all England. The hum and clatter of ships and wharves gave place to the crash and rattle of machinery in the factories and machine-shops of such vast enterprises as those of Colman and Boulton and Paul.

No one who visits the Broads today should miss Norwich. It is not only the capital city of Norfolk and for that matter of Broadland, but it has a unique quality and fascination of its own. Norwich is not only very English—it is very Norfolk. And Norfolk is perhaps the most independent part of all England. We in the rest of the eastern counties, particularly in my native Fens, like to think that we share the same dogged, perverse, hard-headed independent spirit of the Norfolkers. I think we do. It was well put, in a few words, by Sir Thomas Dugdale, now Lord Crathorne, when he was Minister of Agriculture during the latter part of the Second World War before he resigned because of the unforgivable actions behind his back of some of his officials over the infamous Crichel Down case. Tom Dugdale, as a gentleman, took the full blame for tyrannic actions which had been misrepresented to him by his subordinates. All that is now legal history.

I went to see him at the Ministry to fight a battle for many scores of farmers who were being evicted from their land, or threatened with eviction, in the eastern counties by the various War Agricultural Executive Committees. I told Tom Dugdale, whom I happened to know personally, that we would fight to the bitter end.

"I know you chaps will," he laughed. "If ever a revolt blows up concerning this Ministry, we always know that ten to one it comes from East Anglia. You chaps are the most stiff-necked lot in England. You can't be sat on and you don't give an inch. But I must say I admire you for it." That was the tribute to East Anglia and, incidentally, to the Norfolk spirit, from a man who was one of the greatest Ministers of Agriculture we have had this century. Norwich is the shrine of that sort of spirit.

If you want to see it in one unforgettable picture, climb the stone steps on a day of bright sun, sharp winds and white high clouds to the top of the Keep of Norwich Castle, that square, squat tower which the Normans called, prettily 'Blanchtower'. Many years ago, on the advice of an old explosive friend, the late Sir Alfred Munnings, that superb artist, I climbed the tower. The view today is much the same as when I wrote of it then save that the outskirts of the city, like all other cities, are now rimmed with a red rash of new houses.

Stand on that battlemented roof and you gaze upon a city and a landscape which are of the heart and soul of England. No city in this kingdom is more truly English than Norwich. For it is a place of great industries and yet, withal, great beauty. It is a country city, set in an unspoiled countryside. Yet it produces great wealth from trade and manufacturers. It has a lovely soaring cathedral, yet is bound by none of those decorous ecclesiastical spiders which spin their stifling web about the streets of Durham and Ely, of Canterbury and Salisbury. It has barracks and this squat and lowering castle keep, but there is none of the air of a garrison

town. It is a port to which come sea-going ships, their iron hulls
blistered with salt spray—yet it is 'The City of Gardens' through
which rivers run, sparkling like swords.

Stand, as I stood, upon the battlements of this ancient castle of
the Bigods, when the sun swims low in the west in a wild wrack
of wind-blown clouds. The sky is apple green, fading into umber
and yellow with a last blood-red flare to light the upper clouds,
where gulls are winnowing seaward. Gazing thus, from a lonely
height there lies below a tumbled sea of medieval roofs and stark
factory chimneys, the spires and towers of churches, the almost
ethereal beauty of the cathedral, the billow of green tree-tops.
Through the smoke and glitter of evening fires and early lights
come the sudden flashes of the rivers which gave birth to this city
of the Eastern Angles nearly 2,000 years ago, before Christ walked
in Galilee. Looking upon it you will cease to wonder how it is
that Norfolk is perhaps the most individual of all English counties
and Norwich the mother of great English artists.

For within the compass of a man's vision from the top of this
castle keep, there lie wild and shaggy heaths, heaths that inspired
Borrow to immortal prose, that gave birth to the shining genius
of Old Crome and the Norwich School of Painting—and, beyond
the heaths are massed woodlands, chequered fields of green and
gold, the flashing shields of water which are the Broads, whose
like is nowhere else in England, and, beyond it all, far to the east,
the smoking chimneys and spidery masts of Yarmouth, the ancient
town of herrings and ships, that 'sits full upon the Maine Sea'.
In front of Yarmouth, glittering in the sun, is the long sweep of
Breydon Water, the last echo of that great vanished estuary of
Gariensis which, when Norwich was born, stretched well-nigh
from the foot of the Castle Mound to the now-distant sweep and
glitter of the North Sea.

The Yare, with its three tributaries, the Wensum, the Tud and
the Tas, is the heart of the picture. Its sea-going coasters are its
acolytes. Their screws churn its waters daily. Their salt-encrusted
hulls smell of the North Sea. Small beer in London or Liverpool,
these squat, low-waisted, high-pooped coasters of 800 to 900 tons,
but in their setting of reed-fringed river, flat marshes, waterside
villages and whispering willow trees, they are impressive in their
marshland frame. Some go up to Norwich, and so the river
preserves the illusion that Norwich is still a busy port.

The Yare is part of the very soul of the city. Above Norwich it becomes two rivers, the Wensum which flows through the heart of the city—being joined at Hellesdon on its upper reaches by the pretty little River Tud—whilst the Yare, disdaining urban contamination, takes a bold sweep southwards round the outskirts of the city and goes winding through woods and buttercup-yellow meadows past Old Lakenham, Keswick, Earlham—immortal as the setting of Percy Lubbock's picture of Quaker peace in Victorian days—past Colney with its park and hall, and so into the rural heart of Norfolk.

These rivers above Norwich are too shallow for the Broadland cruiser, but they are waterways of pure delight to the man in a small boat. They flow by ancient halls too many of which, alas, like Costessey, the old seat of the Jerninghams and of the Lords Stafford, are now dismantled or derelict; by red-roofed, flint-walled villages with ancient churches; under great hanging woods and through meads which have all the quiet and coloured beauty which gave life and breadth to the great school of Norwich painters.

Below Norwich the Yare flows under the high woods of Crownpoint Park, past the ruined church at Whitlingham, under the low fir-crowned hills of Postwick and then, in a bold sweep round Postwick Marsh, beneath that tapestry of tall trees at Bramerton Woods End.

Opposite Crownpoint lies Thorpe-next-Norwich which someone a century or more ago christened the Richmond of Norwich, and so it is. A pleasant water-side village, with some good Georgian houses and something of the bold vistas of Richmond. Its houses look down on white sails, lush green meadows, full of cattle, the shining river and a long island clad in willows. There for years they held that historic water picnic 'Thorpe Water Frolic'. Stannard, one of the greatest of Norwich painters, painted here his superb picture of the Water Frolic which you may see in Norwich Castle Museum. One has the vision, through the eyes of Stannard, of the river crowded with every sort of craft. Huge wherries bearing gaily uniformed 'bands of music' jostled with hoys, shallops, skiffs, barges, punts, beamy old rowing boats, each with its load of rustics 'garping and cackling', with here and there one of those double-ended, flat-bottomed marshmen's boats which, in Norfolk are used for every purpose from eel-bobbing to reed-cutting and duck-shooting.

Whilst the sedate City Fathers of Norwich would enjoy their

bottles of French wine and German hocks and moselles aboard a great pleasure wherry, resplendent with strings of bunting, a four-oared barge manned by tipsy soldiers from the garrison, blazing in scarlet and pipe-clay and ballasted with bouncing damsels, as likely as not would ram the wherry amidst the shouts and screams of the multitude, the thumping of the big drum, and the eldritch scrapings of the fiddler, punctuated by the boom of the starting gun as another race began.

The Frolic was, in fine, a sort of water carousel and, as the late afternoon turned to summer dusk, more and more people poured out from Norwich, beer flowed like water into the stream itself, bumping matches became more frequent, and lucky was the citizen who was not shot into the river or drenched with water from the resounding splash of a flattened oar. Altogether a time of gaiety. In the end it died a natural death, probably because the City Fathers had been bumped once too often.

Below Crownpoint you come to the Whitlingham Sewage Farm. I regard it with envy and with loathing. Envy because there, on 20th December, 1927, the record one day bag of snipe for all England, 231 of them, was made by five guns, Messrs. J. H. Colman, Geoffrey Colman, H. J. Cator, R. G. Buxton and D. G. Wigan. They picked up 226 snipe in the day and five more were gathered next morning. The total included thirty-one jack-snipe. The birds were driven across the snow-covered marsh by four or five men under the direction of one keeper and were high and difficult shots. Picking up was none too easy as the snow was about three inches deep.

On the same marsh a bag of 144 snipe was made by six guns on 5th December, 1925.

Envy turns to loathing when I read in a letter from a friend who lives nearby: "This river, the Yare, on which I have lived all my life, is now becoming first cousin to a sewer. The waves of detergent foam from the sewage farm and presumably from houses up-river, have killed a tremendous lot of under-water vegetation and weed in the Surlingham Broad and down-river. I would not dream of bathing here. Heaven knows what one might catch. In any case the water is too filthy some days for one to look at it without shuddering. I shudder in any case to think of what it is doing to the fish."

The Nature Conservancy has a few terse comments on the matter. Referring specifically to the outfall from Whitlingham and other small sewage works which release effluents as, for example, North Walsham and Beccles, it says that they will cause serious "damage to amenities, fish stocks and scientific interests of waterways unless Royal Commission standards imposed by the River Authority are strictly observed. Unsightly frothing near outfalls owing to detergents in effluent . . ." and it goes on to recommend "stringent enforcement of Royal Commission standards by frequent site inspections. Regular maintenance of sewage works. Replacement of out-of-date equipment with modern plant. More research on effects of detergents on fauna and flora."

Something must be done and done swiftly to tighten up the regulations at Whitlingham. Otherwise, sooner or later, either the river will be ruined entirely for many miles down or a local householder, landowner, fishery owner or other interested party is going to bring an action at law which will wake up the pundits of the Norwich City Council. Norwich cannot expect to earn money from holiday-makers if it poisons the waters which attract them.

Beyond Whitlingham the river bends to the right. On the left you will see a bold little hill with a crown of firs, wild and challenging against the sky. That is Postwick, which, true to the English tradition of making the English language is called 'Possick'. Then you come to the pretty, pretty water-side hamlet of Bramerton Woods End which is becoming very like any other water-side village whose houses have been 'titivated up' as they say in East Anglia by busy little business 'executives', each with his brace of shiny motor-cars, his shiny little wife and his Sunday cocktail parties. It could be worse.

Beyond on the right-hand bank a mile or two down river, there lies a reedy jungle of bogs and waters, a place of mosquito-ridden mysteries. It is no more than a mile long and about half a mile wide, but the reeds rise fourteen feet or so above the water and the dykes and channels which thread through them, remind one of a miniature 'sudd' on the Upper Nile. One almost expects a mamba to drop from a willow tree into the well of your boat.

In this ancient swamp, which is no more than the grown-up remains of what, some hundreds of years ago, was a great broad, there lies the shallow, forgotten little mere that is Surlingham Broad. Nowhere is Surlingham more than a few feet deep and, since the river-level rises and falls with the pull of the tides at

Yarmouth, much of it, at times, is no more than a few inches deep. It is no place for any boat that will not sail in the track of a snail or in the dew upon the grass. For that reason you will probably have Surlingham Broad entirely to yourself. You may see there wild ducks spattering in the reeds, coots swimming in dignity, moorhens flicking their white tails with perky importance and, if you are lucky, you will hear on nights of spring and summer the ghostly booming of the bittern.

Surlingham Broad is a classic example of a big broad that has now shrunken to little or nothing. With its little sister, Bargate Broad, it covered seventy-two acres of open water in 1840. The Ordnance Survey Maps of 1881 to 1938 showed only seventeen acres of open water. In 1946 aerial photography showed eight acres of open water. Further aerial photography in 1962 showed practically no open water except a number of channels. The main channel is five feet deep and the others are two to three feet deep. When I was last there a few years ago, I found a few open areas of shallow water, much of which became bare mud when the river dropped a few inches at low tide. This broad is a nature reserve and shooting is strictly forbidden.

Yet it is not so many years since Surlingham was a famous place for pike and also for wildfowl and rare birds. Charlie Gibbs, one of the old time Broadsmen, who kept the pub at Brundall, was 'King' of Surlingham Broad. I shall never forget the story he told me one night of how a local big-wig tried to claim the broad as his own private property. Charlie, who was young and full of fire, rose in his wrath as defender of the rights of the common man. He bought an old ship's boat in Yarmouth, anchored it on the broad and lived aboard in the tiny cabin for an entire winter, with his rod and gun and net, existing on what he caught and shot.

Charlie's version of the manner in which, single-handed, he conducted his war and won it, is illuminating and pungent. Setting his pint pot firmly down on the counter of the Yare Hotel one evening, beneath the glassy eye of his monster pike, he stroked his Viking moustache with a hand brown and seamed as leather and, fixing me with a benign blue eye, said: "I told 'em the broad allus had been public and I was goin' to stop there and see it stayed public. If they wanted to shift me they'd have to do it by force. Then I'd have the lot of them up before the magistrits! I told 'em I'd loaded me owd gun full o' swan-shot and that she was liable to go off on her own account if any b—— come nigh of my boat! They kept away all right!

"But, lor', what a winter I had. That snew. That fruz. That hailed. That rined! Some nights I was suffin' cold, I tell ye. But I stuck it even if me fitten (feet) felt as if they'd been frawned (frozen) off.

"I took stones on stones of eels and masterful lot of big owd pike, and shot a few score of ducks, so, one way an' another, I didn't do too bad.

"Arter a year or two they give it up as a bad job and the gennelman what reckon'd he owned the broad told me, nice as pie, that I could fish there any time I liked, perwided I went up to the house and asked permission!

"So up I goes to the big house one night and told the gennleman, polite as you like, that he could have a share in the broad along wi' me an' the rest of the public.

"Then I invited him to come and have a day's fishin' with me and promised him that he'd have some rare good fish too. I told him I knowed where all the fish were and the big 'uns had got my mark on 'em—jest the same as the nick in the tail o' that big owd boy up in the glass case yinder.

"Well, the gennleman he laughed. He gives me a damn great whisky. Ha! three or fower on 'em!—and he says: 'All right, Gibbs, you win! We'll call it our broad in future. Now show me how to catch these private fish o' yourn.'

"Well, we parted good pals an' I took him out an' we soon had a tidy fish in the boat. He was happy an' so was I. But, lor', bless yer, that owd broad ain't half the place it was. That used to be thick wi' fish. Now it's thick wi' mud. What that broad needs is not so much argument but more dredgin'!"

That wise old Broadsman spoke that last mouthful of common sense to me fifteen years ago. They are still arguing. The dredging has not yet started. The sooner the better. Surlingham is a classic example of a great grown up broad which could be opened up to the advantage of all, yachtsman, fisherman and naturalists. Plenty of reed beds would still remain to harbour nesting birds and to hide the secretive bittern, the grasshopper warbler, the bearded tit and others.

Below Surlingham, a little way lies Brundall, where lives that wise man of the Broads, Mr. Alan Savory. Alan Savory is that rare type of sportsman which the eighteenth century produced and in which this century is singularly poor. He is a naturalist whose observations are not only acute, but are made with the eye of an artist. He writes with the pen of a poet, but he shoots his wild geese with a mighty eight bore that would flatten lesser men on their backs. He is a great pike fisher in a land of great pike fishers, but he will never equal the feat of a man named Halliday, a one armed angler at that. Charlie Gibbs told me the story. Halliday came to fish off Coldham Hall, the anglers' inn, in 1939. He was left-handed, but somehow he managed to put his live bait on the hook single-handed and fish it single-handed. God looks after such men. On that day benediction was given to one-armed Halliday. He hooked a thirty-six-pound pike, played it one-handed and landed it one-handed. As Charlie put it tersely: "If that ain't a record it damn well ought to be."

Below Brundall to the left lie wild acres of wild marsh with a little private broad cut off from the river. It all belongs to Alan Savory who here has a unique wild life sanctuary and *inter alia* a rare home of the swallow-tail butterfly. If it were not for such tiny private broads and such land-owning naturalists, of whom thank heaven, there are many in Broadland, the area would not be one tenth as rich in bird life. Savory's books *Norfolk Fowler* and *Lazy Rivers* are a 'must' for anyone who wants to read aboard his Broadland boat or stock his library with the literature of this enchanting half-land of reeds and water.

Below Brundal, the river valley opens into a wide, marshland vista. Acres upon acres of reed and sedge sigh in the wind and ripple in sunlight like the waves of a green sea. Reed warblers chitter their endless tiny songs. Sometimes the marsh harrier or Montagu's harrier beats the lonely level like a setter—flap and glide, flap and glide—and then an airy swing with the ease of an eagle. Wild duck pass over on quick wing or quack softly in hidden dykes. Water-rails squeal suddenly like stuck pigs in green jungles. The bittern creeps, a brown gnome, through secret runways in the reeds or takes to wing, flapping, brown and moth-like, above ancient morasses that knew his kind a thousand years ago. Overhead peewits weep and wail and stumble in airy acrobatics. From the river's edge the heron, grey-blue and ghostly as a shadow, lumbers up on huge wings and flaps like a blown rag into the far flat distances that run on to the salt tides of Breydon and the beckoning of the outer sea. It is an ancient and unspoilt valley of great skyscapes and green and brown landscapes where clouds sail like huge galleon. By night the grasshopper warbler, the 'reeler' bird of the old Fenmen, reels his endless thin song in the brooding silences.

Away to the right of the river lies a wild, bottomless, succession of marshes. Acres of reeds and sedge, criss-crossed by dykes, many of which have grown up and lie in wait to trap the blithe explorer. Sallow bushes stand up like little islands, above the reeds. Here and there a hairy-headed willow or a thin silver birch holds its watching carrion crow. Much of this wild marsh, largely useless even for reed harvest, is Tarlow Fen. Surely here is a place where a new broad could be created by dredging and excavation. There should be a market for the peat which would be dug out. Beyond the fen lies the lonely broad of Rockland, home for many years of that redoubtable character 'Old Scientific' Fuller, who smelt of beer, sweat, eel-slime and duck's blood and proclaimed himself King of Rockland Broad. He was too. More of him in a moment.

On the left-hand bank of the river are more rough cattle marshes and beyond them the woods of Strumpshaw Hall where that good old sportsman-naturalist Squire Holmes lived for many years. He kept a marsh-harrier, which Charlie Gibbs had caught in a rabbit trap, as a pet and used to feed it from his hand. Strumpshaw Broad is another example of a broad which has grown up almost to vanishing point. In 1840 it covered twenty-two acres of open water. By 1938 or earlier, it was only six acres of water. When I went there in 1950 it was about a couple of acres. Now according to aerial photography, there is little or no open water at all and what there is is between two and three feet deep. These marshes, with the consent of the owner and probably the broad, could be respectively excavated and opened up to form a new broad of say fifty acres. Part of this area is a National Nature Reserve.

Rockland Broad, which lies to the right of the river, up a long and fairly broad dyke which strikes straight as a sword through the heart of the reed-beds for half a mile or more, was, until recently, the least spoilt of all the broads and, to my mind, the one which most nearly presented the true character of the old vanished meres of the Cambridgeshire Fens. I spent an enchanted few days on it in a boat not so long ago and wrote at the time: "One or two small islands of reeds, where coots and crested grebes nest, stand up. To the left are a few scattered wind-blown willows. At the foot of the nearest one to the dyke-mouth you are almost certain to find the 'spraint' of an otter, the fish-scales and bones of his last breakfast. For the roots of that old tree for long years have been an 'otter's altar'. To the right the broad spreads to a far, low shore of reeds and sedge. Somewhere amid those reed-beds a narrow channel goes winding through quaking swamps where the grey South American marsh-rat or nutria, bigger than an otter, has his home, to the tiny hidden pool which is Wheatfen Broad, the private preserve of that excellent naturalist, Dr. E. A. Ellis. The great clump of thorns and willows and mixed trees looming above the reed-beds behind Wheatfen holds a heronry. The heron is the daily familiar of these wet wastes and windy skies—the bird in whose shadowy ghostliness is typified something of the mystery, the grace and the aerial beauty of the Broadland waters and skies.

"That evening I remember going up a narrow channel in the punt, silent as a shadow, to watch a heron's nest in a low marsh 'carr', just beyond the tiny hidden waters of Wheatfen Broad. Black-headed gulls laughed above the reeds. There were mallard in a reedy bay. A heron standing like a Grey Eminence in the shadows fished pensively. Through the glasses I watched the marsh-harrier sweep far over the quiet fen with the grace of an eagle. One would have said that the world and all the horrors in it were a million miles away. Then quietly the wall of reeds parted and a bird-like face with piercing eyes eyed me with no little distaste. It was Ted Ellis, the most erudite naturalist in Broadland who in his own right is King of Wheatfen Broad, just as Old Scientific was King of Rockland in the not so long ago. Which just shows you that you cannot go into the quietest corner of the Broadland without the eye of gamekeeper, naturalist, angler or watchful farmer being upon you. It took me a little time and no small eloquence to convince Ted Ellis that I was relatively harmless. Since then we have been good friends. There indeed is a man from whom are hidden none of the mysteries of Broadland from the minutest insect to the rarest migrant bird."

Now let us consider Old Scientific who is still a potent memory in the land. He lived in an old houseboat on the Broads with his gun-punt and his long muzzle loading punt-gun, his 'hand guns' and bow-nets, his eel glaives and 'grigs', and his dog. He was short, bearded and broad-shouldered with fierce eyes, wild hair and wilder whiskers. He had a great barrel of a chest and he could fight like an old time pugilist. He upheld the public right to shoot and fish free on Rockland Broad which, since it is a tidal broad, is a right in law. Nonetheless, I hear that there is a movement on foot to declare this broad a National Nature Reserve. If that comes about those who lose their right to shoot can thank the armed hooligans or 'marsh cowboys' who swarm out to the broad from Norwich and elsewhere as soon as duck shooting begins. They shoot at anything that moves, including other gunners. They even shot Alan Savory's wooden decoy ducks! He himself escaped by inches, an ounce of shot which peppered his punt and hissed into the water by the gunwale. If Scientific were alive today he would put the whole pack to flight.

I wrote of this splendid, smelly, lovable old man many years ago that he "could skate at full speed across the broad, travelling at express speed with his gun in his hand, suddenly throw the gun to his shoulder and shoot stone-dead a gull wheeling and swooping overhead.

"He caught an immense number of fish, shot thousands of wild-fowl and, in his time, collected many rare birds for wealthy collectors when such reprehensible practices were winked at. I shudder to think how many bitterns, bearded tits, harriers, rare warblers and uncommon ducks went into the great, blood-stained, canvas 'side-bag' which swung on a broad strap from his shoulders.

"This uncouth, lovable, pugnacious old man would swallow incredible quantities of beer at the inn which stands at the head of Rockland Dyke, and then, rattling his hob-nailed leather water-boots on the stone floor, he would dance a wild jig which struck sparks from the flags and end up by challenging any man there to fight him for a quart. None did unless they were very young or very drunk.

"In winter, when the punt-guns boomed through the snowy mist far away on the tidal flats of Breydon Water, Scientific would be afloat in his little, low, grey-painted duck-punt, the great muzzle-loader, with its barrel six feet long, lying flat and menacing in its cradle. A few minutes after the booming echoes sounded from Breydon, teams of duck and widgeon with some-times skeins of grey geese would whistle overhead and plunge in sheets of foam on to the surface of the broad.

"Like a shadow the old man's punt crept silently out of its little bay among the reeds and floated flat and ghostly towards the resting fowl. Foot by foot he spritted or paddled silently forward. Then the trigger was pulled. There came a red, searing flame, a foot long, from the muzzle, a billowing cloud of grey smoke, a thudding boom that echoed across the lonely fen and, in a frenzy of wings, the fowl were up and away, skirling with fright. On the water floated a dozen, perhaps a score, of dead and wounded. That was the old man's harvest in winter.

"In summer he caught and netted fish, speared eels and took them in his great funnel-shaped 'grigs' woven by hand from thin osiers.

"If anyone poached on Scientific's preserves, he would shoot at them as soon as look at them. Yet he was universally loved, a sort of uncouth cross between 'Bloody Morgan' and Thoreau. When he died half Norfolk mourned him and men of science who had enjoyed his company and bought his rare specimens knew that a last link with the primitive race of Broadsmen had gone for ever."

Today, a young, solid, Saxon-looking, beefy-faced Broadsman named 'Fudgey' Stone, a famous marshland name, treads in the footsteps of Scientific. He, too, shoots for a living and fishes for profit, but 'Fudgey' is an archangel of innocence compared with the rip-roaring rumbustiousness of Old Scientific.

In many ways, except perhaps at weekends and in the height of summer, Rockland has not changed a lot since Christopher Davies wrote of it in 1833: "You are now in the haunt of heron and fowl and the silence is only broken by the bleating of snipes in the clear air above you . . ." And he goes on to say: "As far as poor humanity is concerned there is a floating palace, and there are its king and its queen. True, the palace is but a large old sea-boat, with a hut built up in the centre third of it, and roofed with planks and tarred felt; but within, all is neat and snug, and spacious enough for the wants of its occupants. And he who sits mending his nets is more free than any monarch. His gun and his nets bring him enough for his needs, his house is his own, his time is his own, he calls no man master, and he pays neither rent nor taxes. What more could you have? His wife is cleaning her crockery, and it is evident that she knows not the need or worry of a servant. Verily, the sobriety of advancing years and the cares of paternity do not prevent me from indulging in a dream of how free and idyllic such a life would be if one could take to it, together with an educated love of nature, a stomach for dirty work—such as hauling in that long eel-net, which is now hung out to dry along the top of the boat. Between a couple of poles on the rond (which is very soft and wet) a casting-net is drying in the wind. Alongside the larger craft is a gunning-punt, with a couple of single-barrelled guns lying ready loaded in it. A few yards away is a group of floating boxes or trunks, perforated with holes, in which the eels, tench, pike and other fish are kept alive until there are sufficient to send to Billingsgate.

"The whole establishment is moored in a little reedy bay close by the mouth of the dyke.

"Presently the man looks up. His keen eye has detected something moving at the far side of the lake. He gets into his punt, and sculls it with one oar worked in side rowlock in a singular and rather inexplicable way, with great rapidity, and noiselessly. Skirting the reeds, and keeping as much as possible within the shelter of the straggling fringe of them which has advanced beyond the main body, he nears the spot where he has marked his quarry. The sun gleams on the barrel of his gun, there is a puff of white smoke, and the report comes loudly over the water, and he has picked up a coot, with which he returns to his hut.

"He is a human spider. The broad is his web; and when anything eatable touches it, he sallies out of his cell bent on destruction. Day and night he follows his pursuit; and though there are two or three others of his kind on the broad, yet it is naturally a place so favourable in all its conditions to bird-life, that he says there is no dimunition of fish or fowl attributable to his pursuits.

"Indeed I take it that two or three amateur sportsmen spending a day on the water would, by their noise and racket about, do far more to frighten fowl away than he with all his slaughter; for he goes to work so unobtrusively, that only the fowl and fish which are killed find out how dangerous he is—(this last phrase sounds rather Irish, but let it pass).

"His pursuits vary a little with the seasons, and this is the course of them. In the spring, when netting for roach and bream is forbidden, he keeps a good look-out for rare birds' nests and eggs, which find a ready sale among the many collectors in Norfolk. Perchance he finds some nests of the bearded tit, with their delicate little eggs, or he notes the nests of the heron, of which there are several scattered colonies about the Broads, and one small heronry close by, at Surlingham. If he does not take the eggs, he waits until the young birds are nearly able to fly, and then secures them alive. Occasionally, too, he shoots an otter, which are plentiful enough on the Broads, making their 'hovers' in a beaver-like nest among the reeds.

"In the summer he goes eel-picking or spearing, or bobbing for eels at night with a ball of worms strung on worsted, by which means he takes large quantities. Then, when the tench sun themselves in the shallow water on hot still days, he 'tickles' them absolutely lifting them out of the water with his hands. The silly fish simply hide their heads in the weeds when they are disturbed, and ostrich-like imagine they are safe.

"With the 1st of August the wildfowl season opens and then for a day or two Rockland Broad becomes populous with visitors. Before midnight on the last day of July, gentle and simple, professional and amateur, come in boats and take up their position, waiting patiently until the dawn brings flight-time, when some lucky ones will get seven or eight ducks before the flight is over. After that, the coots and water-hens find the day an unlucky one for them. The whizzing of shot about the broad makes a nervous man feel uncomfortable. After the opening of the season, however, the professional has it pretty much his own way. In October the eels begin to move towards the estuary, and the eel-net is set across the dyke to catch them in its long 'poke' as they pour off the broad.

"Eel-picking is an art in which some men attain considerable skill. They move gently along in their boats until they see the 'blowing' of an eel, as the bubbles issuing from the mud are termed, and then they strike where the bubbles come from. They can distinguish between the blowing of a large or small eel, and tell both from the blowing of a tench. They do not often strike at random. A still, fine day, during hot weather, is the most suitable time for this sort of work. On such days the wherrymen seize the opportunity when their vessel nears the bank to plunge the spears into the mud, and so get a good many eels. The strokes of the spear are called 'jowles'. Sometimes an eel-picking match takes place on the broad, between two rival champions, under conditions such as the following: The match to be finished in two hours; each man to have thirty jowles, each time calling out, 'Here's a go!' first lifting the spear in the air to show that it is clear of eels, then making one stroke, and then lifting the spear clean out

Hickling Broad—once peat diggings

of the water. The stakes are a sovereign aside, and the match to be decided by numbers, not weight. Each picker has in his boat a mate of his rival's to see fair play, and a boat with two referees in it accompanies the match.

"Hanging up to dry by the eel-hut you will see numerous bundles of reeds, each the size of a rolling-pin, and tightly and neatly tied up. These are the Broadsman's 'liggers', or trimmers, which he sets for pike all over the broad. The line is rolled round the ligger with a foot or two free, and the double hook is baited with a roach. These are often set in water not a foot deep, and really do not seem to do much harm to angling. The pike are too numerous at present, and hence are very small. A friend of the writer's caught thirty with a spoon-bait one day in the river close by, nineteen of which had to be put back again. The liggering on Rockland, therefore, does not interfere with the pike-fishing in the river. There is too great a craze in Norfolk just now for preserving. The consequence is that the rivers are over-stocked; and the fish run short of food, and are necessarily small. People complain that they catch no large fish now as they used to do in the old days before netting in the river was abolished, but that they catch numbers of fingerlings. They have not yet learned that either you must have a medium stock of fish and large ones, or a teeming stock and small ones."

I have quoted these views of Christopher Davies on fish preservation at length because, to my mind he is absolutely right. Too much emphasis can too easily be placed on preservation. Netting if carried out within reason can be of great benefit to any fishery. Many small broads are over-stocked with little fish, half of which ought to be cleared out and taken elsewhere where they are needed.

A perfect example of this was provided in 1948 when Mr. Alan Savory netted a small area of his little private broad, an area of not more than one and a quarter acres. He took 110 fish, all of which were small; but many of the perch had very large heads. This was a clear case of too many fish with not enough food to feed on. Had the perch had more food their bodies would have matched their heads. One can sometimes see the same phenomenon when a very long thin pike with an enormous head is taken out of a remote pool of which he has been the solitary lord and master.

There is usually a bittern or two in the Rockland Fens and I understand that a marsh harrier nested in the neighbourhood in

5

Duck shooting before the Second World War

Crossing the Yare on the Reedham

1949, whilst the Montagu's harrier is a more or less regular nesting species. Marsh harriers turned up in quite considerable numbers on migration in the spring and autumn of 1948 and at least two bitterns were booming in mid-April.

V

WAVENEY—RIVER OF BEAUTY

And a Plan Which Can Ruin It

THE Waveney is a gentlemanly sort of river. Quiet, peaceful, lit with beauty, born in the deep heart of East Anglia, enriched by history and alive with birds and fish. It is a river for the artist, the angler and the small boat sailor who likes peace upon the waters. It has little or none of the garish gaiety of the Bure and the lower reaches of the Thurne. It remains, largely, unspoiled.

If, however, the proposed 'chalet village' for a thousand trippers, complete with motel—and no doubt bingo hall, bowling alley, dance hall, fish and chip bar and the rest of the trappings, becomes a fact at Beccles, the Waveney can say goodbye to its unique qualities of attraction. It will become as vulgar as the rest.

If you can get hold of a little book called *Waveney* by Lieut.-Colonel Granville Baker, which was published in 1934, it gives a perfect picture of this loveliest of Broadland rivers as it was and as it may soon cease to be. He describes its birth thus:

"The Waveney rises in a quiet, gentlemanly way, out of an attractive bed of reeds and rushes fenced about with hawthorn bushes, o'ertopped by groups of trees, oak, beech, birch, with here and there the sterner note of the pine (which) seems to watch it with friendly interest, no doubt recognizing that a well-conducted river is an undisguised blessing."

It is not the sort of river to rise in wrath, flood the countryside, drown the widows and orphans and bankrupt the farmers. It behaves itself. The Yare, the Bure and the Thurne have all done that sort of thing and no doubt will do it again.

On the Waveney, more than on any other river one knows, one can catch, in sudden visions of beauty, the space and light, the background of peace and the clear atmosphere which have been the secret of the Norwich School of Painters from 'Old Crome' to the present. Swift and sudden, nuances of sunlit greens, of translucent effect of light and wind and sun, with splashes of vivid colour that for a second of time rivals anything you may see on the Mediterranean.

In its wide river valleys with its bold and sudden changes of light, its shifting cloud masses, its chasing shadows, under the high sun and in the sea winds, there was born the genius of those great artists of the Norwich School whose works are like a peal of trumpets, a chime of bells, down the lofty aisles of pure art.

Crome and Cotman, Stannard and Freeman, Munnings and Arnesby Brown, Yeend King and Bertram Priestman, and now, in our own modern time, Edward Seago and Roland Green, have all caught the spirit of pure beauty and of good painting from its broad marshland rivers with its wide green marsh pastures, its cattle and horses knee-deep in meadow-sweet and kingcups, the willows blowing in the winds, and the skies—always the skies—those skies that are palettes of all the colours, of all the light and shade and vivid beauty of far distances, skies that are oceans of colour.

It would require the brush of an Algernon Newton to catch those incredible greens—green of emerald and green of moss, apple-green and sea-green which chased each other across the upland fields.

You can come at the Waveney from three different directions. First, you may begin at the beginning and enter this delectable river at its mouth where it debouches into Breydon Water, under the high bluff on which stand the mighty walls of that great Roman camp castle, Burgh Castle, of which, more in a moment. Or you can voyage to it from the Yare if you turn up the New Cut which leaves the Yare at Reedham, travels for three straight miles through the flat, Thurlton Marshes and joins the Waveney at St. Olaves, under the fir-clad Herringfleet Hills. There are the remains of an ancient abbey there and a good inn and various modern 'developments' which will please the man with a caravan mind and a shiny boat. Fortunately you can still escape from it. Thirdly, you can join the Waveney by sailing up from Oulton Broad at the back of Lowestoft where George Borrow once dwelt in peace and wrote his immortal English and where now hydroplanes make the daylight hours hideous. You escape them by going up Oulton Dyke which joins the Waveney a few miles upstream from St. Olaves.

Let us start from Breydon Water. First of all, go ashore, moor your boat and climb the steep and wooded scarp of the bluff on the top of which stands boldly the ghostly remains of the largest Roman walled camp castle in Britain. From that high vantage point you may gaze out, on a clear day, over almost the whole bright and glittering panorama of Broadland. From its massive walls, fifteen feet thick at the base and fifteen feet in height, built of flint and bastioned with towers, you will see shining rivers; white sails gliding above green marshes; windmills standing immobile as forgotten sentinels; brown acres of reed where the bittern creep; and, behind you, the gorse-yellow, fir-crowned line of the Herringfleet Hills.

At one's feet, immediately beneath the tree-clad scarp of the bluff on which stands boldly this ghostly castle, there lie purple saltings where the sea-lavender blooms, shining shallows where sheduck paddle and sandpipers whistle their thin song. And beyond, a few yards only, the hurrying waters of Waveney joint here with the broad deep stream of the Yare. The two widen immediately into Breydon Water and then, all to the east in a bright flash of silver, lies the glittering bosom of Breydon with, on the far skyline of the sea, the smoky chimneys, the huddled roofs, the masts and funnels of Yarmouth, ancient city of the herring fleets.

Burgh Castle was built about a hundred years after Christ was born. The Roman general, Publius Ostorius Scapula, is supposed to have been its architect and builder. Tactically it linked with those other Roman stations at Caister, Reedham, Burgh St. Peter and Tasburgh, each built at a strategic spot which could command the bays and inlets of Gariensis—the Roman name for Breydon.

Burgh was under the command of the Count of the Saxon Shore, that land-admiral whose Roman fortresses dominated the south-east coast from Porchester on Portsmouth Harbour to Brancaster on the Wash. It had three walls to the north, east and south with the river as its main defence on the west. Just over six acres lie within these walls today, an area 640 feet long and 413 feet wide. It was in fact a walled village, a cavalry station of the Stablesian Horse. Today the walls are fifteen feet thick at the bottom, about fifteen feet high and five feet wide at the top. They are built of flints, with towers or bastions at each corner and in the middle. Each wall is bonded by six tiers of narrow red Roman tiles, with seven tiers to each bastion. On the top of each bastion can be seen a depression in which was mounted, we assume, a ballista, or giant catapult, for casting great stone balls at the enemy. It is unlikely that the walls were ever very much higher, but it is probable that they were surmounted by a wooden gangway with protecting wooden walls behind which the archers and spearmen, the slingers and javelin-throwers could stand in safety and hurl their missiles at the enemy.

I have said that the river was the main western defence but there is no doubt that some sort of a western wall existed and has now vanished. Harrod, the eminent Victorian archaeologist, who excavated here in 1850 and 1855, found traces of a western wall 200 feet long or more. He also found oak piles which had been driven into the marshy ground on the west, and remains of two guard-houses which had existed on either side of the main gateway which was in the centre of the east wall. That gateway was only eleven feet eight inches wide, just the width for a chariot to pass through. Today it is a mere gap in the walls. Two other posterns, each five feet wide, can be traced in the centre of the north and south wall. Mr. Harrod also found remains of what probably was a bath house, sixteen and a half feet square.

I know few places where, in the quiet of a moonlit night, one can recapture the sense of past centuries so vividly as in this walled castle. Stand within its grey and glimmering walls on a summer night or under the chill moon of winter when the owls call, the curlew whistle like spectres on the mudflats and the otter moves stealthily in the reeds and it is easy to imagine the stir and hum of the Roman camp, the clink of armour, the stamp and snuffle of war-horses, to see the dancing flicker of camp fires and to hear the lusty Roman choruses sung by men who had campaigned under every moon in Europe from the Tiber to the far, grey rampart of Hadrian's Wall.

Long after the splendour of Rome had faded and the Saxon king Sigebert ruled East Anglia, an Irish monk, Furseus the Hermit, took possession of the Roman ruins and built within its walls a monastery to the Glory of God. It may have been little more than a one-storey place of clay lump walls, reed-thatched, with an altar. None of it remains. Palgrave, the historian, says: "Furseus, who had the poetic temperament, when darkness came on would sit and brood in his cell at Burgh Castle over the doings of angels, the joys of the blessed, and the conflict of evil spirits for the souls of men. These imaginings by the side of the Waveney were destined to bear wonderful fruit, for they kindled the spark which occasioned the first of the metrical compositions from whose combinations, centuries later, the *Divina Commedia* of Dante arose."

Today, the bronze eagles no longer swing in the van of clanking phalanxes over the lip of the corn-golden upland. The long galleys sail no more upon the Breydon tides. The trumpet blasts are stilled. The armourers' hammers clang only in dreams. And Furseus, the silent monk, is but a brown, forgotten moth in the grey and ghostly alleys of Early Christian history.

Beneath the empty walls of the dreaming castle the sea-going cargo boats from Norwich rusty and salt-stained, thud across the bosom of Breydon, throwing up a rolling creamy wash which year in, year out, scours away the mounting mud that is slowly, inexorably swallowing up the salt waters of Breydon. White-sailed yachts pass like butterflies beneath the silent castle walls. The wherries still ply upon their trading occasions. And under the moons of winter and in the grey dawns the fowlers sprit like sliding shadows over the mud-flats. Their big guns boom over the estuary. Curlew cry and the wild geese flight over in clanging multitudes. The castle stands silent, a place of ghosts. Alone the kestrel hovers where the eagles of Rome flew in brazen triumph.

Burgh Castle is the proper sort of introduction to the Waveney for the river is rich in history on almost every mile. St. Edmund the King and Martyr, hid, they say, among the reed-beds of the lower Waveney marshes for weeks on end, hunted by the Danes. Burgh St. Peter Church has a tower red-brick ancient and telescopic, unlike any other church tower in England. They will tell you that the whole thing shuts up like a telescope the moment the yachting season comes to an end and pops out again with the first flicker of a burgee in spring. The whole area is full of ancient farmhouses, many of them moated, from Wade Hall, with its memories of St. Edmund, to Wheatacre Hall, Aldeby Priory standing on its little hump of rising ground above the Haddiscoe Marshes which for years were the subject of successive pictures in the Royal Academy. Sail up the river to Beccles and you sail through a land of marshes and woods, of buttercup-yellow fields and uplands bright with corn. Beccles stands on a hill and commands river and marsh. A town with fine houses of Georgian and Queen Anne, cottages and inns that were built in Tudor times and a church that was begun in 1455. These old houses of Beccles stand in bee-murmurous gardens which slope to the shining river. They preserve the peace and tranquil beauty of a more civilized England which built to please the eye and not for mere cheapness sake. Even the streets of Beccles have an embattled, robust quality for there are Blyburgate, Ingate, Hungate, Northgate, Smallgate, Saltgate, and others which give the authentic flavour of a once-walled and defended town. If the plan to create a new, large 'chalet village' near Beccles goes through, the whole of this river can be so popularized that it will be vulgarized and ruined. One such development can lead to another. The plan must be stopped. It is the prelude to spoliation of the loveliest river in Broadland.

Nowadays it is a town of anglers and men who live by corn and cattle. It has its own Town Fen where in Tudor times, more than once the burghers of Beccles fought bloodily with the armed retainers of the Rede Family, who claimed to have a grant of the fen whereas the townsfolk maintained they had free rights on it.

Some years ago that charming and erudite B.B.C. broadcaster, Wynford Vaughan Thomas, went for a cruise up the Waveney in that splendid old Edwardian yacht *Enchantress* in which King Edward VII had entertained the lighter ladies of his Court. Our business was to broadcast for a week in the Norfolk Broads Week which was organized for the first time by my old friend, Godfrey Baseley, of Midland Region, whose genius since then has produced 'The Archers' programme. Wynford paid the most spontaneous and charming compliment to Beccles as our Edwardian craft swished silkily under the bridge and, in the setting sun, we saw the peaked gables of Tudor houses, the bland red-brick façades of Queen Anne mansions and the white gracious windows of Georgian houses huddled in the most orderly confusion above green lawns and walled gardens which sloped down to Victorian boat-houses and discreet little landing stages built assuredly for small, shy feet hid beneath crinolines.

"That," said Wynford quietly, "makes me believe that England still is England."

We spent a jolly evening of discreet revelry in the low, beamed bar of 'The Cambridge Inn', where the talk was all of duck shooting and coursing matches, of yachting and of angling, for at Beccles they caught a pike of twenty six and a half pounds a year or two ago while several of over twenty pounds have been taken at intervals.

Next morning, while the mist was still on the low marshes that lie on either side of the causeway road from Beccles to Gillingham, I walked to Gillingham to look at the Hall, for it is a house of some note. It was built by the first Sir Nicholas Bacon, the Lord Keeper, who was premier baronet of England.

Gillingham Hall is a medium-sized Elizabethan house with an excellent frontage, and typical cupola-topped towers, set in a grove of stately trees, with its back to the marshes and its face to the causeway or 'Carnsey'.

Along this straight causeway for many years rattled the Yarmouth to London coach driven by that first-rate coachman and natural gentleman, the late Will Salter, who lies buried by Haddiscoe church, whose round tower rises above the marshes a few miles away.

Salter was a real horseman and horse-lover, one of the sort whom we in East Anglia call a 'horse-gentler'. Such men do not 'break' horses. They 'gentle' them. There is a world of meaning and of difference between the two methods. His epitaph in Haddiscoe church, ingenuous but charming, tells the manner of the man.

> True to his business and his trust,
> Always punctual, always just,
> His horses could they speak, would tell
> They lov'd their good old master well.
> His up-hill work is chiefly done;
> His stage is ended—race is run.
> One journey is remaining still,—
> To climb up Zion's holy hill.
> And now his faults are all forgiv'n
> Elijah-like drives up to heav'n;
> Takes the reward for all his pains,
> And leaves to other hands the reins.

About three miles from Gillingham by the road to the left is the ancient hall of Kirby Cane, standing a hundred feet above sea level. Rising from the moat, starred with water lilies, the old Hall, with its mullioned windows, tall chimneys, ancient brickwork and climbing roses, is a picture and a poem of ancient peace. The yew hedges, the grass walks, and the gardens drenched in lilies, sentinelled by sunflowers and sharp-tanged with sage and rue, hyssop and mint, make a setting of colour and scent to a house all too little known but far too lovely and peaceful to miss.

Two other houses in the neighbourhood are worth visiting; the first, Geldeston Hall, where lives General Sir Francis Lloyd, and the second, Hales Old Hall, a mile or two away, the old home of Attorney-General Hobart. The remains of that moated mansion are picturesque in the extreme whilst Hales Green, as Dutt has said, "is a little bit of rural England of the past—of England as it was in the days of the highwaymen, of stagecoaches and romance of the road, of almost impassable byroads, and of rural isolation."

Just outside Beccles is one of the most enchanting small Elizabethan mansions in the whole of East Anglia, Roos Hall. Its twisted chimneys, red-brick gables and high mullioned windows overlook cattle-dappled meadows. It rises tall and rose-red, small and infinitely beautiful, against a frieze of grey-green willows. This little manor house with its mullioned windows, crowstepped gables, graceful corner turrets, and twisted chimneys was built in the heyday of Elizabethan architecture. Two centuries before the first brick was laid, Sir William de Roos, Lord of this ancient Manor, fought at the battle of Caerlaverock with such fire and courage that Edward I made him his Knight Banneret.

Not far from this pearl of a house stands the ancient roundtowered, reed-thatched church and the old rectory of Barsham. There in the Jacobean rectory was born Catherine Suckling, the mother of Nelson. She and her husband, Edmund Nelson, were married in St. Michael's Church at Beccles. There have been Sucklings at Barsham for many hundreds of years, but alas, I hear that Barsham Hall, their ancient moated house which stood amidst the marshes is down, demolished, like so many other fine English homes for which the arid creed of Socialism has no use.

In Barsham church is a memorial to a fourteenth-century knight of no small renown, Sir Robert Atte Tye who, on his death bed, raised himself and with his last breath said: "I command that you, my friends and children, shall drink four dozen bottles of wine over my coffin before the earth is thrown upon it." On which excellent gesture he expired.

All this reach of the Waveney is rich in history. Great and ancient names ring down the centuries like trumpet blasts—de Vaux, de Barsham, de Roos, Blennerhasset, Suckling and Nelson. But surely the most ancient of all was that standard bearer of the Tenth Legion, whose portrait, showing him leaping into the sea to lead Roman soldiers to attack the Britons, was engraved on a gold ring which a woman found when she was weeding a field on Barsham Hall Farm, about 120 years ago. Suckling, the historian, acquired the ring and it is, I believe, with his descendants today.

Beyond Roos Hall the woods of Dunburgh Hill come down to the river and beyond them the scarp of Bigods Hill. Here you have a combination of Danish and Norman for Hugh Bigod, Earl of Norfolk and Lord of Bungay Castle owned 200 manors in Norfolk and was powerful enough to revolt against King Stephen and against Henry II. The remains of his castle at Bungay, higher up the river are well worth visiting.

Geldeston village is charming. Beyond it and round a bend the river opens up into a willow shaded idyllic reach of reed-bordered waters which end at the moss-covered timbers of Geldeston Lock. Now Geldeston Lock is a place of fauns and dryads. It is "far from the madding crowd" in a true and most Victorian sense. Time passes it by and even the motor-car must halt. Here is an island, an island of peace and reeds where the reed-warblers swing and chatter. An island of willows where the pigeons coo, and of May bushes where the cuckoo flirts his tail. An island, too, which has ducks asleep upon its grassy banks, the stealthy stir of an otter in its reed-bed, the springtime drumming of snipe in ecstasy above the surrounding marshes—marshes, flat and emerald, that surround this willow-shaded little paradise like a green sea on which move slow cattle. There is a house, small and old, secret and independent, set upon this island, a house where once dwelt the miller when the waters of Waveney turned the great wheel of the vanished mill. Today it is an inn.

In that inn you may hear many tales. First they tell you of the eel-catcher who murdered his sweetheart, put the body in a sack, weighted it with stones and dumped it in the mouth of a dyke which joins the main river. He had record catches of eels for months afterwards. The story only came out when his nephew, to whom he had bequeathed the secret got drunk in the Kings Arms at Beccles and boasted. The man who told me that macabre tale pointed across the river and went on: "That's the old Shipmeadow over there where they used to have the prize fights in the old days. Many a big turn-up with bare fists they've had on this island in the Corinthian days. You see, if the Norfolk police came after them they could just hop over the river into Suffolk and if the Suffolk coppers were on their track, well, they just hopped back across the mill-stream into Norfolk! It's seen some funny things going on in its time, this old lock house—prize fighters, smugglers, poachers and Lord knows what. There were always plenty of poachers up this old river."

Geldeston is out of this world. In winter it is doubly out of it, for I have been there when you could only reach the Lock Inn from the village by boat. The marshes were a sea of flood waters.

You cannot, unless you have a canoe or a duck-punt which you can haul out of the river and carry round the lock, go beyond Geldeston Lock. It cuts off the upper waters of the Waveney. If the plan to open up the river to Bungay is proceeded with, it will undoubtedly add several miles of enchanting waterway, but one shudders to think how easily the peace and beauty of this comparatively unspoilt river could be ruined if it becomes too popular and too commercialized.

Nonetheless, the upper waters of the Waveney are wide open to the man with a small boat who has the initiative to launch it just beyond Geldeston Lock and go on his ways. The old enchanting town of Bungay, with its castle, the famous Outney Common which lies within a loop of the river, and has seen rumbustious race meetings; memories of the gypsies at Bungay Horse Fair whom Alfred Munnings immortalized in pictures which will live as part of the English tradition. Above Bungay is Ditchingham Hall where Rider Haggard lived for many years and wrote not only many of his novels, but that little known book *A Farmer's Year* which is a perfect, day by day diary of his life as a gentleman farmer in this enchanting valley, when the plough team was still a fresco of beauty on the upland fields. There too you will find the cottage in which dwelt that grand old man 'The King of the Norfolk Poachers' whom Lilias Rider Haggard has described superbly in those two sagas of country life *I Walked by Night* and *The Rabbit Skin Cat*.

Bungay also has the Black Dog, who is supposed to haunt certain lanes thereabouts and is the devil on four legs. The last time he was definitely seen was on Sunday, 4th August, 1577, when, during a frightful storm, the Black Dog suddenly appeared in the church of St. Mary at Bungay "running all along down the body of the church with great swiftnesse and incredible haste among the people, in a visible fourm and shape, passed between two persons, as they were kneeling uppon their knees, and occupied in prayer as it seemed, wrung the necks of them bothe at one instant clene backward, insomuch that even at a moment where they kneeled they strangely dyed." It was said of a hardened sinner that he could no more blush than the Black Dog of Bungay.

This Black Dog, like 'Old Shuck', who haunts the cliff paths between Sheringham and Cromer, and Old Scarp, who haunts Southtown Road in Yarmouth, is merely a legendary survival of the Danish sea-rovers' Black Hound of Thor. A similar animal, "as large as a calf and with eyes like saucers", haunts a few inland Norfolk villages, where he is known for some odd reason unexplained as 'Owd Rugusan'.

Not a lot remains of Bungay Castle, but there are two fine, round, stout towers and considerable portions of the walls still left. Three sides of the castle walls remain, varying in height from fifteen to seventeen feet and in thickness from six feet to eleven feet. The dark shaft in the centre of the castle mound was never a dungeon, but was much more probably the bottom of a well.

Hugh Bigod was the most turbulent of all this warlike family. He rebelled against King Stephen in 1170 and his castle was taken from him. He regained it a year or two later, but when Henry II succeeded he had most of it destroyed. Bigod rebuilt it in 1163, and again most of it was destroyed in 1174, when, after another revolt, all his estates were taken from him. Richard I restored them to Roger Bigod, and in 1294 Edward I granted another Roger, fifth Earl of Norfolk, leave to fortify the present castle.

The man of adventure in his canoe, duck-punt or small double ended shallow-draught Norfolk marsh boat, can push upstream beyond Bungay, past the great park of Flixton. When I used to shoot there, twenty years ago, the Elizabethan Hall of the Adairs stood in many windowed splendour with herds of glancing deer to lighten the scene. Now the estate, which once covered 15,000 acres is split up, the hall demolished, the deer have gone and the beneficient influence of a family who were good squires for centuries has vanished. This is called progress.

Beyond Flixton is the charming little village of Homersfield. Then comes Wortwell and then Mendham and beyond that, the road bridge which leads you up to Harleston where I recommend The Magpies as a first-class hotel. The river runs on to Brockdish and beyond that I doubt if you could go. It is all a land of peace, of corn and woods and grazing cattle with villages of thatched houses and moated farms, with the heron fishing like a silver-grey ghost in the shallows, reed-warblers reeling their thin song in the summer dusk and swallows dipping on the stream. The land of water lilies, of tasseled reeds, where, so far, pollution is unknown. For how long?

VI

THE BURE AND ITS BROADS

Ghosts, Bird Sanctuaries, Big Fish and Pollution

". . . A REEDY river, fifty feet wide with a maximum depth of four feet, and it was bung full of houseboats, motor-boats, swans, lounge lizards, presumably male, and a giggling crowd of near-nudes, most obviously female. Harris's boat was moored to a petrol pump and her name was *Perfect Lady*. She looked to me like a perfect bitch because she had (a) a fifty-foot mast in a tabernacle and no preventer backstays, (b) a maximum draft of two feet with six feet six inches minimum headroom, (c) she was painted pink with chromium fittings, (d) her cockpit was full of silk cushions."

This is Wroxham. Wroxham is the capital of Broadland. *Perfect Lady* is a thirty-five-foot Bermuda sloop, with four spring beds and a pressure gas cooker. A good type of a Broadland sailing yacht.

The words which introduce this little picture are not mine. They are the winged wisdom of Mr. Weston Martyr, an internationally famous yachtsman, who has won all sorts of deep sea races, in the dirtiest of seas and the filthiest of weather. His immortal book *The £100 Millionaire*, if you can get hold of it, will make you chuck up your job, throw your bowler hat over the yardarm, desert your wife, shoot your mother-in-law and go to sea with the office cash, embezzled in toto. Weston Martyr is also an archer of national fame. A toxopholite who draws the long bow.

He was not drawing the long bow when he described Wroxham in the unflattering words which I quote from that endearing anthology of sailing *Down the Wind* by Jack H. Coote.

Weston Martyr went to the Broads with a deep-sea sailor's scornful foreboding. He was bribed to do so, by the promise of a jar of Navy rum, a case of pre-war gin and a Suffolk cured ham of indecent proportions.

He sailed from Wroxham with his nose in the air. Within minutes he had rammed "a gold-plated houseboat heavily laden with blondes". The international ace, standing superbly at the tiller of the *Perfect Lady* then "carried away her radio mast and a string of Chinese lanterns". The owner of the boat roared down the river at him: "Why didn't you bring your nurse."

The deep-sea-dog cocked his nose more snootily and swore to "sail her out of here or bust". He did. His sea experience had not taught him "that one cannot pass a fifty-foot mast beneath the overhanging branch of a forty-five foot tree". Meekly, he said: "I hadn't seen the darn thing anyhow." His two shipmates there-upon, as he records: "quanted us to hell out of there. I was glad . . . because there was a sound in my ears as of a herd of plastered jackasses hee-hawing. It was those despised Broads boys and girls laughing." They made three miles in the next three hours. Then they had to heave to to let the jib sheets cool. They were red hot.

"If you do not believe this," says Weston Martyr stoutly, "try working a thirty-five-foot skimming dish with no keel along a fifty-foot wide river around whose every bend the wind keeps dead ahead. During those three hours we tacked ship every nine seconds, or well over a thousand times. And if the Bermuda or Fastnet courses can provide any tougher job than that, I am glad to have missed it. I also understand now, fully, why Broads yachtsmen managed to get along without preventer backstays."

Later in the day Mr. Weston Martyr, who thinks much the same of motor yachts and motor-boats as I do, kept one of them waiting for quite a long time, whilst he insisted on trying to tack the *Perfect Lady* across his bows. Finally decency got the better of obstinacy and he let the motor-boat pass. The latter, being a per-fect gentleman, quietly pointed out that the next reach was three miles long, full of mosquitoes, the wind dead ahead and it was coming on dark, so would he please accept a tow to the next broad which had a decent pub and no mosquitoes. Mr. Martyr accepted. Moreover he admitted to his two sailing buddies "the man's a sailor and a gentleman, dammit! And I've been going about for years saying all motor-boatists were no-sailors and cads".

A day or two later our Mr. Martyr challenged an elderly gent

Charlie Gibbs, one of the last of the old Broadland fishermen and fowlers

A grown-up Broad on the Yare

to a race, since the latter was sailing the twin of *Perfect Lady*. The elderly gent had never sailed anywhere except on the Broads, whereas Mr. Martyr, has, as all the world knows, sailed in the Fastnet Race, the Harwich-Hook of Holland and all the other acts of deep-sea martyrdom in which the Royal Ocean Racing Club gang indulge. The old gent beat the deep-sea wizard by fifteen minutes.

Mr. Martyr is now a changed man who no longer says "I spit on the Broads! I wouldn't be seen dead there." The moral of this little tale, which, incidentally is true, is that Broads sailing is an art in itself, peculiar to its surroundings and made more difficult by all the things which this present scribe, no great shakes as a yachtsman anyway, heartily dislikes, e.g. gold painted houseboats, lounge lizards, giggling blondes, radio masts and Chinese lanterns. You get the lot at Wroxham. You will find a heavy backwash of them at Horning. And not a few scattered up and down the rest of the Bure between Coltishall and Yarmouth.

That does not alter the fact that there are some remarkably fine small-boat sailors among them and that nobody but a very good small-boat sailor can hope to sail either the Bure, the Thurne or what that eminent lawyer, Mr. Peter Carter-Ruck, another deep-sea man of no little fame, has described as "the antiferous waters of the Ant". He learnt to sail on the Ant. Now he is pretty well in the Weston Martyr class.

The Bure rises deep in the heart of Norfolk, beyond Blickling Hall, that superb Jacobean home of Anne Boleyn, which no intelligent visitor to the Broads should miss seeing. I have slept in it, but never saw her ghost walk which is not surprising because the present house was rebuilt after her death.

Those headwaters of the Bure are small, sweet, full of trout, jealously guarded by a fly-fishing club and, like so many other English rivers, rich in the colours of history. The river flows by the last ruins and inhabited remains of Oxnead Hall where dwelt the Pastons and by Little Hautboys and so down to Horstead Mill at Coltishall, which was a perfect poem of beauty until it was burnt down in 1966. Coltishall marks the end of the cruising waters of the Bure so far as they are open to fairly large boats. Above Coltishall you must go, as you would go on the headwaters of the Waveney, in a canoe or a small sailing dinghy, or better still a duck-punt which will float in the dew on the grass.

The reaches between Wroxham and Coltishall are rural and

6

pretty-pretty. First there is Bridge Broad, below the railway bridge at Wroxham which is neither town nor country but a bit of both. Then you come to Belaugh Broad rapidly growing up, small but pretty and after that the wooded bluffs and steep little hills which they call 'Little Switzerland'. Belaugh is a fascinating riverside village and indeed all these twists and bends of the river up to Coltishall are more reminiscent of the Thames than the flat marshes and reedy fens of so much of Broadland. So you may regard this stretch of the river from Wroxham to Coltishall as ideal for a family party with Aunt Jane included.

Wroxham itself is a little Venice of trim thatched bungalows, straight dykes arched with willows, endless boat docks and a great and lovely broad just down the river. Old Mr. Loynes, who had a mighty great spade beard, a patriarchal figure and built good boats, was the father and the beginner of Wroxham. He went there in 1878 and started the business which was the pioneer of Broadland boat-building. He died at the age of ninety-six having worn a yachting cap from dawn to dusk on each day of the year. They will tell you in Norfolk that the Loynes family came over with the Vikings. I do not doubt it. His son carries on the tradition.

Wroxham is also notable for that amazing village store known as Roys which claims to be "the world's largest village store". There is also Mr. Jack Powles, a boat builder of note, a mighty man with a gun and a good chap to know. I have happy memories also of the Broads Hotel at Wroxham for they gave us a hot bath, a hot dinner and a warm welcome on a bitter night in mid-winter when other men and women had spurned us elsewhere.

Wroxham owes a good deal to Major S. W. Trafford of Wroxham Hall for he threw open the whole noble expanse of Wroxham Broad to the public, whereas a previous owner Parson Blake-Humfrey, had the place chained off and forbidden to all boats. Wroxham is an ideal broad for sailing with a well-run yacht club, first-class fishing and charmingly wooded surroundings. The trouble is that too many people go there. Personally, I prefer Wroxham or, indeed, any other broad in autumn after the first sharp frosts have sent the majority of the 'water-hikers' home and have turned the reed-beds and marshland levels into seas of glowing colour, orange and rusty red, yellow and gold. Sometimes in winter one has seen hundreds of wild duck rise from the empty waters of Wroxham where, on a busy weekend in summer, a moorhen dare hardly show its beak.

Nonetheless, if you want to sail a boat in well-conducted races, Wroxham is the place and if you want to stock your boat with anything from cigars to caviare, from butcher's meat to children's clothes, the ingenious Mr. Roy will have the answer.

Downstream, below Wroxham Broad on the left, lies Hoveton Great Broad to part of which the owner Captain T. C. R. Blofield allows access. Most of the broads and marshes here are a Nature Reserve but the angler has a good chance of catching a good twenty pike.

Opposite Hoveton Great Broad is that charming little piece of water Salhouse Broad, quite idyllically pretty. Parklike meadows rise in a green slope from one end whilst the other end is shadowed by a tapestry of wood. Salhouse Hall in a park near the church has a fifteenth-century door, whilst the church tower is 600 years old, the font is medieval and the stone coffins under the tower are 700 years old. You can catch good rudd on the fly in Salhouse Broad, so one way and another Salhouse offers everything for the angler, archaeologist and artist.

The Rising Sun is a pleasant inn where you will hear local talk worth listening to and country common sense. It was there that I heard the immortal story of that famous old yacht skipper, 'Shucksher' Moore.

"He was a rum owd boy. He could drink a brewery dry and fight a rigiment o' Grenadiers. He come home one night, half-seas over, an' see the old double-handed pump standin' in his yard in the moonlight.

"Shucksher orf with his jacket, puts up his fists, squares up to this owd pump, and says: 'Now, yer b——. I'er got yer where I want yer. I'll tan the bloody hide orf yer!' And he lets drive with both fists."

"What happened?" asked the landlord.

"Happened! He damn nearly bruk both fists, skinned his knuckles raw, and lets fly agin. 'Hit me! Yer would, would yer? yer rotten hodmedod!' he yells. And he pasted that owd pump till the neighbours come out and hauled him orf!

"Ha! A rum owd bor he was. He went in the owd steam-boat *Vivid* to Wroxham regatta one day. Full o' beer he was. The owd *Vivid* was chuggin' along, keepin' a steady course, when Shucksher yells out to the engine-man:

" 'This ain't no pace! Shove 'er along! Bung on the coal, bor, hot up yar bilers—I'll keep the bloody steam in!'

"And he wops himself down, starn fust, on the steam safety-valve, and sot there though that nearly scorched the hide orf him. Lor! That owd steam-boat she shot round and round in a circle like one o'clock till they hauled him orf."

Coltishall is a long straggling village with a good hotel called The Anchor, an equally good boatyard, a noble church which greets you with a skull and crossbones in stone on its entrance gate, several delectable inns, one of which bears the unusual sign of The Recruiting Sergeant—a bibulous warrior in a three-cornered lace hat of Waterloo vintage with a pint pot in one hand and a dirty leer on his face.

There are some Carolean houses in Coltishall, a common dappled with donkeys and geese, the legend of a thirty-two-pound pike caught in the river and a bridge over the river which has its own particular up-to-date legend.

About 1933 I helped my friend, Malcolm Freegard, that scholarly B.B.C. producer, who from Norwich has put out many excellent Norfolk programmes, to produce a programme on East Anglian ghosts and witches, entitled 'The Dark Shore'. Black Shuck, the ghostly hound of Odin, who is said to haunt so many miles of East Anglian coast and elsewhere, naturally figured large in the programme. Old legends of him were legion.

Lo, who should turn up but a respectable middle-aged man of Coltishall with his 'young lady', equally respectable and middle-aged. Both had been 'walking-out' one fine evening, as had been their wont for many years. They crossed Coltishall Bridge. As they were walking over it they were conscious that something followed them. He stopped to strike a match to light her cigarette. At that instant, Black Shuck "as big as a calf and as noiseless as death" passed them by within a foot. They had no doubt whatsoever that it *was* Black Shuck.

Oddly enough, a young farmer from the Sheringham area turned up on the same programme to say, quite flatly, that he too had seen Black Shuck cross the road in front of him. He had not only crossed the road but had gone clean through a five-barred gate. And it was in the clear light of a summer evening. None of these three people were in the slightest degree neurotic, nervy or, one would have said, particularly imaginative. They were just plain common sense citizens. Make what you like of that.

If you like good old houses, there are several in the village. Old House *c.* 1710–20; the Limes, a really splendid house dated

1692; Hazelwood, 1766; and Coltishall Hall, *c.* 1700. There are many lesser good houses, mainly in eighteenth-century brick. Horstead House *c.* 1620. Horstead Hall *c.* 1835 and Heggatt Hall part Tudor, are nearby.

Down river through marshes, by woods, by shock-headed willows and through flat fens you come to Horning. Now all this right bank of the river is part of the Woodbastwick estate of some 9,000 acres which belongs to the Cator family—good landlords, good naturalists, preservers of wild birds, and adored by their tenantry. This great estate includes Decoy Broad, Cockshoot Broad, Ranworth Broad, Malthouse Broad and the whole of the Ranworth fens and marshes which are dotted with a large number of small pools and 'pulks'. Much of it has been declared a Nature Reserve and it is indeed one of the most important wild life sanctuaries in the Kingdom. Here bitterns, marsh harriers, hen harriers, ruffs and reeves, the occasional osprey, rare waders and it may even be that most enchanting of all, the avocet, delicate as porcelain, are sure of a home and a safe resting place.

Ranworth Great Broad and Malthouse Broad are open to the public. Ranworth Inner Broad is preserved for bird life but fishing is allowed by permit. A few years ago, when it was thrown open to the public, the usual hooligans ruined everything for everyone else by robbing the nests of rare birds. So permission was withdrawn. That is the sort of thing which happens too often. The pretty little Maltsters' Broad, with an inn, a green and grassy landing-stage, a boat dock and a colony of 'wild' ducks so tame that they eat out of one's hand is a favourite place to anchor for the night or for a day or two.

If you do so, walk up the village street to Ranworth church. The man who misses seeing this superb church, the loveliest in the whole of Broadland, has missed something in this life. It possesses a unique treasure in the shape of the famous Ranworth Missal or Sarum Antiphoner, a superbly illuminated book of early medieval workmanship. I doubt if it is surpassed by any similar work in England other than the Luttrell Psalter. The church contains a painted screen of incredible beauty, which has been described as "suggestive of a great initial page of some splendidly illuminated manuscript". The paintings are said to have been the work of German members of the School of Meister Wilhelm of Cologne, who settled in Norwich during the fifteenth century at a time when this church was building.

Ranworth church has been well restored within recent years. It owes much of its stately beauty to the generosity of Flemish weavers who had a colony in the village more than 400 years ago. There is an attractive Elizabethan manor-house in the village, many charming old cottages and a parson who is justly proud of his lovely church and its Missal. The Missal, incidentally, was written by the monks of Langley Abbey and consists of 285 pages of sheepskin illustrated by twenty brilliant pictures coloured with vegetable dyes and gold leaf. It was stolen in the reign of Henry VI and was lost until about 1850, when a collector bought it for fifty guineas. At his death it came into the possession of a Bond Street bookseller, who asked the vicar £500 for it. The sum was raised within eighteen months. The Missal and the painted screen between them attract as many as 20,000 people in a year to the church.

The ghost of a monk, the man who painted the Ranworth screen is said to row up Ranworth Dyke at night in a boat of medieval design with the friendly spectre of his little dog sitting beside him. Ranworth is indeed a village of ghosts. First and worst is Colonel the Hon. Thomas Sidney, who, on 31st December, 1770, is said to have been kidnapped by the Devil, who threw him over the pommel of his saddle on a seventeen-hand ghostly hunter and then galloped madly across the broad, each hoof-mark on the water raising a jet of steam! This ghastly steeplechase takes place each year at midnight on the last day of the year, for those who have eyes to see.

Then there is the 'whistling' ghost, in a certain house which shall be nameless, but which my friend, Mr. Alan Savory, declares he has heard.

The Ranworth Fens where the late King George VI spent some of the happiest days of his life duck-shooting at dawn and dusk, were for long feared as the home of Wills o' Wisp or Jack o' Lanterns which were said to "haunt these marshes and torment homeward bound farmers, knocking them down and dismounting them".

I suppose I am one of the few people who has seen a Will o' the Wisp. They were common on hot midsummer nights, on my own drowned fen, known as Adventurers' Fen in the parish of Burwell in Cambridgeshire—bubbles of marsh gas which rise to the surface of the water, burst, immediately ignite and then float airily and crazily over the deeper rotten bogs. Those who have followed them have obviously met an uncommonly unpleasant death. Hence the superstition which has grown up round them.

The Horning and Ranworth farmers who were 'dismounted' by them a century ago had clearly made a night of it at the Horning Ferry Inn, and fell off their horses with fright or were thrown when the animals reared on their hind-legs as any horse would do if one put a ball of fire under its nose. I like much better the story of the Horning Donkey, told by Suffling in *The Innocents on the Broads*, to wit:

"I can't say as I've seen a human ghost, but I have seen the Horning ghost in the Long Lane—that's the ghost of a dickey (donkey) yer know.

"I wuz coming from Walsham one night in the winter time, and I don't know how it wuz, but suthin' fare tu say to me—'Look behind'.

"Well, I must, fule like, look roun', 'cause I fancied I could hear sumthin' go clickerty click, clickerty click, behind me. Sure nuff there came a white dickey lopin' along the road, all alone. I felt a bit scart and my old hobby pricked up har lugs as much as to say 'Hello, hu's this a follerin' me?' Presently I pulled up short like and the white dickey he pull up tu. Then when I go on, he go on, and we'en I stop, he stop. So thinks I, yew ain't no ghost anyhow. Then a bright idea cum inter me hid. 'I'll go back and see whose donkey 'tis.'

"So I tarned round and back I go, and when I'd got almost up to the white dickey who stud right in the middle o' the road facin' me, my old hobby stopped short and nearly hulled me outer the cart. Poor ole girl she whinney'd wi' fright and roun' she came of her own accord and along the lane she go as hard as she could clap her fower huffs to the ground.

"But it worn't no use; this here white dickey sune began to shorten the distance and every time I looked roun' it wuz nigher. Lord, I felt all of a muck sweat and I know me eyeballs stood out so that any one might ha' chopped 'em out wi' a hook. Closer it cum, and close; an' when I looked roun' again, it wuz just behin' with smoke comin' outer its nosterels like out of a furnace, and I du believe there wuz a little pink flame with it, but thet I ain't sure about, cuz I wuz upset. But this I du know the smell o' sulphur was right powerful.

"I pulled old Cally—short for California—inter the deek (dyke) and past came this here white dickey and sure nuff it wuz a ghost arter all, for I could see every bar of a gate by the rodeside rite trew its maizey body.

"My ha'r must 'av' riz on me hid, for orf went me hat. Away went the dickey up the Long Lane leading past the church to the village, and away went old Cally arter it, full tare, and think's I wot's agoen to happen nixt.

"Why it came to an ind like a flash. When the dickey come to the churchyard wall it plumped trew jest as easy as I could poke my finger trew a pat of butter and wot's more it didn't distarb a single stoon of the thick wall.

"Yew may laff, but nex' mornin' when I went ter look for my hat—'cause I dussen't goo back that night—I took a good view o' the churchyard wall, and there worn't a hole in it nowhere, and not a single print of a dickey's huff in the roadway."

Horning village, just across the river from Ranworth is notable for big fish, bigger fish-liars and the Swan Hotel which had and I hope still has a collection of stuffed fish which confound even the local liars. There is a thirteenth-century church of some distinction whilst the barn at Horning Hall was the medieval chapel of the vanished 'Hospital of St. James'. The village itself is an architectural chaos of conflicting styles. There are lovely local cottages with the simple beauty of Norfolk flint and thatch. Then you come across the most banal suburban villas which would be suited to the outskirts of Birmingham or Coventry. I suspect that retired Midlanders who have always had a hankering for the Broads, live in some of them.

The river here is polluted, not only by oil and sewage from boats, but as Dr. Hoather rightly reports, by "the highly polluted dyke passing behind the hotel" at Horning Ferry "and receiving its sewage effluent". There he found "an objectionable sewage odour from the water". Nothing would induce me to bathe in the river at Horning. The Nature Conservancy also draws attention to the nuisance of "sewage effluents from river craft, houseboats and riverside dwellings . . . between Wroxham and Horning". You have been warned. The highly picturesque Horning Ferry Inn was bombed and almost entirely destroyed during the war, but it has arisen Phoenix-like from its ashes and is as popular as ever. The owner told me that the older part of the inn still left standing is haunted by the ghost of a monk which has been seen several times by himself and others. Could this be Pacificus, the monk who redecorated Ranworth rood screen in 1538 and, as I have said elsewhere, rows up the Dyke in summer with his ghostly little dog beside him.

Those stuffed fish in the Swan Hotel provoked a typical Norfolk contest of tall tales one winter's day when I walked in to gaze upon them. There they were, sailing round the bar in stately procession, nose to tail, glassy-eyed. Full length pike, head and shoulders pike, pike rampant, pike about to pounce, pike quiescent, pike with their mouths shut and others about to leap from their glass cases upon you with yawning jaws, glittering with teeth. I remarked upon the monster of them all, a thirty-three and a half-pounder and, as a born Fenman, said to Mr. Oakes, then the landlord: "pretty good that one—but a tiddler compared with the fifty-two-pounder which they took out of Whittlesey Mere in Huntingdonshire when they drained it in 1849."

"Fish!" said Mr. Oakes airily as he exercised his strong right arm. "There they are. Pretty good, they tell me. But there, I don't know anything about fresh-water fish. They tell me they catch 'em here as big as dogs. I jes' listen. Takes a bit o' listenin' to, sometimes, I can tell you. Lor, how them fishermen do go on. Wonder is, they ain't struck dead!

"You see why, I come from Gorleston. We catch *fish* there. Not jes' one at a time, but millions of 'em. Ah! Millions, I tell you. Shipfuls! Yarmouth herrin's. Finest fish in the world. Worth a guinea apiece!"

"Ha! Yu orter come down on the Yare," said a listening wherryman. "They bin a-ketchin' fish there lately that damn near pulled 'em in. Every time they ketched 'em they raised a wave that nearly sank the blessed boat. Telly what it was—a damned old seal. They got him last week at Cantley. Over foive fut long he was, and now he's gone up to Norridge to be stuffed. Got whiskers on him like the Lord Mayor, and a grey owd hid like an owd parson. He'd make yar owd fish look silly!"

Whilst in the Horning district, it is worth paying a visit to Hoveton Little Broad part of which is open for cruising only. The rest is a Nature Reserve.

Downstream, past Ranworth Dyke on the right and past the private dyke on the left which leads to Horning Hall Farm, you come then, still on the left, to the mouth of the river Ant which will lead you to the wild waste of Barton Broad and the wasted wilds of Sutton Broad. Before, however, you take this voyage, it is worthwhile sailing a little further downstream and then going up the dyke to the right which leads to South Walsham Broad. This is an enchanting sheet of water, shaded by trees and therefore no place for sailing. It is full of ducks, its woods noisy with pheasants and if you get there at midnight on 1st May the broad is suddenly alive with Viking longships. Before your eyes, if you have the right sort of eyes, you will see the body of Oscar, the son of Saturn, burned aboard his ship to a wild fanfare of the Seakings' horn. If you are so disastrously myopic as to miss this spectacle, there is a good inn in South Walsham, with a noble signboard of a ship in full sail which will console you.

South Walsham Hall is a good, modern red-brick medium-sized mansion of Elizabethan style, standing above smooth lawns and overlooking a wooded arm of the broad. The whole estate, broad, woods, plantations, marshes and farmlands, runs to about 800 acres and used to belong to a delightful friend of mine, the late Sir Bartle Frere, who was beloved by everyone who knew him. When the estate came up for sale, it was fortunately bought by Major the Hon. Henry Broughton, brother of Lord Fairhaven. The two brothers have spent most of their lives protecting and enhancing the rural beauty and artistic treasures of their two estates. That is a rare thing to come across in these days when penal taxation breaks up one well-run estate after another, forces art treasure onto the market and turns shoddy little building speculators into get-rich-quick millionaires. Had the South Walsham estate fallen into speculative hands it could so easily have been ruined.

Here let me tell a little story which concerns a unique set of pictures now in South Walsham Hall. A certain peer who shall be nameless once remarked to me one day that he had a collection of flower pictures by a Dutch artist which showed an appropriate set of flowers for each month of the year. He wanted to get rid of them and asked my advice. I found them standing racked on the floor in his private chapel which had a leaking roof, rotting floorboards and perpetual damp. The pictures were by Jan van Huysun (1682–1749), the celebrated Dutch painter who was probably the greatest artist of flowers of all times. *The Dictionary of Painters* by Daryl says "the most curious florists in Holland vied in supplying him with the choicest models for his pictures and he succeeded in painting the best flower pieces ever produced. His works are highly valued especially those on a clear or yellow ground".

I told my inquisitive peer, who happens to be a personal friend, that his set of pictures was probably worth £9,000 or £10,000 and I added that a friend and myself would scrape up the money to buy them. He gave me a quizzical look.

"If you'll go to ten thousand here in the country," he grinned, "I'll bet you I'll get a damn sight more in London." Up to London they went. There they fetched, if I remember rightly, either £13,000 or £15,000. Major Broughton has them today and being a true connoisseur, hangs a different picture every month in his dining room, to portray the flowers of the month. Meanwhile, my noble friend and neighbour put the money thus received into field drains, farm fences and re-seeding grass pastures. He is a farmer first and foremost.

South Walsham has two churches in the same churchyard. This is not because they were built by two jealous sisters, but merely because a heap of dry manure caught fire, set light to a barn and a house and ended by burning down half the church as well. That is the truth, but the legend of the sisters will endure.

When you return downstream from South Walsham Broad to the River Bure you are back in a country of open marshland, flat cattle marshes, seamed with dykes and the reedy wastes of Ranworth Fens. A lonely country of sun and wind, of carrion crows and feeding rooks with gulls like snowflakes against the sky and a heron standing on the bank, musing a fish. Ahead on the opposite bank stands up the black humped mass of the last poor ruin of the once mighty Abbey of St. Benet. It is not much to look at today. Once it was one of the most powerful abbeys in the kingdom. It was powerful enough to defy the King. The Bishop of Norwich sits in the House of Lords today, not as Bishop of Norwich but as Bishop of St. Benet-at-Holm.

I know no place in all Broadland which is more poignantly impressive to any man of imagination than the few gaunt stone walls enclosing a ruined drainage mill which are all that are left of this mighty abbey. You must see it at dusk when mists rise, the sunset sky is a bale-fire of black and scarlet and gold, with the high rays of the dying sun against a marching rampart of thunderous clouds. That is how I saw it the first time.

I wrote of it then: "St. Benet's is infinitely pathetic, a place of sad dignity. Nothing remains but a great archway, a tall fragment of flint-built wall, and, within it, the round brick tower of a ruined mill from which a barn owl flew. Away to the right, on higher ground, stood another lump of grey wall, like a dolmen lost on a moor. And, beyond it, a long fragment of flinty walls, rubbed by cattle, the playground of rabbits.

"These walls are all that remain of the cruciform abbey church, in which was buried the mighty Sir John Fastolff, that doughty soldier, who under Henry V, fought at Agincourt, Caen, and Rouen, was at the taking of Harfleur, and became Governor of that town. Later he was Governor of the Bastille, Seneschal, Lieutenant, and Regent of Normandy, and Governor of Anjou and Maine. He came home from his many battles to build Caister Castle, which he made one of the largest and finest buildings in England. Then he died, and they buried him here in the abbey church of St. Benet at Holm. And today the cattle graze, the rabbits play, and the carrion crows strut like ravens over the coarse turf between walls beneath which lie the bones of that great English soldier.

"Stand on the river bank at dusk and you may see, in the mind's eye, the soaring towers, the glittering stone pinnacles, the winking windows, the terraced chapels, houses, and granaries which once rose above the vanished walls of this great abbey that stood like a fortress-village, high-walled and girt about by waters, on its little island amid the meres and foggy fens.

"There were quays and walls, with sea-going ships tied up or riding at anchor. There were monks going about their business, cowled and belted. There was singing and high music in the high abbey church. And the chime of bells at evening, ringing far out across the lonely, glittering fen.

"It was a place of sanctity and great beauty, a hive of human life, and a centre of great goodness, this walled island-village of the monks which sprang from that small chapel founded by Suneman, the hermit, some time before 816. The Danes sailed up this river in 866, burned the hermit's chapel, and slew him and his followers. A hundred years later Wolfric, a holy man, retired to the island of Suneman and built there a holy cell.

"But the tide of Danish arms swept over all East Anglia, and Wolfric's cell grew, under Canute, into the great Benedictine monastery of St. Benet-at-Holm. That was in 1034. Canute made it a walled and fortified place. You can still see to the east, by a ragged line of hawthorns and blackthorns where magpies nest and winter blackbirds roost, the foundations of his buttressed walls and the footing-stones of the towers which stood at the angles of those walls.

"Then came the Norman Conquest. Duke William's mailed soldiers were sent in a fleet of boats against the island-fortress of the monks, which covered no less than thirty-eight acres of ground. They besieged it on all sides. The high flint walls and the deep moat to north, east, and west, with the river to the south, defied them for weeks.

"Then one day a captured monk, Ethelwald, was brought into the Norman camp. He promised to re-enter the abbey and open the great gate to the besiegers if the Normans would make him Abbot. Such was the price of treachery.

"The Normans promised and released him. Ethelwald returned to the abbey and, on the appointed night, threw open the great gate. The Norman soldiers surged in, and, amid the flare of torches, the wild clanging of bells, the whistling of arrows, clash of swords, and screams of the wounded and dying, the abbey was taken and the defenders slain.

"Then Ethelwald was led by sardonic Norman knights to the High Altar in the great abbey church, dim-lit by swealing candles and smoking torches, and there, dressed in the Abbot's robe, the mitre was placed on his head and he was installed as Abbot of the monastery while, without, the dying monks lay writhing in their blood, and the Fenmen who had aided their defence kicked in halters from the battlements.

"Then, on that night of high and bloody tragedy, the Normans led the new Abbot, proud in his Judas pride, to the topmost tower of the high church. They snatched the mitre from his head. They stripped the cope from his shoulders. They put a halter about his neck. And the pale traitor, screaming in his base agony, was thrown from the tower to dangle kicking at the end of the rope. That is the tale.

"And they say that if you go ashore on Cowholm Marshes, alone on a cold night of moon, you will see a black figure, choking and kicking at a rope's end from the high arch that still stands —the traitor, his robes flapping in death like a black crow in a snare.

"For long centuries after that bitter night of flames and blood the abbey flourished under the new Norman lords of England. All through the Middle Ages it was strong and powerful. It escaped even the general suppression of 1537. In that year William Rugge, the Abbot, was translated to the See of Norwich, and the revenues of the abbey were also transferred. With the Abbot went the

Barony of St. Benet-at-Holm, by right of which dignity the present Bishop of Norwich has a seat in the House of Lords.

"Later the abbey was pulled down. Tower and wall, chapel and dwelling-house, dormitory and frater, granaries and barns—all alike were demolished. Their stones were loaded in long lines of great boats and towed up to Norwich there to build the great Duke's palace of the Dukes of Norfolk.

"That palace, for many years, was the feudal hub and centre of the city's life. The Dukes lived there as little kings. Their state was magnificent, their generosity munificent, their retainers like unto an army, their entertainments princely.

"Then came a day when the citizens of Norwich obstructed the Duke's will. They made churlish objections to a great pageant proposed. So the Duke razed his palace to the ground, and the stones of St. Benet's were scattered to the winds. Who knows but that today some humble dwelling-house in the back streets of the city is not builded of them, that some wall is not cornered with their fine quoins, or that the very street that you walk upon is not founded upon their buried remains? Thus the Dukes 'cast their shoon' in the face of Norwich, and Norwich was none the better, for they were good overlords. There are some who say that this final demolishing of the palace was the fulfilment of that curse which follows all who build their houses from the sacred stones of churches."

I cannot discover that 'Old Crome', that superb artist, ever painted a picture of St. Benet's. He of all men would have captured the bold majesty of the place as it was and, as a contrast, the sad ruins of today.

There is another place across the marshes of a lesser note but with its own little legend of good works by forgotten men. That is the tall and lonely tower of Thurne church. Donald Applegate told me the story one night as we lay at anchor in Thurne Dyke:

"The old men say that a light shines from the top window of that tower sometimes on dark nights. When the monks were about over there in St. Benet's and there was illness in Thurne village, or at Oby, or Clippesby—little, lonely old places, all of 'em—they used to light a torch in the top room of the church tower. That light shined across the waters to the abbey. And then the monks knew there was sickness, and need of a doctor. So they'd come rowing in their little boat, a mile and a half across the fens, to tend whoever needed them. They must have been good old boys, them old monks. But all that was hundreds o' years ago."

There is another legend of these marshes of a very different sort —the Ludham Serpent. The *Norfolk Chronicle* for 28th September, 1722, told the tale:

"On Monday the 14th inst. a snake of an enormous size was destroyed at Ludham in this County by Jasper Andrews of that place. It measured five feet eight inches long, was almost three feet in circumference and had a very long snout. What is remarkable there were two excrescences on the forepart of the head which very much resembled horns. The creature seldom made its appearance in the day time, but kept concealed in subterranean retreats several of which have been discovered in the town, one near the bake-office and another on the premises of the Revd. N. V. Jeffrey and another in the land occupied by Mr. Popple at the Hall. The skin of the above surprising reptile is now in the possession of Mr. J. Garrod, a wealthy farmer in the neighbourhood."

The chances are that these serpents were foreign snakes which had escaped from ships that had docked at Yarmouth. There is a similar story of a great snake which haunted Bulphan Fen in Essex, not far from the Thames estuary where it might easily have been brought from abroad by ship. It was slain at Herongate by Sir John Tyrell of Heron Hall. You will see nothing worse on the Ludham Marshes today than a blonde in a bikini with, possibly, a bull seeing her off.

VII

WATERS OF THE ANT

The Beauty of Barton Broad—And a Tale of Nelson

THE Ant is an entrancing, irritating, defeating and seductive little river. It twists and bends. It convolutes and curves until it almost doubles on itself. If, as the deep-sea sailor Carter-Ruck has said, you can sail "the antiferous waters of the Ant" without ramming a reed-bed, mounting a bank, gybing your ship or sinking the next boat you can sail anything anywhere. The Ant joins the Bure just below Horning Hall and just above St. Benet's Abbey. This unique little river is less well-known than most of the Broadland rivers. You can almost get away from people. It flows for the first half mile through Ludham cattle-marshes where I have pursued wild geese in winter under the protective wing of the late Jim Vincent of Hickling, the greatest marshland gamekeeper that Norfolk ever knew, and where in summer one has been pursued smartly by a Friesian bull. Ludham Old Hall was originally a seat of the Abbots of St. Benet's. Then the Bishops of Norwich had it as a country-house. It was burnt down in 1611. The old brick chapel is still used as a barn. You may see it if you walk a short way from Ludham Bridge which spans the Ant and boasts a store where you can buy anything that man, woman or boat may need.

Beyond the bridge you are in a land of wild marshes and reed-beds, of willow carrs where woodcock lurk and a little hill crowned with a biggish thatched house known as How Hill. For sixty years or more this was the home of the Boardman family who on their 334 acres of land created a unique small marshland estate, alive with wildfowl and rare birds. In 1966 it was bought by the Norfolk County Council. The property includes Cromes' Broad, small and private and packed with wild duck. Not far off is the little land-locked Alderfen Broad, which I am told is now

Even the yachts were different—sixty years ago

Sailing on Oulton Broad in the mid-1960s

almost grown-up. You can walk to it from the hamlet of Irstead Street.

Now as you cannot get away from ghosts, witches, Wills o' the Wisp and bogles in this marsh country, keep clear of Alderfen Broad after dark. The Reverend John Gunn, who was parson of Irstead, got the story from an old parishioner, Mrs. Lubbock, in 1849. He had heard a lot in the village about a ghostly light known as 'Neatishead Jack'. Mrs. Lubbock enlightened his darkness and Parson Gunn published it in Volume II of *Norfolk Archaeology* thus:

"Before the Irstead Enclosure in 1810 Jack o' Lantern was frequently seen here on a roky night, and almost always at a place called 'Heard's Hole' in Alder Carr Fen Broad on the Neatishead side, where a man of that name, who was guilty of some unmentionable crimes, was drowned. I have often seen it there, rising up and falling and twisting about and then up again. It looked exactly like a candle in a lantern.

"She evidently connected the *ignis fatuus* in that spot with the unhappy man's spirit, as if it were still hovering about; and Jack o' Lantern was, in her apprehension, endued with volition and intelligence; for she affirms that if any one were walking along the road with a lantern, at the time when he appeared and did not put out the light immediately, Jack would come up against it and dash it to pieces; and that a gentleman who made a mock of him and called him 'Will of the Wisp' was riding on horseback one evening in the adjoining parish of Horning, when he came at him and knocked him off his horse.

"She remembers, when a child, hearing her father say that he was returning home from a large (largess) money-spending at the finish of harvest, in company with an old man, who whistled and jeered at Jack; but he followed them all the way home, and when they entered the house he torched up at the windows.

"The Neatishead people were desirous to lay Heard's spirit, so annoyed were they by it; for it came at certain times and to certain places which he frequented when alive. Three gentlemen (she could not tell who or what they were, she supposed they were learned) attempted to lay the ghost by reading verses of Scripture. But he always kept a verse ahead of them. And they could do nothing, till a boy brought a couple of pigeons and laid them down before him. He looked at them and lost his verse; and then they bound his spirit."

7

Quiet waters—reed-lined bank at St. Olaves

Irstead is small, charming, shaded by trees and possesses a church with the unique distinction that William of Wykeham was once vicar. Not far off lies one of those enchanting small Elizabethan manor-houses which are the jewels of the English scene—Irstead Hall. It is a farmhouse, built in about 1580 as the home of a village squireling, the local Lord of the Manor, who probably owned and farmed not more than about 400 acres. Like all such houses it was built with grace, with an eye for beauty and equally for common sense comfort, with twin-walled gardens to hold the sun, to grow pears and nectarines, where the lady of the house, her children and handmaids, could sun themselves in peace at needlework on quiet afternoons.

The house-builders of today could learn a lot from those of the age of Elizabeth I. These little village manor-houses, although they enshrine the principle of such vast mansions as Hatfield, Longleat and Blicking, are neither large nor grand. There is no ornate Italian decoration but they have grace and proportion and dignity in a small but fine style. Compare them with the cheap-jack matchbox dwellings of today, built of breeze blocks, concrete, formica and sheets of glass to sell at fantastic prices—and last perhaps fifty years. One may well ask if we have progressed so very far, although central heating, plumbing, electric lights and gadgets are trimmings which the Elizabethans never knew. They built to last. We build to sell—fast.

The late Walter Rye of Norwich, who was perhaps the most erudite county historian that Norfolk has known in the last century and a genealogist of national repute who torpedoed more than one pretentious pedigree of the Norwich and Norfolk plutocracy of bankers and brewers, told an engaging story concerning Irstead. You will find it in his rare *Norfolk Songs, Stories and Sayings* published in 1897.

"Jimmy Cox (all Coxes come from Barton, the only other inhabitants of that village being Watts) who kept an eel-sett near Irstead Shoals, died, as even Coxes must. Three weeks after, Waters, a great big wherryman from up the end of the Barton river by Ebridge Mill, and about as strong and good a waterman as there is on the river, was coming down with his laden wherry from the canal, and stopped for the night at Irstead Shoals.

"He was just going out to empty the leaves from his teapot before going to bed, when who should he see but Jimmy Cox sitting on the tiller, and looking as comfortable and as homelike as never was.

" 'Why, Jimmy, I thowt you was dead', said Waters, but Jimmy he say niver a word, and then, Waters, he bobbed into the cabin again and wondered what he shewd dew, till he got that frightened that he dashed out with his eyes shut not tew see Jimmy, and he up with his quant and away he shoved out of the shoals till he was right away, and then in he bobbed again and covered his head till the morning came, and never again will he lay in Irstead Shoals."

Beyond Irstead there opens up the wild waste of Barton Broad —a waste of once open waters, now largely grown up with floating 'hovers', anchored 'bolders' and encroaching reeds and sedges. Once it was 284 acres of open water. That was in 1840. Between 1881 and 1938 it covered roughly 259 acres of open water. Since then it has shrunk alarmingly to 162 acres with an average navigable depth of little more than three feet. They will tell you locally, as I was told, that this shrinkage has been caused deliberately, to a large extent, by one or two small and cunning landowners who, over the years, have deliberately anchored bolders (fragments of floating bog) in the shallower waters in order that the reed roots should spread out, attach themselves and thus expand, until whole stretches of shallow water are covered in a few years by reed growth and become 'hovers' (riverside bogs). These, in time, become solid land. Thus the landowner acquires more land at no cost to himself. It is as simple as that.

This great broad, one of the noblest in all Norfolk, has been nibbled at until it has lost pretty well a hundred acres of water in the last hundred years.

This, they tell me locally, is due entirely to the fact that the Lords of the Manor, the Prestons of Beeston Hall, sold out their rights on the broad many years ago. Newcomers who bought relatively small acreages of land fringing the broad, were the niggers in the woodpile. No blame whatsoever attaches to the Preston family, who for 300 years or more, have been squires and landowners, with a great sense of responsibility.

I came across an old man, Tom Cautman, one windy day at that enchanting little broad-side huddle of cottages called Gay's Staithe, who put the matter in a nutshell:

"I lived under Sir Edward Preston," said old Tom. "And a better gentleman never walked. When times got bad in the last war Sir Edward knocked my rent down. He reckoned I had only got a pension to live on, and prices was goin' up so he lowered my rent to help me out. One of the rale owd Norfolk gentry he is. And his grandad, old Sir Jacob, was the same sort. They've had to sell orf bits of the estate, but the workin' man's no better orf for it. Allus friends of the workin' man, them squires, and good 'uns too. I go brushin' for him at his pheasant-shoots, and he allus gives us beaters eighteen bob a day and a pheasant apiece."

Barton Broad is about a mile long and, after Hickling, the largest broad in Norfolk. It has the same remote quality of unspoiled marshland, of primeval wildness. The swamps which fringe it are wide, deep and dangerous. Away to the right, as you enter the broad, lies the wilderness of the Catfield Fens where you can lose yourself and drown with the greatest of ease. Small boys should be tied to the mast with ropes if they attempt to go ashore. The Catfield Fens are a wilderness of hidden pulk-holes, narrow reedy channels, bottomless mud and jungles of sedge.

In these fens, that erudite naturalist, Lord William Percy, who lived for many years at Catfield Hall, carried out his patient investigations into the odd habits of the bittern, that mysterious gnome of the reed-beds. I remember sitting with him one day by the fire in Catfield Hall whilst he described how he sat for hours, day after day, in a stinking swamp, watching a bittern catching eels and then using the 'powder puff' which the bird conceals beneath its feathers. It dusts itself with the powder in order to clean its feathers of the slime gathered during a busy morning catching eels. Lord William does not burst into print or smirk from the television screen on every possible occasion as do some of the 'birdy boys' who impress upon us that they alone are the experts. Yet I doubt if any man alive today knows more about wildfowl and their habits than this tall, retiring brother of the Duke of Northumberland who has been to most of the out-of-the-way corners of the world to watch and study rare birds. His photographs of bitterns which he took in Catfield Fen constitute a unique collection and a most valuable addition to our knowledge of the habits of the bird.

Barton is a home of great pike. You can catch a twenty-pounder if you are moderately lucky. Wise or lucky men have caught thirty-pounders. Shooting, once free to the local villagers, is now prohibited. Barton is, rightly, a Nature Reserve administered by the Norfolk Naturalists' Trust.

The charm of Barton lies in its diversity. Within half a mile you may sail out of a wet, wild reedy wilderness up the wooded water-way which leads to an idyllic farmhouse, a few cottages and a roadside pub at Gays Staithe. The sort of place that Constable or Morland would have adored to paint. Barton Staithe, the hamlet which lies below the village of Barton Turf, is a place of equal charm. Under two oak trees there sits an ancient yellow-fronted off-licence where they will sell you beer out of the back window in the back-yard. It all belongs to 1850 or earlier.

The Barton families who have made local history in their quiet, enduring way over the centuries as boat-builders, wherry owners, wildfowlers, fishermen and broadsmen, are the Hewitts, the Hayletts and the Coxes. They have been sailing these waters, catching fish, shooting wildfowl, harvesting reeds, generation after generation for the last four or five centuries.

One day I called on an old friend, Mr. William Hewitt, head of a family who have been about these parts for at least 500 years. He represents that type of English yeoman whose integrity and pedi-gree would shame the claims of half the gimcrack peerages of today. His great-grandfather, Robert Hewitt, who died in his sixtieth year in 1838, was the man who first taught Nelson to sail a boat. Nelson was a schoolboy, twelve years of age, at the Paston Grammar School at North Walsham. His sister rented Barton Broad, from a Mr. Morse and the admiral-to-be used to come down and stay with her. Here is the tale as Mr. Hewitt told it to me:

"My great-grandfather didn't teach Nelson to sail as far as I know, but he rowed him across the broad on a right rough day according to a letter I've got in my desk. The tale is that he also taught him to sail on another occasion but that I don't know. Nelson's sister rented Barton Broad in those days from a Mr. Morse and Nelson used to come down here to see her when he was on leave from the Navy. In fact, my great-grandfather drove him away from the Hall to catch his stagecoach to London the last time he ever came here.

"But as to the tale about great-grandfather taking him for a row, I'll give you a copy of a letter which appeared in the *Eastern Daily Press* from a Mr. Loraine, who looked up all the facts, and if you like to print that letter you can."

So here, with Mr. Hewitt's permission, is the letter which records what was possibly the young Nelson's first experience of a passage by boat in rough weather. It may well be that he did, indeed, first learn to sail on Barton Broad, and if so it is more than possible that a Hewitt was the man who taught him the feel of the wind and the way of the sheets.

Sir,

A few paces from the main entrance to the church of Barton Turf is the grave of Robert Hewitt. The inscription upon the tombstone records that he died in 1838, aged 60 years. Hewitt, it appears, was one of those rare men whose simple words and deeds are remembered. The great occasion of his life, as related by him, was when he rowed Horatio Nelson across Barton Broad.

The facts as I gathered them recently are these. On a day when the wind blew strong and keen, young Nelson, then a slight boy, delicate to see, appeared at the waterside, accompanied by a friend, possibly his tutor, and observing a boat ready there at once expressed a wish to cross the broad.

His companion, careful for the boy, raised objections—it was too cold, the conditions were stormy and the water much disturbed—a day, in fact, quite unsuitable (and, if I may make a guess, the boat was not a very trim craft).

Pooh, the boy would have none of it. "I'll be a man or a mouse", he protested. The victory was won on Barton Staithe; young Nelson crossed Barton Broad, perhaps even now dreaming of some decisive Trafalgar. Hewitt rowed.

Pleased with the narrative as told me, and trying to satisfy an inquiring mind as to material dates, upon my return home I consulted authority, to find that Nelson and Hewitt must have been born the same year, Nelson born 1758, entered the Navy in 1770 and therefore could have been no more than twelve years of age when at Barton, or rather younger supposing him still at Paston School, North Walsham.

Now Hewitt was of the same year, and though a sturdy boy living at the waterside may early become a waterman, 'tis unlikely that he sculled the two passengers across the broad; probably he and a companion each took an oar. Anyway Robert Hewitt accompanied young Nelson upon that early adventure, was present at the victory of Barton Staithe, and sleeps now in Barton Turf churchyard.

Yours, etc.

H. LORAINE

Mr. Hewitt went on: "I remember the time when any man in this village could shoot or fish on Barton Broad without let or hindrance. It was the common right of all of us. The Prestons never denied it. They were good squires and proper gentlemen—and still are. Many a man hereabouts got his living at shooting and fishing. Now you can't shoot, and the fishing is by ticket. We used to shoot everywhere except on the bit we call Irstead Broad, which lies below Irstead Lodge and extends up to the Pleasure Hill. There was another little broad in the plantation called the Turkey Broad but that's all grown up now.

"All the rest was free. Sir Jacob claimed only the reeds and the growth round the broad, but never the water, as far as I knew.

"The Coxes and Hayletts and the Hewitts all used to go gunning, some of them for a living in winter time. They used punts, and there were five or six swivel-guns—regular punt-guns—that fired half a pound of shot each. And they used to get some good bags, too—sometimes thirty or forty ducks in a morning.

"But, Lord Bless you, the broad was then about 600 acres of water. It was as big or bigger than Hickling is today.

"Now it is about half the size, and there are half the birds. We used to get wild geese then, and the ruffs and reeves nested here then, but you don't see many geese here now in winter, and the ruffs and reeves haven't nested for years. But there are as many bitterns about now as there were then, I will say that.

"Old 'Pinney' Cox was about the last man who ever used a swivel-gun, and that would be sixty years ago, when I was a boy. There was an amateur gentleman called Paul and two or three other locals, who all used swivels—but if you fired a swivel today you would probably kill a couple of pike-fishers and get half a dozen gamekeepers down on you. Anyway, there aren't the ducks to shoot at.

"My father loved his gun and his dog, and he used to have the shooting on Irstead Holmes and on the fens round Catfield Hall where old Mr. John Lubbock lived in those days. His wife was a sort of 'wise woman', old Mrs. Lubbock, and full of prophecies about war and famine, most of which never came true. My father shot every sort of bird on those fens—and wild geese too.

"My great-uncle, William Hewitt, was gamekeeper a hundred years ago at Burnley Hall, over at West Somerton, where you once had the shooting. Old Skelton was the decoy-man, and he was supposed to be the head man at the job in all England. He used to tell me how he stopped up all one night to keep open a 'wake' in the ice when the old decoy-pond was frozen so that the ducks could come in for a drink. That was when Joseph Hume, the M.P., had the Hall—about 1850. Another Hewitt was keeper at Hoveton Hall with the Burroughs, and another at Westwick Hall with old Captain Petre—so you see we've all loved the gun."

It is only by talking—and listening—to the older race of Broadsmen that one can get a true picture of the Broads as they were before the rash of commercialization and mounting vulgarity set in. The picture of the past is too good to be lost. The picture of the future is anybody's guess.

You can go up the Ant from Barton Broad through a forest of reeds which was once Sutton Broad to the Staithe Hotel and Country Club which was once the old Wherryman's Arms. In those days it was a humble beer-house where wherry skippers drank and fought and smuggled cargoes were disposed of. In the end the place was shut up. A few years ago it was re-born, modernized and turned into a place of good food and all 'mod cons'.

If Sutton Broad was dredged out and the fringes of Barton Broad were cleansed of the encroachments of reed and floating swamp, Barton would undoubtedly become a highly popular place for the holiday-maker. This need not interfere with the bird life of the district, since the Catfield Fens, Middle Marsh and the marshes round How Hill would always be a sanctuary for them.

The other obvious improvement is to restore Dilham Broad which lies further up the Ant and to re-open the North Walsham and Dilham Canal. This would give the small-boat sailor the open sesame to the upper reaches of the Ant, through wooded and agricultural scenery, past Honing and North Walsham right up to Antingham Ponds which lie within a mile or so of Gunton Park where a bygone Lord Suffield entertained Edward VII in state. There is no doubt about it that if these schemes are not taken in hand, Barton Broad will continue to shrink, Sutton and Dilham Broads will become dry land and the upper reaches of the river will be of little value to the Broadland economy or indeed to anyone else.

If the holiday industry—and that is what it is—is to be catered for and the increasing demand for more sailing water met, these waters of the upper Ant offer an immediate and a practical solution.

VIII

THE WILD CHARM OF HICKLING AND HORSEY

From 'Slumdom' to a Marshland Idyll

HICKLING BROAD and its satellite, Heigham Sounds, Horsey Mere and its forgotten neighbour, Martham Broad, with that lost and seldom visited little broad, Blackfleet, give, to my mind, the last true picture of the older unspoiled Broadland which a few Victorians knew and none wrote about until Christopher Davies sailed these waters.

There are the same wide, wind-whipped, steely waters in winter that Colonel Peter Hawker, 'the Father of Shooting', saw and marvelled at when he visited this out-of-the-way corner of wilder England in 1816. The same wide reed-beds rustling in the wind. The same shifting play of light and colour over long miles of cattle marshes, dyke-seamed and lonely. The same undertone of the sea in the night silence, thundering forever along miles of lonely beaches and hairy sandhills.

In summer the shallowness of most of Hickling and almost all of Martham means that holiday craft are confined to a few channels. The rest of Hickling Broad is left to the dragonflies and reed-warblers, nesting coots and the water rail squealing like a piglet in his fastness of reeds.

This wild country of wind and waters, of quaking bogs and tussocky marsh, is much today as it was 300 years ago with the difference that the cattle marshes are better drained and the low uplands better cultivated. Great pike still plunge in the deep bays of Heigham Sounds where you may catch a thirty-five-pounder, if God is on your side, and no man will wonder greatly. Teams of mallard etch their evening way across the apple-green and pale yellow of sunset skies that Canaletto might have painted. The marsh-harrier beats the levels like a questing hound. The Montagu's harrier, the blue-hawk of the old Fenmen, nests here, more rarely than a few years ago. As for the bittern, that ghostly voice of the night, the black tern, the bearded tit or reedling, the short-eared owl soaring like a buzzard, or ruffs and reeves, delicate in spring, this is their sanctuary. You may see almost any rare species of wildfowl or wader on the British list at Hickling or Horsey if the wind is right and your eyes are bright.

Fortunately, practically the whole area is strictly preserved as a National Nature Reserve. This was due, in the first place, to the late Lord Lucas and the late Lord Desborough. Lord Lucas lived at Horsey Hall and loved all birds and was loved by most men until he was lost mysteriously in an aeroplane during the 1914–18 war. He went out of his way to protect the bittern which, by about 1911, had become practically extinct as a British breeding species. After his death, the late Lord Desborough, whom I had the good fortune to know well, succeeded as owner of much of Hickling and its marshes. He carried out a deliberate and well-planned policy of preservation. Major Anthony Buxton, who became owner of Horsey Hall and its estate of 1,600 acres, which includes the whole of Horsey Mere, did the same. Then he handed over the Horsey estate to the National Trust to ensure that the policy of bird preservation was maintained for all foreseeable time.

The greater part of the Hickling-Whiteslea-Heigham Sounds chain of broads is now a National Nature Reserve administered jointly by the Norfolk Naturalists' Trust and the Nature Conservancy. It is free to river craft but shooting as elsewhere on the Broads is strictly prohibited. Gamekeepers and marshkeepers keep a sharp eye on the vandal and the hooligan.

Martham Broad is private and with the little South Broad forms part of the Burnley Hall estate now of some 2,000 acres which has had a succession of owners this century. For some years it belonged to my friend, the late Sir Gerald Talbot, a keen shooting man, who took infinite pains to preserve rare birds. Woe betide the man who shot a bittern. After his death I was fortunate enough to have the tenancy of the shooting for some years. Since then the estate has passed through three different ownerships in less than twenty years. Fortunately, it is still intact.

You come to this group of broads by way of the River Thurne, broad, deep and slow. The Thurne joins the Bure, not unnaturally, at Thurne Mouth. From thence until you reach Potter Heigham bridge it is as well to keep your eyes shut, mentally. Far too much of this stretch of river suffers from cheap-jack developments. Potter Heigham, once a pleasant village, is now, on the riverside at least, little better than an urbanized slum. Fortunately, the low arches of Potter Heigham bridge and the swift current which occasionally races through them, deter many of the more aggressively large river craft from going upstream. Long may the bridge remain.

Little more than a mile upstream from Potter bridge, one comes to Kendal Dyke, the 'Candle Deek' of the marshmen. This leads directly into the wilderness of fens and meres which are the Hickling-Heigham Sounds and Whiteslea area, three continuous broads which cover more than a square mile and form the largest open area of water in Broadland. For miles one sees nothing but tasseled reeds, the brown heads of bulrushes, sedge and reed-mace, with here and there the gleam of hidden pools, where wildfowl dwell in thousands.

I have many vivid memories of days and nights spent on these waters and amid the wild, surrounding fens at all times and seasons of the year; winter days when one has seen two or three thousand wildfowl in the air at once, heard wild swans trumpeting in the mist and seen lordly skeins of wild geese come in on their far aerial voyage from the Baltic and beyond; summer days when the swallowtail butterflies were out and every flower was in bloom; autumn days when the reeds were turning from green to gold, from gold to crimson, pheasants crowing in the reed-beds, snipe springing by the dyke-side, and duck sibilant in the dawn.

It is a place of incredible beauty, a wild, untamed and desolate beauty, at every turn of the year.

When you sail across Hickling the surrounding marshes are so low that the broad seems to be twice its size. In autumn mist or summer haze it seems shoreless. You have the sensation of sailing through an unreal land of water and crying birds.

The navigable channel across the broad is marked by posts. Stick to it if you are in a deep-draught cruiser or sailing boat. Otherwise you will stick in the mud and stay there.

The true way in which to explore this enchanting broad is either in a sailing dinghy or better still in a flatbottomed duck-punt which will go anywhere. Catfield River which leads to Catfield Staithe and the interesting collection of old wattle and daub cottages on Catfield Common, referred to elsewhere, is a broad dyke running through reedy fens, seldom explored by anyone. I have never been up it yet without seeing an enchantment of bird life, from snipe to bittern, from teal to tern. Occasionally the osprey turns up and fishes the wide waters, the lord of the skies. He usually makes his headquarters on the top branches of a dead oak in Wagon Hill Plantation, a low copse at one end of the broad.

The old-fashioned Pleasure Boat Inn, immortalized by Oliver Ready, is, apart from a few additions and a little modernization, much the same as it was in his day. A place not to be missed. There are a few picturesque cottages at that end of the broad, now mainly converted into highly expensive houses, one or two drainage mills and, overlooking Whiteslea, the thatched roof of Whiteslea Lodge, once the home of Lord Desborough. Otherwise you will not see another house on the broad itself.

Hidden in a reed-bed, however, at the Hickling Staithe end of the broad, is a little reed-thatched house with its feet almost in the water. There lives my friend Roland Green one of the most remarkable bird artists of this century. He does not advertise himself or his pictures but they have been bought by royalty. If you can acquire one you have an investment in beauty.

When one has seen all that Hickling has to offer—and it deserves at least two or three days of calm and leisured appreciation—go up the Meadow Dyke from Heigham Sounds, through a wilderness of reeds to Horsey Mere, a mile away. Horsey is an enchanting little lake, of about a hundred acres, with a character entirely its own. It lies so near to the sound and scent of the sea that it seems almost to be of the sea. It is almost circular, with an island in the middle, and, on a sunny day, it is as blue as the Mediterranean.

Horsey is a charming, bleak little village lying between the broad and the sandhills which, for miles, fringe the sea like a miniature mountain range. It has a reed-thatched church of simple but unforgettable beauty, an inn, the Nelson Head, and a village shop which sells everything from buttons to postcards.

Seventy years ago Horsey was practically cut off from the rest of the world during the entire winter months, for the road across the marshes to West Somerton was so appalling that when carts attempted to travel by it the drivers took bundles of reeds and faggots with them to place under the wheels to prevent them from sinking in the softer spots.

Horsey is a paradise of rare birds, and the stronghold of the

marsh harrier which Major Buxton strictly protects. I have seen
as many as five in the course of a day, and a pair of bitterns at the
same time. Crees, Major Buxton's keeper, who lives in a thatched
cottage hard by the belt of trees which surrounds the tiny grass
park in which stands the tall, whitewashed Georgian hall, is a
first-class naturalist and a most interesting man with whom to have
an hour of intelligent and instructive conversation. He has an eye
like a hawk and an uncanny knowledge of the movements of every
poacher and so-called bird-watcher within five square miles.

In the far corner of Horsey Mere lies a wild reedland of about a
hundred acres called Braydon, once part of the mere and now a
dense reed jungle. Otters live there. The bittern nests there.
Harriers sweep over it, gliding shadows of menace. Beyond lies
the flat prairie of the Waxham Marshes on which I rented the
shooting for a few delectable seasons.

If you have a small boat you may go from Horsey Mere up the
Cut which is a broad dyke until you come to Waxham Hall.
That, indeed, is a house of history, built somewhere about mid-
fifteenth century of faced flints with stone quoins. It is one of
those middle-sized manor houses which have a lasting dignity of
their own. There lives a good Norfolk yeoman who farms his
land well, under the constant threat of the sea. Indeed, the hall,
standing within its embattled walls, is no more than a hundred
yards from the tide-edge. The great barn is one of the largest in
Norfolk. The church which stands beyond the duck pond is cold
and noble with, alas, too much of it in ruins. It stands in austere
dignity among the bitter sea-fields with a few scattered cottages
and the hall alone to owe it spiritual allegiance. This was the church
in which Oliver Ready's father ministered to his lonely parish for
so many years. Within, there is a good Early Elizabeth monument
to Thomas Wodehouse, date 1571, for Waxham was originally
the seat of the Wodehouse family who at one time owned manors
which now lie far beneath the encroaching sea. Of it Blomefield
in his history of Norfolk, published in 1775, says:

"Oliver de Ingham was Lord of it in 1183, (when the 3d. part
of his great tithe belonging to it was confirmed to the monks
of St. Benet) as was Sir John de Ingham in the reign of King
John.

"From this family it came by marriage, to Sir Miles Stapleton,
and from that family, by marriage to Sir William Calthorp, whose
grandson, William Calthorpe, Esq. sold it to Sir Thomas Wode-

house, who was lord in the reign of Queen Elizabeth, and of the manor of Ingham, as may be seen there at large.

"This family of the Wodehouses is a distinct family from that of Kimberley, and bore, for their arms, quarterly, azure and ermin, in the first quarter a leopard or; which arms belong to the family of Power, and I find these Wodehouses to be formerly stiled Woodhouse, alias Power."

Half a mile southerly of the hall, lies Brograve Farm in the marshes not far from the sea-wall. All this long and lonely level of marshland is known as the Brograve Level and on Waxham Marshes stands the brick-built Brograve Mill, a round towered draining mill with, if I remember rightly, an eighteenth-century date in the brickwork. This commemorates the Brograve family who owned Waxham at some time after the Wodehouses had gone.

The hall is said to be haunted by the unshriven spirits of the Brograves who died violently. First, Sir Ralph who died in the Crusades on a Saracen's spear, then Sir Edmund who fell in the Barons' Wars. Sir John was killed by an arrow at Agincourt and Sir Francis in the Wars of the Roses, fighting for the Lancastrians. Sir Thomas was slain at Marston Moor and Sir Charles fell at Ramillies under Marlborough.

Sir Barney died a bachelor, although he dotted the countryside with his portrait. On New Year's Eve he gave a banquet to the shades of his departed ancestors, when covers, and nothing else, were laid for the six ghostly visitants. The seventh was more substantially supplied. Glasses were filled for each guest and their toasts solemnly drunk. At midnight the wraiths vanished and later Sir Barney awoke, tired, cold, and with a hangover.

His fights and bets were fantastic. When a sweep overcharged him for cleaning the Hall chimneys, he fought the man but got the worst of it because he knocked so much soot out of the sweep's clothes that it nearly choked him. It took a week's hard drinking to remove the taste of it.

The late Walter Rye had an enchanting tale of a local marshman's verdict on Sir Barney in these words:

"Owd Sir Barney Brograve he wur a werry bad old man and he sold his sould to the Davil and guv him a parchment bond. When he died he went and called on the Davil and say to him, 'Here I be' and the Davil he say: 'Sir Barney, I allus sed you was a perfect gennleman' and Sir Barney he say: 'Well, you might ask me to set down' but the Davil he say: 'I've been looking trew your account and it fare to me if I hev you in here 'twon't be a sennight[1] afore yew'll be top-dog and I shall hev to play second fiddle, so there's your writin' back, and now be off!' And Sir Barney, he say: 'Where am I to go tew?' and the owd Davil he forgot hisself and got angry and he say: 'Go to hell!' Sir Barney he had no idea of wanderin' all about nowhere, so he tuk him at his word and he sat down and stayed. And they du say there's tew Davils there now."

Waxham Hall is mainly notable for the tall, embattled wall with a square pinnacled gateway, which encloses the whole of the forecourt on the side that faces the towering sandhills and the imminent menace of the sea. Stand on those sandhills, upon a hairy crested rampart of hills and valleys, and you look for miles on either side upon the loneliest, bleakest and most austerely beautiful stretch of coast on all the eastern sea-line of Norfolk.

If the proposed 'chalet town' for 8,000 trippers at Sea Palling which lies only a mile up the coast from Waxham, becomes a nightmare fact, the whole character of this lovely stretch of coast will be vulgarized and lost forever.

In summer it is a place of infinite peace and sunlit horizons. In winter a bitter land of bitter spaces. A land of ghostly mists and sea fogs stealing like grey armies. A land of shouting gales and thunderous surges. A land, too, of wide, quiet meres and secret waterways, of sighing reed-beds and the whimper of endless wings of old, small woods of oak and monstrous fern, and of blown, stinging sand and the whipping feet of sleet before the strong sea gales.

Stand on the high sandhills looking down on the old hall of Waxham and the long Brograve Level of marsh and fen beyond, and you will see a land which has not changed a lot since Colonel Hawker came here to shoot wildfowl in 1816.

Imagine it, however, as it was when the sea broke through in the winter of 1937–8 and 'The Great Flood' put back the clock. I have described that flood elsewhere[2] but since it is a matter of Broadland history I take leave to repeat the picture as one knew it then on that Saturday in February:

"It was six o'clock on a dark night. All day the sea had pounded

[1] Sennight—seven nights, a week.
[2] *Harvest Adventure*, Harrap, 1946.

Caister Castle, a famous Broadland ruin

hollowly through hours of shouting gales against the thin sand-hills. Then, in the beginning of the dark hours, it broke through at Horsey Gap. First a trickle, then a swirl of curdled waters, and, when the next great roller flung itself, white-crested, at the hills, the whole bank collapsed with a rumble and a roar.

"A hell's-pool of water poured through—a deep, wide millrace with all the North Sea behind it in power and volume. The sand-hills crumbled to left and right. Great mountains of sand fell into the flood and were tossed away. The marshes became, first, a thin film of glistening water. Next, a racing succession of spreading pools. Within an hour they were a lake as far as eye could see. And still the sea poured in. But there was no man to see, no eye to witness, this high drama. For drama it was, since the sea had come back to claim its own again, to open up the ancient harbour where once the Hundred Stream flowed without hindrance into the North Sea. That was the haven where the Vikings laid up their long-ships. And on that night in February 1938 the sea came back.

"In the dark night the waters spread from Somerton to Hick-ling, from Martham Holms to Waxham, Horsey, its church, hall, and village, became an island again. Those lonely farmhouses of Somerton Holm and Winterton Holm were again what they had been—'holms', or islands amid the waters.

"Cattle stampeded for the high lands. Hares made for the islets and the upland fields. Rabbits were drowned by the thousand. Moles, voles, rats, field-mice, and worms were slaughtered in thousands. For a year or more there was no worm in the soil. Between ten and fifteen thousand acres were all either one great lake or poisoned by salt. When morning came a glittering inland sea stretched as far as the eye could see. Draining mills stood up like black lighthouses. Tens of thousands of coarse fish floated, belly-up. Huge pike up to thirty pounds in weight, perch, roach, rudd and shoal beyond shoal of great slab-sided bream were killed.

"Two men in a punt went out with their guns on the Waxham Marshes. They found 104 hares huddled like sheep on an islet. They shot the lot. Their punt could scarce carry the carcasses home. Even snakes were drowned out, and found coiled in death round gate-posts and bushes or washed up with the tide-line far inland. Great clouds of gulls fought and clamoured over the dead. It was a feast for them and for the harriers, the hawks, for the

8

The lonely ruin of St. Benets Abbey on the Bure

carrions crows, the jackdaws—for every ghoul and scavenger that walked or flew—but a tragedy for all else.

"When Arthur Dove, the millman of Horsey, walked downstairs on that dark Sunday morning he stepped up to his knees in salt water in his own kitchen.

"Then men began to count the tale of themselves and see which man was missing. In half a dozen villages there were anxious whispers. Was So-and-So at home? Had this or that man been seen the night before? Had Bill been down on the marsh after the cattle? Or had Tom been 'under the hills' after illicit rabbits? And, behold, one man was missing. He was a milkman. He and his lorry were lost.

"Away inland, at Potter Heigham, which in far centuries gone was once a tiny seaport, the butcher told Herbert Woods, who is uncrowned king of that village, Lord High Admiral of his fleet of yachts and pleasure boats. The missing man had not been seen for near a day at Martham or Palling or Horsey or Somerton. And between all those four villages the water stretched for miles. Somewhere out in that wilderness of water he was lost, perhaps drowned.

"So Herbert Woods took his most powerful motor-boat, and, with three of his men, and a dinghy in tow, with hot soup and rugs and brandy, they set out up-river towards the sea. It was a wild day of gales and running tide, of white-capped waves and rising waters. No other boat faced the river that day. For miles they cruised over hedges and marshes, scanning the waters with field-glasses. At last, halfway between Horsey and Somerton, they spied the top of the lorry sticking up above the seawater. A huddled figure waved feebly. He was marooned on that lonely marsh road which runs from Somerton to Horsey.

"The motor-boat could not reach the lorry. So they anchored and set off in the dinghy, four men rowing desperately against an easterly gale that tossed their boat like a cork. Time and again the dinghy was blown off her course, and, said Herbert, telling me the tale, 'I think that poor chap must have been near hysteria, for every time we were swept off our course he screamed terribly. It was a dreadful thing to hear. When we got to him he was so frozen with cold and so weak that we had to lift him off the top of the lorry slowly, lower him into the boat, which was tossing up and down on the waves in the gale, and then rub him down and give him hot soup.

" 'He was a young man, only about thirty, but he was so weak and cold that I think he'd have collapsed and died within another couple of hours. Luckily we were in time, and he pulled round. He was blue with cold, and his feet were only just above the water.' "

From Waxham to Horsey Mere by the Meadow Dyke, through flat marshes where reeds sigh in the wind to Heigham Sounds and thus down Kendal Dyke to the slow waters of the Thurne, is no more than half a morning's sail—less if you choose to pollute the silence with a motor-boat. Turn left—since we are not at sea I refuse to be nautical—and you will come to Martham Ferry which may hold you up for a brief moment. Pass that and eventually, in peace and quiet, you will come to the Hundred Stream, now an insignificant dyke. It goes snaking off to the left through cattle marshes, under the Horsey road, to Bramble Hills on the coast which, when I had the shooting, was a deadly place, full of un-exploded bombs and things waiting to blow you up. Once, centuries ago, the Hundred Stream was a harbour wherein the King's ships rode at anchor. Today it is only fit for a gun-punt.

Keep therefore to the right, along that deep, broad dyke, edged by tall reeds which they called the Dungeon. It is full of great eels and whacking pike. There you come upon the opening to Martham Broad on the left and a dyke which leads into the little South Broad on the right. Martham Broad you may navigate in a small boat, but not with ease for in summer it is thick with weed and at any time of the year it is shallow. The South Broad is private and a nature reserve and for that reason it is barred by a great chain.

To me it is a place of infinite nostalgic charm for when I was lucky enough to be the shooting tenant of this estate of Burnley Hall the little South Broad was, for a few enchanted years, one's private paradise.

Upland corn stubbles march down to the southern shore where a little grove of oaks, twisted by North Sea winds, stand solemnly, their feet in lipping waters. A tiny green beach, a little woodland plat scarce twenty yards long, an oasis of green grass and autumn-gilded oaks in a flat sea of rustling reeds, of rippled water that lies blue as the Mediterranean under the high Norfolk sky.

You will not see another boat from month's end to month's end on that small secret broad, locked away behind its dense reed beds, behind the padlocked rusty chain which spans the narrow entrance dyke.

Little waves race away, a running glint and gleam in the autumn sun, across the broad and into far bays, hidden channels and tiny islands of tall reeds. If you lie down in the sun, eyes almost level with the water, you get a duck's eye view of this enchanting tiny lake. For it is tiny, yet, under the high sky, lying flat and gleaming amid the marching reeds, it seems vast, vast as a small sea, lonely as a Saxon echo. Flotillas of coots ride black and bobbing on the running wavelets. Mallard and teal rise with a rush, swing round in high airy circles, plane down again on bent wings, hit the water, paddles first, and ride the surface like alert destroyers.

Lie low, let the punt slide grey and ghostly before the marsh winds, that wind which sings and smells of the sea, the sea that beats and grumbles for ever beyond tawny sandhills across a mile of marshes where dykes gleam like crossed swords, and you will see much more.

Lie low and let the punt ride, a sliding creature of wave and wind, and the birds come to you.

That gliding ragged shape that comes low over the reed-beds, glide and flap, flap and glide, is a marsh harrier, half as big as an eagle. They breed here. It is almost their last home in all England. They pluck young partridges from the sandhills, whip up the crouching pheasant poult from the linseed field by the far wood of drowned skeleton oaks, scare the ducks and send the coots into a frenzy of thrashing feet and unflung whitened spray. They are killers. No friends of the shooting man, no friends of the game preserver, no friends of birds great or small, these gliding shapes with the dove-grey wings, the tawny heads, the yellow, reaching claws, and the bright tiger eyes. But we do not shoot them. Theirs is a beauty too old, too ancient, too savage an echo of the medieval England that hides shyly in such forgotten corners, too rare and windy a beauty to be shot. They are worth a partridge chick, a pheasant poult or a wounded duck. For of such forgotten echoes of past beauty is compounded the present beauty of this lost little lake among the whispering reeds and the flat marshes that lie within constant threat of the sea.

In the middle of the broad is an island. A tiny plat of green grass with a fringe of reed. On it sits a flint-built Victorian boat-house with a thatched roof where swallows nest and a kingfisher lends lambent grace. They call it the Pleasure Hill. The name evokes an undying picture of Victorian ladies in crinolines and wide straw hats with coquettish parasols, boating down from the Hall with a vast luncheon hamper and plaid rugs to spread upon the grass. An afternoon in the sun with the water lilies and the glancing dragonflies. The swirl of a basking fish. Sharp and thin, the cry of terns, snowflake-white, plunging like plummets into the water. The slow, wavering dip and roll of black terns, blue and indigo in the sharp light. The Victorians were content with quiet beauty and laughed at little things. Perhaps that was why they lived long lives and died with a happy faith.

Go quietly up the dyke from the broad towards the thatched roofs and waddling white geese of the little village of West Somerton and you pass, on the right, the tall brick tower of Somerton draining mill.

That mill is something of a monument to the lonely lives and quiet heroism of the race of Norfolk millmen. For centuries these men have tended their mills in the loneliest parts of eastern England. They knew the rise and fall of the waters over thousands of acres of marshes. They knew exactly what the easterly gale would do in the North Sea and how the bore of the tide upriver might bring death in the night to sleeping villagers, their cattle and sheep. They were the guardians of the marshland.

Such a one was my old friend, Dick Jettens of West Somerton. A typical marshman, short and broad, shrewd of eye and of infinite wisdom. He lived in a thatched cottage near the Staithe where he farmed twenty or thirty acres of land, kept his cow and fattened his pigs. A good man in a boat, a dead shot with a gun and a tireless walker through shoulder-high reeds, over quaking fens and on the heavy clay of the uplands.

One wild night of gale and lashing rain, death almost came to Dick Jettens in Somerton draining mill. Alone, in the dark, he climbed to the top of the tall brick tower to set the sails. The wind roared and buffeted in from the North Sea, trumpeted in great gusts across the marshes, and flung itself with shuddering fury upon the tall, lonely mill, standing there in the starlight by the dark waters of that stream they call the Dungeon. The sails whirled madly in the wind with a great rushing hooroosh, with that sweep and fine frenzy which is irresistible, terrifying to watch.

Inside, the tall dark mill shook and shuddered. The machinery clattered, clanked and groaned. The wind screamed like ten thousand devils in the wooden top and clawed at the balcony as though it would wrench it away. Far below, brown flood waters from the marshes churned and gurgled over the paddle wheel, pouring white-crested into the Dungeon.

And in that inferno of screaming winds and clattering machinery, high in the dark top of the mill, fifty feet above the ground, a wheel caught Dick Jettens by the coat. It tossed him back and forth. It banged him on the floor, flailed him up and down like a terrier with a rat. It punched him into unconsciousness. It stifled his screams, the screams which none would have heard, for the nearest cottage, that of old Di Thain, the Broadsman, was near half a mile away. It would, in another brutal minute or two, have killed him.

Mercifully, his coat ripped up the back seam and, bruised and unconscious, he was flung into a corner.

That is why one of Dick's arms always carried ghastly wounds. Flesh and bone were shrunken. The arm was bound in leather.

West Somerton village is small, old and quiet. The people do not change a lot. The Thains, marsh farmers, eel-catchers and wherrymen, have been there or thereabouts since the dawn of time—or, as I guess, since the Vikings. What, after all, is Thain but an anglicization of the Norse Thegn, which became the Scottish Thane? Dionysius Franklin Thain is, in himself, a fine marriage of the Greek philosopher, the Saxon freeman and the Danish rebel, an old friend of earlier days. Harry Thain is one of the best eel fishermen in Norfolk. I have known him catch a six-pounder and a four and a half-pounder and he had another of five and a half pounds which I did not see. He has had tench of that weight in his net and plenty of big perch of a couple of pounds or so. Percy Thain owned that good old wherry the *Fir* whilst 'Blucher' Thain was one of the greatest wherry skippers in this century. Sidney Thain used to keep the Nelson Head at Horsey. Walking along the shore one wintry morning he picked up a Brent goose, alive. Its wings were not broken. It was undamaged by shot. It was free of oil. Yet it made no attempt to fly or swim from him.

'Sydda' took home the small, dark wild goose with the burnished breast of purplish black and the broken white ring round its neck. Like enough it had been bred in Spitzbergen or on the snow-whitened wastes of Franz Joseph Land in the Arctic, where bull seals roar. Yet it adopted 'Sydda' and his wife as a lost child will adopt those who give it a home. For a few days it was shy and frightened. Then it started to eat grass. After that corn. Then it fed with the chickens on chicken meal, bread crusts and kitchen scraps. To show her gratitude the little goose laid a nest full of small white, round eggs for Mrs. Thain.

When spring came the little goose, stirred by primitive urge flew up out of the hen-run and straight out to sea. 'Sydda' and his wife mourned her. Next morning the goose was back among the chickens in the hen-run. And 'Sydda' and his wife were as happy as though the prodigal son had come home.

Burnley Hall, where lived my old friend, Sir Gerald Talbot, is the Manor House of the village. A warm, red-brick, Georgian house, with six or eight bedrooms, a walled garden, a tiny park and a belt of trees at the back to shelter it from the sea wind. In those trees stands a ruined church. From the floor of the chancel springs a straight oak tree, thirty feet high or more. It tops the roofless church wall, rustles its leaves in the sharp sea winds and spills its acorns for feeding pheasants.

"Years ago an old woman up and died" Dick Jettens told me. "She had a wooden leg and allus went hoppity. They buried the owd gal under the chancel floor. Her owd leg took root. That sprouted. And up came the oak tree. But the owd gal she didn't sprout. She lays quiet—proud of her leg, I reckon."

Beyond Somerton, towards Winterton, a cold ridge of plough sweeps up to the sky. They call it the Blood Hills, since here was fought one of those many dateless battles between Saxon and Viking. The hills ran red with blood.

All this coast from Winterton to Somerton, from Horsey to Happisburgh and far beyond is smugglers' country. The sandy farm track from Winterton Holmes Farm on the Burnley estate down to Somerton Gap at Winterton Ness—the most easterly point of England—is still called by farm labourers "the owd Smugglers' Road" for at the Gap many a cargo was landed and carried inland by wherry. That was when the millmen would set their sails at certain angles over fifty square miles of flat marshes to warn the smugglers and their receivers that a cargo had been landed or that the coastguards were on the prowl.

Hickling has its own stock of legends. You will hear of the Hickling Skater. You will see him on a winter night of ice and white moon, speeding across the broad, sparks flying from the soundless cut and clip of his flashing skates. He wears the uniform of one of Wellington's grenadiers. For it was on a bitter winter night of the Napoleonic Wars that the young Hickling soldier skated across the broad to meet his village sweetheart by the War Bush—a little marshy island where the local boys hid from the press gang. Suddenly there was a loud crack and the young soldier went through a patch of 'stock ice' into the bitter water. Weeks later the body was found when the ice broke up.

When all Norfolk was deep in snow with drifts fifteen feet deep in the winter of 1946, a pony drawing a horse sled belonging to Ned Bell of Hickling suddenly went through the ice. Two men skated off and came back with a ladder and ropes. The horse was lassoed, pulled to the surface, the ladder was pushed under its belly and with twenty men pulling, sledge and pony reappeared and were driven off dripping across the ice. They take those sort of things for granted.

Donald Applegate once told me an inspiring story of old George Applegate the Elder who had an eel-sett in Candle Dyke. Old George was hauling in his nets one dark November night with young Donald hauling the end of the net on the bank. Donald shouted to the old man and got no answer. So he jumped into his dinghy, rowed down the dyke and bumped into a drifting punt in the darkness. "I heard a sort of a squawk", says he, "so I ran my fingers round the gunwale of the punt, and came on the old man's paws a-holdin' on".

"Gimme a leg out a-here, booy," says he. "I'm none tu warm, and I don't want tu hev tu walk home along the bottom of this here old dyke. Thass tu mucky!"

"I got the old boy aboard my boat," said Donald. "And, do you believe me, he wouldn't let me rub him down or take him ashore. He jest hopped into his punt and rowed back to Potter best part of two miles, although that was so dark you couldn't see your ten fingers spread out six inches in front of your nose. He was eighty-five then, but that never worried him. He lived till he was ninety-two and then he only died of old age.

"Ill? He never had no more than a toothache all of his life."

Here in the Hickling and Horsey fens the old Broadland traditions, customs and way of life still survive. The landscape is unspoiled. Wildlife is protected. The waters are unpolluted. No brash development ruins the scenery.

How long this state of affairs can endure elsewhere in Broadland is a moot point. The visible forces of destruction increase each year. If an overall plan to preserve and develop the Broadland scene is not put into force within the next few years, England will lose a unique part of her rural heritage of beauty.

IX

GLORY OF THE WHERRY

The Sailing Ship of the Marshes—Skippers, Cargoes and Races

THE Norfolk wherry was unique among boats. There was nothing quite like it in Holland. Nothing approached it in design or appearance upon the once-wide meres and great rivers of the Fens. That, in itself, is remarkable for the wherry was primarily a trading ship in the not-far-off days when marsh-farmers and those whose land abutted on coastal creeks and estuaries, sent, perhaps, three-quarters of their produce by water. Roads were deep in mud for six months of the year. Farm roads were 'bottomless'. At Horsey, for example, the road to Somerton was over quaking bogs in which farm wagons could sink to their axles. Bundles of faggots and reeds lashed together were laid in the wetter parts of the road in the days when Robert Rising was Squire of Horsey.

At home in the Fens in my great-uncle's time, which was about 1870–80, it took eight hours for a four-wheeled wagon, laden with wheat and pulled by three to four horses, to reach Newmarket only ten miles away. That was the state of secondary country roads. In the sodden marsh country of the Broads, the wherry was the obvious answer. Within my own life-time they were an everyday sight. To see a wherry, long, low with broad-bosomed bows, sweeping huge and batlike down a river or through a reedy channel, with its great sail towering high above the marshland scene and touching the reeds was more than impressive—almost awe-inspiring. They were, in fine, the fresh-water equivalent of the great sailing barges of the Medway, the Thames, the Essex Blackwater and the Suffolk estuaries. Those were the greatest sailing ships in the world to be worked solely by a man and a boy. The wherry, of somewhat different construction, was their younger inland brother, although occasionally they took to salt water.

The average wherry was long and shallow with a towering mast and a vast sail rigged on the principle of the old-fashion Una rig, but without a boom. They were from seventy to twenty tons burden and crewed by two men, a man and a boy, sometimes the wherry-man and his wife and, occasionally, by one man only. They could sail very fast, extremely close to the wind and were so handy that they could be navigated among other craft in a narrow river reach, to within an inch or so without scraping paint. There was a tiny cabin in the stern. The steersman stood abaft of this against the tiller with the sheet working on the 'horse' on the cabin top in front of him. The mast moved on a fulcrum. The lower end was weighted so that one man, working the foresail, could easily lower it or raise it.

If the wind fell away the wherryman and his mate pushed the craft along with a quant. This is a long, slender pole with a knob at one end and a spike and shoulder at the other. The shoulder was to stop it sinking in the mud. A quant is not unlike the 'spread' which was used by Fenmen to propel the turf barges on the Wicken and Burwell Fens in my youth.

The wherryman first went forward to the bows of his craft and then plunged the quant into the water, put the knob against his shoulder and walked aft along the plank-ways or catwalk, shoving as hard as he could. This part is easy enough. The amateur can do it—but when he tries to pull the quant out of the mud he may easily find that it pulls him in. Those who have fallen overboard from a punt on the Thames, the Cam or the Isis will sympathize.

One odd little superstition among the old wherrymen was that a quant must always be laid on deck with its point towards the stern whilst the boat hook should be laid with its point towards the bows. Otherwise the voyage would have bad luck. In practice this is, of course, plain common sense. The average quant had a wonderful quality of bend and spring. They were made of the best natural-grown pine and would bend like a sword-blade.

I have been lucky enough to see, and occasionally sail with, some of the last of the wherries. Today what few trading wherries are left on the Broads have auxiliary motors. The old *Albion* which was saved by the Norfolk Wherry Trust is, I believe, the last one still propelled solely by sail.

I learnt what little I know about wherries from that splendid old Broadsman, the late Donald Applegate of Repps, fifteen years or more ago when we sailed our boat up the 'Catfield River' to Catfield Staithe. This is what I wrote of it at the time:

"For centuries the wherries sailed up the Catfield River bearing cargoes of coal and stone, granite and marl, and taking away corn, roots and wood. The Riches family who own the Staithe, were famous wherry-owners, and from it sailed those famous wherries, *The Two Brothers*, *The Zulu*, and *The Violet*. They were all trading up to 1910, carrying cargoes of up to thirty and forty tons each.

"Old Skipper Childs and 'Dodger' Bob Miller were famous wherrymen who used this river. 'Dodger' lived and died in a tiny brick cottage standing on the banks of the Thurne, in Repps parish between Potter Heigham and Thurne Mouth, not far from Repps Mill.

"When the old man lay dying on a couch his last thought was of his beloved wherry, and they still tell the tale of how the aged Broadsman raised himself with his last gasp and tried to push an imaginary quant with his shoulder. And, falling back, he died. 'Dodger' was a very fine skater in his day, as was old Ted Beales of Hickling, who sailed a wherry called *The Emily*.

"Beales was a very religious man and would never sail on a Sunday. No matter where he might be anchored on that day, he would always leave his ship and trudge across the marshes to worship at the nearest village chapel.

"In the end his wherry was run down by another in a high wind on the Bure between Runham and Yarmouth in the Six Mile Reach, where she sunk with a load of about twenty-five tons of corn. This led to a bitterly contested lawsuit, which was enlivened by much nautical knowledge and hard swearing by wherrymen witnesses before they could decide who had committed the error in helmsmanship.

"Now, since I have talked a good deal about wherries, it is as well, sitting here at Catfield Staithe where one old warrior lies sunk, to describe them. They are unique. No other part of England or the world can show any precisely similar boat.

"To begin with, a wherry is no more than a cargo barge, locally built for local waters and uses. They are usually fifty to sixty feet in length, with a beam of from ten to twelve feet, and only draw from two to three feet of water, so that they can sail almost in the track of a snail. They are usually from twenty to twenty-five tons' burthen, but there was one monster in the '80s or '90s of no less than eighty-one tons.

"The hull of the wherry is for nineteen-twentieths of its length one long hold, covered by hatchways which take off in two-foot sections. Aft is a tiny cabin about eight feet long, which contains two bunks, a small coal-stove, and two tiny wooden cupboards. There is no table, and you can only just sit upright in it, yet in such an incredible cramped dwelling Donald's grandmother, old Mrs. George Applegate, had three children. They were all born in the cabin, without medical assistance: ' 'Cos the doctor was too darned late.' And there the family lived for months on end, cooking and sleeping in a space about eight or nine feet square. All three children grew to lusty manhood and lived to great ages.

" 'Cripple John', an uncle, who kept the eel-sett in Meadow Dyke, became semi-paralysed in middle life but he still contrived to sail his boat with one arm and his teeth. He used his teeth to pull in his mainsheet! 'Cripple John' lived to the age of eighty-six, while his father reached ninety-two and his mother eighty-six, and as Donald said: 'They only drank the rainwater off the roof.'

"Old George Applegate built the thatched boathouse at Potter Heigham, which still bears his name, and the long, low cottage which stands end-on to the road near Broads-Haven. In 'the great March gale' of eighty years or so ago, when scores of ships were lost at sea, the old man shifted three or four sacks of potatoes to one corner of the house to stop it being blown over!

"Old George would leave Potter Heigham in his wherry at ten in the morning, loaded to the gunwale with corn, and would reach Yarmouth that night—a masterpiece of sailing, for Yarmouth is a good twenty miles and a strong tide often had to be encountered.

"At that time of day as many as sixteen wherries could be seen at one time loading and unloading at Potter Heigham bridge. They carried cargoes of granite, gravel, corn, roots wood, coal, cattle-cake, and anything else that needed transportation. Today if you are lucky you may occasionally see 'Blucher' Thain's *Lord Roberts* taking on or unloading her twenty tons of sugar-beet, and now, thanks to the late Herbert Woods' fine craftsmanship, the old *I'll Try*, rebuilt and repainted, is on the river again, under the Thain flag—but, alas! powered by motor and no longer driven by wind.

"It is doubtful if there are more than six trading wherries plying on the Norfolk rivers today, and I believe that only one of them still goes under sail.

"A wherry sail is an enormous affair of tanned canvas, a loose-footed mainsail with a towering gaff but no boom. The mast, stepped right forward in a tabernacle, and up to forty feet in height, is raised by a number of leaden weights, weighing up to a ton and a half each, attached to its heel. A windlass helps to pull this enormous spar to its full height, but it is an extraordinary fact that there is no standing rigging whatever.

"Although a wherry can sail closer to the wind than any other craft that floats, there are times when a dead head-wind means that she must be shoved along by sheer brute force. Then the quant comes into play.

"When under full sail a wherry fairly swoops down the river, looking like a huge brown bird from another world. The deck-planking in the waist of the ship surges under water for two or three inches, and a continual stream of water washes on to it and off again. It is a thousand pities that such noble craft, noble in their native strength and simplicity and their fitness for the task, should have been elbowed off the rivers by the march of so-called progress.

"Every wherry was sailed by the tell-tale indications of an iron weather-vane fixed to a short two-foot rod at the top of the mast. A three-foot length of silk swallow-tail bunting flew from the end of the vane, showing every whim and eddy of the wind. These vanes often took fantastic forms, the figure of a woman or an animal cut in iron being affixed at one side. Donald had one of a woman. He had painted her skirt green, her blouse red, her legs pink, and given her black shoes on a field of green grass.

" 'Well, I'll change the owd gal's colour-scheme next year,' said he. 'Must keep the gals in the fashion, you know.' This vane came off a wherry called the *Fir*, now owned by Percy Thain, son of 'Blucher'."

The forerunner of the Norfolk wherry was a craft known as the Norfolk Keel. The first wherry is recorded about 1706, so the wherry must have either pre-dated them or the keel was coeval with the birth of the wherry. I remember that patriarch of the Broads, William Hewitt of Barton, whose family have been in Broadland for centuries, saying that his grandfather sailed a Norfolk keel. I pointed out that this would date from 1706 or earlier.

"Yes, there or thereabouts," said William Hewitt. "You see, these old tales run over hundreds of years in old families like ours, especially when every one of us lives to eighty or ninety"—with a laugh.

"You can soon cover a few hundred years with three generations that way. But I don't believe there's a keel left anywhere, unless it's in a museum; and I've never seen a picture of one, although they do tell me there's a pub in Norwich called The Keel and Wherry, in King Street, which has some old pictures of the keel.

"I used to have one or two trading-wherries myself, and I won the silver cup given by your friend, Captain Fanshawe, when he was M.P. for these parts. That was in 1931. A real nice gentleman he was too, and a proper Conservative. We could do with him again.

"I won that cup with the *Lady Violet*, and a lovely wherry she was, but I sold her soon after, and now I hear the Catchment Board have got her and have rigged her with a derrick for dredging up mud. What a come-down for a boat that could sail like a witch!"

Christopher Davies, almost the first historian of the Broads, and certainly the first man to write about them at length as a holiday resort, had a good deal to say about wherries, wherrymen and a highly interesting passing reference to a Norfolk keel. In his classic *Norfolk Broads and Rivers*, published in 1883, he said:

"There are a large number of men employed in this kind of navigation, and as a rule they are sober, honest, and civil men, ready to give any assistance in their power to the yachtsman. A great weakness of theirs is a fondness for tea. This they boil in the kettle, which then never 'furs'. The wherries are built entirely of English oak, and a large one will cost about £500, including the sail and the ton and a half of lead which is bolted on to the heel of the mast, to act as a balance on lowering and raising it. They are so solidly put together, and the ribs are so close and strong that they last a very long time. Their 'lines' are very graceful, with a hollow entrance, and long fine run aft. Those interested in such matters will find drawings and dimensions in an article by the writer in the *Field* of 20th March, 1880. A small wherry of thirty tons burden would be fifty-two feet long by thirteen broad, and would only draw when loaded two feet six inches of water. A wherry's mast, having no stays to support it except a forestay, must be very stout and strong. They are made of spruce fir, and are very massive, yet we have seen a little girl amuse herself by rocking a mast up and down, so carefully was it balanced. A weight of two tons being played with by a little girl, was a curious illustration of the triumph of man's mechanical mind over matter.

"The sail is used without tanning until it gets dirty, when it is dressed with a mixture of seal-oil and tar, and so becomes a rich dark-brown, which in the sunlight often gives the needed warmth of colour to the landscape. The feminine character of vessels is well understood, and most of us have heard of a ship being in stays; but a wherry, when it is fine and the wind is light, puts her bonnet on. This is a strip of canvas which is laced on to the foot of the sail to increase its size, and the sail being hoisted higher up the mast, it is equivalent to setting a top-sail.

"We have often enjoyed a sail in a wherry, and if there is a good breeze it is exciting work steering. Their great length is rather embarrassing to one accustomed to small yachts, and they seem to run away from one. The way the masts are lowered when shooting a bridge is startling. On you go before a strong breeze until within a hundred yards of the bridge, when the sail is sheeted flat; the man goes leisurely forward leaving his wife or son at the helm, lets the windlass run; down comes the sail; the gaff has then to be detached from the mast and laid on the top of the hatches; then, just as you think the mast must crash against the bridge, it falls gently back, and you shoot under; up it goes again without a pause, the forestay is made fast, and under the pressure of the windlass the heavy sail rises aloft, all before you have quite got over your first impulse of alarm.

"Before a strong breeze and with the tide, the wherries will attain a speed of seven or eight miles an hour, and even at that pace, create less disturbance of the water than a small yacht. A laden wherry sails better than an empty one, as the latter carries no ballast except the lead on her mast. Sometimes, but not often, one is upset. Early in the eighteenth century one is recorded as having upset on Breydon Water while coming from Yarmouth, when twenty persons were drowned. She was no doubt bearing a holiday party, as wherries often do now. A year or two back one was upset by a sudden squall near Surlingham, and went so completely over that her masthead stuck several feet into the mud at the bottom of the river, and held her there. There was only one man on board, and he got ashore safely.

"The wherrymen are most civil and careful men, and accidents

Ramworth Broad off the River Bure

rarely happen to other craft through their fault. The yachting men recognize that the wherries are on business while they are on pleasure; and if there is a doubt as to what should be done, they give way to the wherry. In all other respects the more closely you adhere to the rule of the road the better do the men like it, for then they know what to do. We have been in a crowd, composed of seven wherries and two or three yachts, all cross-tacking in the same hundred yards of river, with a steamer threading her way between; and although the steering literally had to be to half an inch, there was no apprehension of any accident.

"The anglers are not by any means considerate towards the wherries. They moor their boats in the channel and at inconvenient corners, and are enraged if the poor wherryman sweeps by close to them, while perhaps it is all he can do to steer his craft so as to avoid running them down.

"In the summer time the life of these men cannot be a very disagreeable one; but in the winter, particularly during frost and snow, when ropes and gear are coated with ice, and the quant is one long icicle, the exposure and hardship is sometimes great. If the rivers are 'laid'—that is, ice-bound—their usual avocation ceases. Many take to ice-gathering for the warehouses which supply ice for the carriage of fish; and at any symptom of a frost, men will lay out with their wherries and collect the ice off the dykes, which of course freeze before the rivers, and a wherry may sometimes earn £30 or £40 in a winter. One of the ice warehouses is at the lower end of Oulton Broad; and on many a hot summer's day you may see the ice pouring in a glittering cataract down a timber-shoot into a vessel beneath.

"On fine days wherries go by sea between Yarmouth and Lowestoft, a distance of about nine miles. Many years ago, during a great depression in the traffic, several of these craft went down the coast to try their fortune on other rivers, but the adventure met with ill-luck.

"The present wherries (1880) are much smarter craft than those of a couple of generations back. At that time there was another class of vessels called 'keels' which were fitted with huge square lug-sails, and were chiefly used for carrying timber. These are now unknown. The last we saw was some ten years back on the Bure. We had moored opposite St. Benedict's Abbey one chilly gloomy evening, when a keel came up the river before the strong easterly breeze. The immense square sail, as she passed us and

9

The wide wild beauty of Barton Broad

drove on, shut out the narrow feeble sunset, and seemed to deepen the gloom around us. She was a very old-looking craft, and so far as we know she has never reappeared from the faint western glow in which she then disappeared.

"Like their close relatives the Dutch, the water-abiders here are fond of bright colours, and a newly-painted wherry is gorgeous with red and blue and yellow. The masthead is always gaily painted, and is further decorated with a vane, cut in the shape of some nautical figure or emblem, and with a red streamer attached. It is a picturesque sight to see a wherry's deck being tarred. Over a roaring fire a caldron of tar is evaporating into pitch. The boiling liquid is poured on to the deck and spread, while it is rapidly covered with sawdust, which is trodden down by a war-dance on the part of the men. The object of this is not only to keep the deck watertight, but to give a better foothold to the men when quanting. Again, we have seen a picture worth painting when a wherry has been canted over by means of a rope from her mast, and in a boat alongside men in the picturesque waterside costume are burning the tar off her bottom with huge torches made of bundles of reeds as big as wheatsheaves. And oh, the delightful smell of the tar! Speaking honestly, a bit of tarred rope has a sweeter fragrance to us, and a greater wealth of association, than the choicest posy of flowers.

"Wherries are often fitted up as yachts, and may be hired for the purpose, and very comfortable cruising craft they make."

The Broads have always bred good small-boat sailors. Sea-going sailors may sneer at them as ditch-crawlers and 'mud-pilots' but the fact remains that anyone who can navigate a small sailing boat in the narrow dykes and overcrowded rivers of the Broadland and sail it with skill and without going aground in some of the shallowest sailing waters in England, is no fool. Nowadays too many people who hire a boat on the Broads know little or nothing of how to handle it. They are the eternal hazards which the real small-boat sailor has to watch like a hawk.

When Nicholas Everitt who was not only a lawyer of considerable eminence but a Broadland landowner—he lived at North Cove Hall for many years—was writing his unique book, *Broadland Sport*, in 1900 and 1901, he included voluminous and detailed notes on yachting, past and present, on these waters. To look back to the lateen-rigged racing craft of his day is a vision into a vanished world. For example, the old *Enchantress*, built about 1850 by Mr. Green of Wroxham, was nineteen feet on the ram with a counter seven feet long, nine feet of beam and she drew four feet. Her foreyard was sixty feet! Later Mr. O. Diver of Yarmouth converted her into a ten-ton cutter. The Lateeners were all the fashion then. Now you never see one.

Nicholas Everitt, however, describes a craft which was the sensation of his day and was obviously a forerunner of the catamaran of today. This is what he ungallantly described as the "racing machine, *Gossip*". Mr. George Mollet of Brundall designed her about 1890. Everitt says: "She was as quaint a looking craft as one could well meet with and looked like a raft raised upon two pontoons. She was a double-hulled boat drawing less than a foot of water, and her middle was hollowed out so that when she rested upon an even keel an undivided waterline extended all round her. In sailing she ran over the water rather than cut through it, and as she carried 450 feet of sail area it is no wonder she left everything else behind. She was very simply rigged with a large lug-foresail and a small mizzen, whilst her stability was assisted by a sliding centre-plate of three feet to four feet exposed area. Her rough measurements were L.W.L. seventeen feet; beam, seven feet; depth, two feet.

"After winning her first race at Oulton Broad on a Whit Monday, she was offered for sale for thirty pounds but purchasers were shy as they did not altogether appreciate her appearance and preferred a safer ship to sail in. She was however sold a few days afterwards, and her new owner, during her first racing season, won prizes equal in value to more than double the purchase money.

"This boat was the forerunner of a class of racing machines which exercised full sway upon the waters of Broadland for the next seven years. These boats have no comfort, even for sailing, much less for cruising; everything is sacrificed for speed."

To my mind the most charming pictures of everyday life on the Broads in the '70s, '80s and '90s is given in that enchanting book by Oliver Ready *Life and Sport on the Norfolk Broads* which was published before the First World War. His father was Rector of Waxham for forty years or so in the days when the whole parish consisted of only fifty or sixty people. His sons, as merry as a pack of hounds, had the run of broads, marshes, farms, boats and sea-going smacks and lifeboats. No children could have had a more idyllic upbringing in a world in which peace and security seemed immutable—for was not Napoleon dead and the Union Jack and the British Navy supreme.

His description of Hickling Water Frolic is a rural cameo of sheer delight. Alongside the staithe at the Pleasure Boat "lay boats of various sizes, shapes, colours and ages, all lateen rigged, with sails hoisted and flapping in the breeze, while aboard or on the path, men and youths with rolled-up sleeves were putting the finishing touches: a new lashing here, a block changed there, a few stitches in the leech to prevent quivering, and throwing up water on to the sails to make them hold the wind.

"It was Hickling water-frolic, and the first match was about to start.

"Berthed nearest the broad lay the Rarverand's *Thorn* with Old Tom, two of his sons, grandson Albert, and big Dick Suggate, the boat-builder, aboard by way of crew.

"It was the day of lateeners in those remote waters. Whence the peculiar model and picturesque rig came I do not know, but both have now long since disappeared, never to return.

"The *Thorn*, winner of many a hard sailed race, embodied all the best points of this curious class.

"Her actual hull was about fourteen feet long, though an enormous square eight-foot counter stern lying almost clear of the water, gave her a length overall of, say, twenty-two feet.

"Half-decked, bows broad and bluff, and a nine-foot beam, she presented a very tubby appearance, though below water her lines were fine, with a two-foot iron keel and a large rudder swinging below the counter.

"Painted, black sides with vermilion streak round gunnel, red bottom, and slate colour on decks and inside well, she looked very smart and impressive.

"Her short, thick foremast, stepped right in the bows with a strong rake forrard, carried an enormous lateen sail with a yard about forty feet long, and an eighteen-foot boom swinging just clear of the mizzen-mast.

"Almost burying herself in the water, throwing up a big bow-wave, and drawing a small mountain astern, that enormous sailspread still forced her along at great speed, and she would roar majestically by with all the power and swell of a steam launch.

"Beating into the wind was her strong point, for besides sailing

very close, she went about like a flash, and without losing hardly
any way; while running before a strong breeze was dangerous
work, as her towering mainsail, pressing down on the foremast
raking right over the bows, forced her further and further into the
water, till she would crash along, bows level, with all hands con-
gregated on the counter to keep her from running under.

"In the first match were the *Thorn*; the *Maria*, another noted
racer belonging to a sporting farmer; the *Ethel*, always down by
the bows and up by the stern; the *B.B.* and several others, though
the *Ethel*'s enormous yard having snapped in two shortly after
starting, the race soon resolved itself into a duel between the
Thorn and the *Maria* of which Old Tom, as usual, just managed to
get the better.

"All the neighbourhood for miles round seemed to be there, for
the broad was thickly dotted with wherries and boat-loads of
sightseers being either sailed or quanted about so as to get good
views of the racing.

"Just before the second match, general attention was claimed by
Harold (aged about seven or eight), who, having borrowed a
large lateen sail from Old Peyton, the inn-keeper, had hoisted it
on his little green boat, which, caught dead aft by a strong puff,
flew out of the front deek at the rate of knots, sheering about and
rolling so wildly from side to side as to alternately ship water
over both gunnels, while Harold worked frantically at the helm
to avoid ramming other craft, till finally she capsized to windward
and sank in open water about a hundred yards out, amidst prolonged cheering.

"On the staithe a troop of niggers provided music and much
merriment, while the continuous roar of voices from the inn
parlour proclaimed a busy day for the trade.

"Sailing races over, excitement centred round a sculling match,
which, after several false starts, numerous fouls, one fight, which
carried both combatants overboard and was continued in five feet
of water, and endless hard language, was won by Tom Goose of
Horsey while a quanting match was carried off by Old Tom's son
Noll, who, in his prime, took a lot of beating.

"Next day we learned that more fights than usual had kept
matters lively at the Pleasure Boat till a late hour, and as several
of the gladiators had been 'pulled', water-frolic interest continued
unabated till fitting pains and penalties had been inflicted by the
local magistrate. . . .

"Barton Broad, four miles from Hickling by road but more than twenty by river, was a fine sheet of water with good depth in those days, though latterly it has become much choked up by dense growths of weed.

"Barton water-frolic was an important annual fixture at which most of the local cracks competed.

"I remember driving over one morning with father and joining the Rarverand and Activity in a large flat-bottomed boat anchored amongst low reeds and in such a position as to command a good view of the whole broad.

"Both the *Thorn* and the *Maria* were sailing in the principal race, together with half a dozen other lateeners and one big white cutter, which, it being the first occasion such a rig had competed in those waters, gave rise to great comment and a good deal of apprehension amongst local owners.

"It was a cloudy day and blowing so hard that most of the boats would have reefed had it not been that an upset in those shallow waters spelt nothing worse than a ducking, for which reason every stitch of canvas was hoisted by all, on the sporting chance.

"The race was four times up and down an S-shaped course, in all about seven miles; starting from fixed moorings and drawing lots for berths.

"The *Thorn* had her usual crew aboard and Old Tom, luckily drawing No. 1, got the windward lay.

"How those boats roared through the water when manœuvring to take up positions, heeling right over beneath their forty-foot spars till even keels could sometimes be seen! It was most exciting, but suddenly they were all in a beautiful line, with snow-white sails fluttering and cracking like whips in the gale, when 'bang' went the starting gun, and they were off.

"At the report the old *Thorn* seemed to shoot right ahead, gaining a lead of perhaps forty yards within the first half minute, and there she stuck for the whole race, with the other eight boats hard on her heels like a pack of hounds, leaving behind them lanes of foam, and sending up a combined roar that carried to the furthest limits of the broad.

"You never saw such a sight! The poor old *Thorn* looked just like a hunted deer, settling down into the water as though straining every nerve to escape, while each minute our hearts were in our mouths as she staggered wildly beneath her towering cloud of canvas; 'She can't live.' 'Yes, she can.' 'Ah-h-h!' as she gibed round the top buoy and half her foresail was in the water, followed by an involuntary cheer as she gathered herself together again.

"Once there seemed no hope, the Rarverand exclaiming, 'She's gone!' and lowering his field-glasses; but lo! with sails almost flat on the water, and all her crew perched on the windward side, she luffed and slowly righted, and then tore on past us like a train, her bows smothered in foam, big Suggate standing right aft, Albert frantically working at the pump, and Old Tom with set face and hand on the tiller, watching her every move, while the swell she rolled broke over and almost swamped our boat.

"The *Maria* and the big white cutter were the worst, for first one and then the other would draw right up, till we thought the *Thorn* must be caught, and then die away again, but only apparently to gather up strength for a fresh attack.

"During the last round the wind, if anything, increased, and several boats came to grief, though everyone was too absorbed in the deadly struggle between the three leaders to pay heed to aught else.

"At last the gun fired, as our good old *Thorn*, twenty yards ahead of the cutter, fled past the winning flag, to be instantly shot up into the wind by Old Tom: the strain over, the race won! Hip, hip, Hooray!!...

"... Two or three days after the water-frolic I again found myself, uninvited, aboard the *Thorn*, in company with the Rarverand and her usual crew, including Activity in charge of the lunch-basket and two gallons of six-ale in a big stone bottle.

"With two reefs in the huge racing mainsail and the cup flag flying proudly at our peak, we bowled across Barton Broad on the twenty-mile sail through beautiful winding rivers, back to Hickling....

"... Shooting by Thurne Mouth, where masses of dark-green bulrushes fringed the broad and tidal stream, we reached Heigham Bridge at about three o'clock, when it began to drizzle, with wind falling light and five miles still to go, though frequent pulls at the stone bottle kept our crew in high spirits, despite the ever present flaky specks.

"Through Candle Deek, Narroways, over the Sounds and Whittlesea, we reached Deep Deek by five o'clock, and could just see Hickling Broad opening out through the now heavy rain, when darting from amongst the reeds, a flat-bottomed boat drew alongside, the dripping occupant, a thin, tallish man with a long beard, holding on to the *Thorn*'s gunnel and showering on the Rarverand a torrent of congratulations.

"It was John Grapes, thatcher, marshman, wildfowler and fisherman.

"When at last the Rarverand could get a word in, it was to ask if Mr. Grapes could drink a glass of beer.

"Mr. Grapes could, certainly he could, though of course he had thought of no such thing when coming alongside.

"Activity looked deeply concerned, holding the enormous bottle to his ear with both hands and shigging it vigorously, while Old Tom thought there might be 'just one more glass if yer squeeze her right tight'.

"Grapes held forth a tumbler, over which Activity turned the bottle upside down, when out shot some dregs of beer together with the mouldering skeleton of a mouse: strong even in death, and origin of those flaky hops!

"Fishing out and holding up the delinquent by its tail, Grapes looked thirstily from the half-tumberful of dregs to the faces of that horror-stricken crew, and then letting go the gunnel, shoved back into the reeds talking as he went.

"As for the crew, they trembled and quaked and brought forth laughter mingled with tears, oblations to that ridiculous mouse."

What a picture this gives us of rustic fun in Broadland villages before the Broads had become commercialized and alive with shiny little boats chugging busily from broad to broad, leaving their films of oil upon the water and scaring the birds with their din.

Oliver Ready gives an equally blithe picture of the visit of Edward VII when Prince of Wales to Great Yarmouth when "a wave of patriotic excitement passed over the whole of Broadland". There was no railway in those days. The famous old 'Goose and Dickey' line through Potter Heigham had not been constructed. We can date the period roughly by the remark made to me by my old Broads skipper, Donald Applegate, in 1948: "That old railway's no older than my brother Bob. That was being made same time as my mum and dad was making my brother Bob at home— that's sixty-seven year ago. When they opened it that ran from North Walsham to Yarmouth and on the first day they took all the Lords and Ladies from the Manors all along the line to Yarmouth an' give 'em a slap-up feed. After that they didn't stop for no one. You could jump on or get chucked off, didn't matter which. The guard always hulled the parcels out at the station as they whizzed through. One day they come thunderin' into Potter Heigham Station at a good twelve miles an hour when he chucked out a big parcel what ketched Simmons, the station-master, on the snout and laid him out flat. They were always impartial on that line." Since then, alas, the Goose and Dickey, like so many other charming little branch lines, has vanished.

In Oliver Ready's youth, since there was no railway, most of the local inhabitants drove by horse and trap or 'dickey and cart' to Yarmouth, but a good few walked. His young brother Harry went by sea with the coastguards after having chased their boat along the beach for five miles, at the end of which they took pity on him, lowered sail, put ashore and took him aboard. Oliver himself got a free passage for the round trip aboard the wherry *Emily* owned by George Deals of Waxham, whose son George went as skipper whilst his young brother Slam, nine years old like the young Oliver, "filled the position of first mate." Mr. Deals, by the way, rented land from the Rector for a quarter of a century on a verbal agreement. He always paid the rent when he liked which was usually before it was due "a lease for the land and receipts for the rent being considered quite unnecessary as between man and man".

The self-contained establishment of Mr. Deals and the voyage which followed is neatly described:

"Mr. Deal's house had been struck by lightning, he kept a cow, a sow, a donkey, a horse named Boxer, and besides the land, did a nice little business in coals and pig foods by means of the wherry.

"Therefore, I embarked early one morning with reliable friends, while a strong breeze from the most favourable quarter, nor'west by north, promised a quick passage.

"Running free, we soon covered the five miles to Heigham Bridge, on approaching which Slam dived down into the forepeak to free the foot of the mast from its retaining clamps, and when within a hundred yards of the massive old-time structure, rapidly lowered the sail; and then, just as we shot under the low, stone arch, our enormous mast swung gracefully down till it lay flat upon the hatches; to as gracefully swing up again the moment we were through, and be instantly clamped below, as well as made fast to the bows by a thick wire fore-stay, after which we both set to work cranking up the sail with all our might, so that the

Emily gathered way again and continued her voyage without making any stop."

Having chased the royal procession through the streets of Yarmouth and caught an ecstatic glance of the Prince of Wales at the moment when "an old lady leaned far out from her carriage window and touched his uniform as he rode by, whereon His Royal Highness turned in the saddle, bowed and smiled, to the old lady's perfect delight," the young Oliver set sail that night in the *Emily* with a full cargo of coals and maize on a voyage home against light headwinds which took nearly three days. Finally they berthed safely in the back dyke of the New Cut at Waxham. Here disaster overtook them, for 'the sail' was still standing, and the skipper being busy in the cabin rounding up, Slam and I took upon ourselves to lower it without orders.

"I was at the winch slowly unwinding, while he clung on to the halliards to ease the strain, which caused my crank to suddenly slip off, with the result that Slam was jerked ten feet up the mast before he could let go, as the enormous sail came down with a crash, snapping the gaff into three pieces and bursting half the cogs off the winch.

"It was all done in a moment, and who would have thought it!

"I noted our skipper's pale face at the cabin door gazing on the wreckage with staring eyes, I observed Mr. Deals, senior, slowly approaching up the lane, and I remember Slam and myself quietly but promptly quitting the scene for our respective homes."

My own last vision of a wherry came one night when we sailed out of the reed-fringed mouth of the Waveney, under Burgh Castle, into the wintry waters of Breydon. Dusk spread its wings above the luminous grey walls of the Roman castle-camp, with pigeons coming in from the marshes to roost in tall, ivied trees about the church and its high, lonely rectory. Starlings wavered in great clouds above reed-beds which stand with their feet in the salt waters, for, in those whispering wildernesses, they roost in chattering thousands, the sound of their wings like waves of the sea as they swoop and wheel.

As the boat turned her bows back into the grey waste of Breydon, a waste of waters which seemed to melt on every side into low, flat marshes so that you could scarce tell where water ended and land began, there came out of the mouth of Norwich river a wherry, her waist almost awash in the running waves. It was that staunch old vessel the *Lord Roberts*, gay even in the dusk with her strakes and stem painted in vivid hues of red, white and blue, a fine, barbaric display of colour utterly in keeping with her surroundings. For a boat is like a farm-wagon; it will glory in bright and garish colours since those colours are usually picked and painted by the native artistry of men who, although they may not be 'book-learned' or ape the pansified affectations of the modern interior decorator, yet derive in their country blood something from the brave imagery of the medieval craftsmen who were their native forebears.

There she drove through the waves, plunging a little on the tide, bold in her red and white and blue, a long, lonely little ship going out in the dying of the day, to the salty jumble of waters and rush of tides at Yarmouth. The lonely, leather-jerkined figure of 'Blucher' Thain, her owner-skipper, stood crook-kneed in the cold wind at the great tiller. So might some noble Thane of the Danish sea-rovers have skippered his long-nosed ship down this grey and bitter tideway when all the seas overflowed this land, and the salt tides lapped the shores of Norwich and flooded the far marshes of Earsham, away up the sinuous waters of Waveney.

'Blucher' waved a slow, wordless greeting as the wherry drew away towards Yarmouth and the sea. Her engine puttered quietly into the dusk, for no tall mast etched its stark spar against the sky, no huge sail bellied in the raw wind. And that is a loss in beauty.

X

ANGLERS' PARADISE

The Finest Coarse Fishing Area in England

BROADLAND is the coarse fisherman's paradise. No comparable area in England can offer such diverse variety of fishing. Every type of coarse fish can be taken. The sea fishing off the coast is superb and the relatively few trout waters are as good as you will get anywhere in the eastern half of England, with the possible exception of the Driffield Beck in Yorkshire. The trouble with trout angling, however, is that since the waters are few they are naturally strictly preserved and membership of a fly fishing club is almost as difficult as the entry of a rich man into the Kingdom of Heaven.

When we come, however, to pike, perch, bream, roach, rudd, tench, dace and monstrous eels, you enter the coarse fisher's Elysium. Why he should be called a 'coarse' fisherman is a mystery. His language is no coarser and his habits no worse than those of the dry-fly purist, when the latter hooks a bush or his own ear.

The fighting qualities of pike and perch are in many ways little inferior to those of salmon and trout—and the weight of fish which you may catch in Broadland waters would make many a trout stream look silly. The popularity of the Broads is best exemplified by the following comparative figures showing the number of licences issued by the East Suffolk and Norfolk River Authority:

	1955	1961	1962	1963
Freshwater (season)	32,642	49,392	51,858	53,021
Freshwater (day)	6,715	19,398	20,950	23,200
Trout (season)	605	749	611	649

The River Authority regulate fishing by the issue of licences; they employ bailiffs to enforce the by-laws and they control pollution by ensuring, or trying to ensure, that the effluents discharged into broads and rivers conform with the required standard of purity. That is an Augean task in itself. Pollution from boats, sewage and riverside development is a vast problem, dealt with at length in another chapter. It can well become a menace to fishing in some areas. It is fortunate therefore that the Authority re-stocks rivers, clears stretches of river bank and buys or leases fishing rights when they become available.[1]

Meanwhile although the anglers increase, the quality and quantity of the fish does not apparently decrease. Pike have been taken up to nearly forty pounds in weight. Perch of two and three pounds upwards are not uncommon. Bream can be caught by the hundredweight—if you like catching that singularly dull fish. Eels, according to Broadland legends have been taken up to nine pounds in weight. I have certainly seen, and eaten, a six-pound eel.

In the last century freshwater fishing on the Broads was as much a commercial business as trawling at sea. Fish were taken in nets by the ton and sent to London and the great Midland cities by rail. Today that has finished. Eel fishing alone remains a commercial big-scale proposition. The size limits of fish laid down by the Authority are as follows: pike twenty-four inches; bream, chub, grayling, trout ten inches; carp, dace, perch, roach, rudd, tench eight inches.

Most anglers today faithfully return to the water those fish which they do not wish to keep. The old wasteful days of killing every fish that was caught and sometimes throwing it away to rot on the bank have largely gone. The present day visiting angler is usually a man who is tied to the office desk, the factory, the workbench or some other form of industrial slavery during the week. He lives too often in a concrete jungle or in a wilderness of small, featureless streets. His escape to the waterside is his moment of truth, his balm of peace, his return to natural things. All honour to him. He deserves the best that this crowded isle can give.

When he is the solitary angler he has the best that the world can offer him. But my heart bleeds for those patient droves of pegged-down club anglers who arrive by the coachload and dot the river banks with mathematical precision. Slavery has pursued them—and caught up.

[1] For practical information about Broadland fishing, see Appendix II.

Consider then the charm of a lake, Fritton Lake, away from the crowds, void of motor-cruisers and transistors, part of a great estate and a place of peace immutable. You have to walk there. It is worth it.

They say it is the best pike lake in England. I have never fished on Slapton Ley or Hornsea Mere, in the Welbeck lakes, in the ducal waters of Blenheim or in any of the Cheshire meres, but I have fished most of the Norfolk Broads, many Fenland waters, the Hampshire Avon, Gailey Pools, and a few other notable pike waters and can fairly say that, splendid though they are, they are not the equal, on a good day, of this long, glittering, tree-embowered lake set in the heart of the lovely Isle of Lothingland. Not one person in a hundred has ever heard of that enchanting Isle. Perhaps not one angler in ten thousand has ever fished Fritton Lake.

It lies a few miles at the back of Hopton which is halfway between Gt. Yarmouth and Lowestoft. You will find it marked on the map as Fritton Decoy. That is because one of the last duck decoys in England is still worked at one end of the lake by Lord Somerleytone's decoy-man. Many of the wildfowl caught there go to stock lakes in public parks.

The Isle of Lothingland is no isle at all, but it was one when Fritton Decoy or lake was an arm of the sea. The lake and the 6,000-acre estate of Somerleyton belong to Lord Somerleyton, a young, far-sighted and progressive landowner. This means that the natural beauty of the lake is preserved and that the land round it cannot be 'developed' by building speculators.

Fritton is about a mile long, very deep in parts and breathtakingly lovely. At one end lies the Old Hall with walled gardens, lakeside lawns—and a hundred yards of bank fishing. It is a sporting hotel of the old type.

Lord Somerleyton allows fishing and boating on the lake during the summer season, but in winter, when the decoy is working, anglers must restrict themselves to the Old Hall water.

Hark to the words of Mr. W. W. Ward as we talked together on the first occasion that I ever visited Fritton some fifteen years ago.

"Pike—we've got 'em—you might say almost too many. One winter we took 443 pike, every one over fifteen pounds, from this little stretch of water in seven weeks from December to February. That same winter we put back no less than 936 fish all under fifteen pounds each. They were the tiddlers."

"What on earth did you do with these fifteen-pound tiddlers whilst you were fishing and before you put them back" I asked. "You couldn't put them in keep nets."

"Ah," said Mr. Ward with a thoughtful smile, "We kept 'em in a keep-boat. We pulled an old boat up on the bank, about sixteen feet long, filled her full of water, and put all the fish into the boat until we'd done. They were splashing round there like a mass of eels on the boil. You never saw such a boat-load of fish. It would have made a taxidermist turn in his grave. Then, when we'd done fishing, we just tipped the boat over on its side and they all slithered back into the lake.

"I had half a boatful another day when his lordship came down to see me. He took one look at 'em and said: 'Those are the devils that kill my ducks. What are you going to do with them?'

" 'Put 'em back in the lake, my lord,' I said.

" 'Oh no, you don't. Knock 'em on the head! Knock 'em on the head! They kill dozens of my ducks.'

"Well, we kept on killing all we took for a time and then we came to the conclusion that if we were going to keep the fish population up we had better shoot the little 'uns back, so now everything under fifteen pounds goes back into the water.

"Big fish! Ah! We've had one or two really big 'uns but we can't beat that thirty-five and a half-pounder that a chap caught on Heigham Sounds near Hickling Broad. But we did have a real whopper of thirty-four pounds three ounces here twenty years ago, and a good runner-up was one of twenty-nine pounds five ounces which was caught here in 1947. I dare say there are several round about that size still waiting to be caught."

Some mighty eels have been caught in the lake, including one of eight and a quarter pounds which Mr. Ward caught on a dead bait. Another of six and a half pounds was taken in 1950. Such large eels are by no means uncommon in the Broads district. I saw an eel of five pounds, another of six pounds, and a third one of over six and a half pounds taken in an eel-sett in the Dungeon Dyke at West Somerton by Harry Thain, the eel catcher, in November 1947. These large eels are almost invariably very dark in colour. And it is supposed that they are "all-the-year-round" residents who do not migrate to the sea.

Is there anywhere else in England where a mere hundred yards of fishable water can show such an astounding record of pike.

Listen to the tale of the Rev. Mr. Stevens. That sporting parson, fishing in the winter of 1947 off the lawn, caught one twenty-five and a half-pounder, one twenty-five-pounder, three twenty-four-pounders and no less than ten sixteen-pounders—all *in one day*! Meditate on that, ye mighty ones of Slapton Ley and Fording-bridge, of Heigham Sounds and Hornsea Mere. And if that tale is not sufficient to stir the blood, what of the exploits of those two local farmers Mr. Noel and Mr. Skoulding? Those two mighty men caught no less than thirty-nine pike totalling 293 pounds between them—*in three hours*!

The great charm of Fritton is not only the size of the pike and the beauty of the scene, but the fact that you may see almost every species of wildfowl known in Britain and pretty well every animal from a red stag to a badger or an otter. I was there one day when an osprey, that lordliest of all anglers, was fishing the lake, a sight for the gods. He remained about the place for quite a time and chose the top of a tall tree for his roost. There are bitterns there also.

Fritton is almost unique as a duck decoy. Most decoy ponds are from an acre and a half to four acres in extent with some three to six 'pipes' radiating in semi-circles from the pond. These pipes are netted tunnels of water which become narrower towards the end away from the pond until finally the water in the pipe diminishes to a mere ditch and finally peters out. Where the water ends a long hooped detachable tunnel net, known as a 'trammel', stretches out across flat grass. This is the final trap into which the ducks are driven, until they are huddled in a dense mass, unable to fly. The decoy-man then takes them one by one in the trammel net.

The entire pipe from its wide lake-side mouth to the trammel net is arched over with iron hoops, covered with netting. Both banks of the pipe are fenced in by overlapping sections of tight-packed reed walls about six feet high. Between the reed walls and the water runs a narrow path with a little fence or 'dog-jump about a foot high set at the points where the reed screens overlap. Each pipe is worked according to the direction of the wind as ducks have a keen sense of smell.

The principal actor in this extraordinary drama is the decoy-man's dog known as a 'piper'. He is trained to trot along the bank-side path, hop over the dog-jump, disappear behind the next reed screen, re-appear in front of the following screen and repeat this jack-in-the-box appearance and re-appearance until he is well

Confusion worse confounded—at Ludham Bridge on the Ant

round the bend, the wild duck following him quacking abuse. It is presumed they think he is a fox. Ducks loathe the fox because he has a caddish habit of sneaking up like a serpent on his belly and leaping on the wild duck as it sits sunning itself on the bank. Many years ago a decoy owner tried out a monkey instead of a dog. The duck followed that also.

The first time I was ever privileged to see the Fritton Decoy work was when Walter Mussett was decoy-man and his dog Copper, a golden retriever, was in his prime as a 'piper'.

Through a peephole in the screen I saw about thirty mallard, teal and wigeon swimming in the mouth of the pipe. Tall reeds made a backcloth of yellow and gold, russet and fading green. The duck were completely unsuspicious. In the mouth of the pipe swam four or five mallard, almost within touching distance. A few yards up the pipe, three hen pintail, uncommon and beautiful, quacked and flapped in a little wired-in cage. They were the decoys.

Musset silently beckoned to Copper. That wise dog trotted unconcernedly around the edge of my screen, appeared in full view of the duck whose head shot up instantly, and loped quietly up the bank towards the next screen. She disappeared behind it, like a red shadow. Instantly a babel of abuse broke out from the duck. They began to swim rapidly towards the mouth of the pipe. Those already in it swam up it after the vanished dog. A second later Copper, at a nod from Walter, appeared silently from behind the next screen, flicked her tail, trotted past the screen and appeared again. It was uncanny. So was the behaviour of the duck. One and all they swam up the pipe, quacking vociferously. Copper appeared again without even giving them the benefit of a glance and as suddenly disappeared.

This was too much for the leading mallard. Two of them half swam, half flew up the pipe, yelling abuse at this jack-in-the-box of a fox. The rest swam on rapidly, cutting V-shaped ripples through the water like a fleet of little destroyers. Copper popped out again higher up. The dog-hunters burst into a fresh frenzy of abuse. They rounded the bend swimming strongly.

And, exactly on the turn in the tunnel, halfway up the pipe, Mussett suddenly stepped from behind a screen. Instantly every duck took to wing, quacking furiously. They poured up the narrowing tunnel in a frenzy of wings until forced by the diminishing netting to come to ground they scuttled one after the other

Tower windmill at Horsey Mere

into the narrow entrance of the trammel net which stretched, pegged out like a gigantic eel trap, on the dry land at the end of the water tunnel.

Walter followed them quietly. They huddled closer and closer in their prison. Long, snaking necks, and beady-eyed heads suddenly stuck out of the netting on either side.

Walter stooped down, unhitched the end of the trammel, gave it a twist and flung it on the ground. There, safely prisoned, were about thirty duck, their bewildered heads sticking out of the netting at all points.

"Easy, isn't it?" he said. "But it isn't as easy as it looks. As often as not something puts them off. Maybe a twig cracks. Maybe a sudden panic for no reason. Why, only the other day it was a sparrow hawk which flew out of the pipe as soon as I got there.

"You never know what you'll catch in these pipes. I've caught a jay, herons, kingfishers, and even snipe and woodcock. My father-in-law caught a bittern and I've heard of an owl being taken in the pipe. Those pintail were caught only three days ago. We shall get ten shillings each for them alive.

"These pipes work best with a north-west or north-west-by-west wind. An east wind kills us. The duck won't wear it.

"You know the old saying: 'When the wind is in the east 'tis good for neither man or beast.' Well, that goes for ducks too."

Fritton is not a true broad. It is, most probably, the last relic of an estuary of the sea, now landlocked. In the Broads area, however, the angler with an inquisitive mind, a large-scale map, and sufficient good manners to get permission from whoever may be the owner, will find small, forgotten broads, often of an acre or two only, set in the middle of a reed-marsh, or pulk-holes cut off from the main river or broad by a belt of reeds. Those are the places for the solitary man. There he can find his little secret kingdom of peace and beauty.

I know such a broad, shallow, no more than two or three acres in extent, at least half a mile from the boat-dyke, set in the middle of reed-beds and litter marshes, within smell of the sea. It is as remote from the world of the raucous holiday-maker, the bleached blonde and the bawling transistor, as the North Pole is from Blackpool beach. Yet, half a mile away, motor-cruisers chug up the river, gangling youths in appalling shorts and knitted skull-

caps display their herring-bone ribs and the hyena chorus of the
pop singers is relayed relentlessly to the unappreciative ears of
grazing cattle. Picture a day there.

I went to my secret broad through waist-high reeds across a
quaking bog which shook at every step. A wind blew sharp off
the North Sea warmed with the scent of meadowsweet and the
September sun. Why is it that September is always the best month
of the year putting 'Flaming June' with its flaming rainstorms to
utter shame?

A great bird, low flying quested the marshland levels like a
ranging Irish Setter. Lonely against the sky in that lonely land
beside a sea where no ship sailed and no smoke trails smudged the
far horizon. It was an echo of medieval England. A wind-borne,
fleeting cameo of beauty. A Montagu's Harrier, the great 'blue
hawk' of the old Fenland. They breed about here. So does the
creeping bittern, that tawny breasted, tiger-eyed gnome of the
reed-bed. I have heard its hollow booming love song echo in
spring across a mile of lonely fen, that witchlike voice of the indigo
night which terrified the Saxons in their turf huts on Fenny Isles
when St. Guthlac wrestled with the 'foul fiends and swart demons'
in his reed-thatched cell, fantasies born of a brain tortured by
malaria and ague.

Well, the malaria has gone and I no longer meet a Fenman yellow with 'the shakes'. Although as a boy I remember
old men, born of the reeds and water, who still dosed themselves with poppy-head tea and laudanum drops to keep ague
at bay.

Today, bittern and harrier, bearded tit and garganey teal,
delicate as fine china still linger in this remote corner of Broadland
where no raucous trippers with transistors pollute the silence.
There are grass snakes on that marshland level three feet six inches
long or more and a great bull that weighs a ton roaming the far
marsh wall and the cattle marsh beyond, emperor of all he surveys.
Between them, the snakes and the bull, help to keep this little bit
of England tidy.

Now the point about my secret broad is that it is full of tench.
Great big bronze golden fellows, who wallow like pigs in the
shallows and nose their way like Dutch barges through the water
lily pads.

Few people ever fish for them because few people know that
this forgotten little broad still exists. Like every other broad it has

'shrunk wunnerfull' in the last hundred years or so. According to the Tithe Award map of 1840 it covered twelve acres of water. By 1881 it had shrunk to nine and a half acres. In 1946 it covered a bare five acres. Today, it is, at a guess, three acres of water with nine surrounding acres of quaking ronds and hovers. If you sink through you are up to the waist, or deeper, in stinking mud and lucky to get out. Nowhere is the water more than three feet deep. Altogether a paradise for tench and hell for the angler who tries to fish for them.

Yet we have had luck. More by good management and hard work than by sheer luck. To begin with, an ancient punt, 'tore-out' but still floating, is the answer to those dangerous man-traps of floating ronds. Weeks ago we used the punt to hook out masses of weed with a Broadsman's 'crome' and thus clear fishable swims. That is the first essential. We started to rake out weed long before the season began and have done it at least once a week since the season got under way.

I like to fish for tench with a lightish rod, a fairly fine line, an ordinary peacock-quill float cocked with one shot only and new ox-blood mixed with bread and bran into stiff balls as ground bait. Work it up into the balls after it has become congealed. Incidentally, ox-blood if you can get enough of it, emptied by the bucketful on to a snipe marsh will draw all the snipe from miles around and give you the finest shooting on earth. It breeds blood-worms and since they are the larvae of chronomid flies which tench adore, that is perhaps why tench like ox-blood in their ground bait.

A somewhat uppish friend who fishes with me when he can tear himself away from Test and Itchin catches tench on this secret little broad with a fly. I am not sure which fly. It looks like an Alexandra, but since I have never caught a tench on a fly and only hooked a wretched swift when I attempted to do so, I am too ashamed to ask him. Me for the ox-blood, a loaf of bread and a tin of worms. Ox-blood is an old, old trick. It was used in the Fens and elsewhere to attract fish centuries ago. Pike go for the smell of it, eels swarm towards it. Years ago in Egypt I remember dosing a marsh down in the Delta with buckets and buckets of it. The result was that with the aid of two subalterns we shot 153 snipe in a morning. Any butcher will fix you up with a bucketful of ox-blood for a bob or two. Then work it up into your ground bait and dump the balls into your cleared swim. If the water is really weedy it is a good plan to clear a few channels through the reed-beds leading into the main swim. Then you will draw tench from the far side of the water.

Mr. Fred Taylor who knows more about tench fishing than most people says that his brother once baited a tench swim with a load of farmyard manure full of brandlings. The idea was that the tench would have to work through the muck to find the worms and this would keep them longer on the spot. It must have worked for on the opening day, says Mr. Taylor, "over fifty tench were taken, the majority of them being over four pounds with a few five-pounders thrown in for luck."

I have never caught a five-pound tench, but I will lay 5 to 1 that a six-pounder waits to be caught in that secret, forgotten little broad among the reedlands of eastern Norfolk. The man who catches him will probably do so early in the morning. That is the real time to catch tench, particularly in shallow water. We have taken them at night many a time, fishing both with worms and bread, and with honey paste. They seem to go into the deep water when the sun becomes really warm. Or shoulder their way into the reed-bed where they pick up any amount of food from the actual stems of the reeds. A lot of it falls off the reeds as the fish move about.

Old angling writers believed that the tench was the 'doctor fish' for the pike and that when the latter was scarred or wounded it rubbed its wounds against the slimy tench and thus gained heal-ing ointment. I regard it as the philosopher's fish for wherever you fish for tench you will usually find solitude, quiet waters, peace—and patience. You need all the patience in the world.

There are rewards even if you catch no fish. The sudden sliding shadow across the broad of the harrier on his piratical beat. The chittering of reed-warblers in the reeds. The clanking of coots and the pert crimson-pated moorhen swimming by a few yards away, jerking its white tail. There was that day too, when a party of ruffs and reeves, now almost the rarest waders in England, swept over like scimitars, swung round in an arc, landed in a muddy shallow not twelve feet away and stood there, long-legged, erect as soldiers, beaks poised as though to repel boarders. The ruff is not much bigger than a large thrush in its body weight, but it has one distinction which makes it unique among marshland birds—its ruff. This collar of feathers round the neck with the prominent feather ear tufts behind the eyes are raised and displayed when in spring the cock bird spars and jousts for the favours of the sober suited little hen bird.

What makes them unique is the fact that if you examined a hundred ruffs in full breeding plumage, you would never find two ruffs exactly similar in colouration. In this respect they resemble the differences between the thumb print of men. I have half a dozen stuffed ruffs a century old or more in my collection of some 400 British birds. One has a white ruff flecked with minute black spots, another an orange and white ruff. The third dark tawny. The fourth almost sulphur yellow. The fifth and sixth are mottled and flecked with marked differences.

Now although the ruff may be almost the rarest of British breeding waders there is a fair chance of seeing them on migration this month or next month on almost any lake in England where you have muddy shallows and a certain amount of marshy verges. The bird is about a foot long, wings seven and a half inches long, the overall plumage brownish grey with darker feather on the back and lighter under parts. The ruff and the ear tufts make it quite unlike any other bird. I have known ruffs which were blue-grey, bright orange, pure white, pale yellow, dark brown and even streaked like a bittern's breast.

The point is that where tench are there you may expect to see the rarer sort of marsh bird from the bittern to the ruff, from the bearded tit to the garganey teal. The London reservoirs know them all and record them almost annually.

Birds and animals are the angler's familiars. Since he is a quiet fellow, they come to him. He is part of the landscape. He promises no menace. Therefore he sees a lot that is denied to the chattering hiker, the petrol-propelled motor-boat fiend, the moronic Beatle-disciple with his long-player and long hair. These people make a noise. Therefore they repel nature. Since they have learned little they see even less. Which is, perhaps, just as well from the angler's point of view. He can get away from the mob.

The mob is at its worst usually in June and July. No power on earth would induce me to go boating for pleasure on any popular broad in mid-summer.

Luckily there are always the hidden corners, the grown-up dykes, the reedy shallows, the out-of-the-way places, such as my secret broad, to which the man of vision can escape. Broadland offers an infinite diversity of little hiding places for the angler in a shallow draught punt or the man who will plod through the reeds and jump the dykes to find some little place that the rest of the world has forgotten.

Coarse fishing begins on 16th June. Then is the time, if the sun shines and you can lose the crowd, to savour the full glory of an English mid-summer.

June, the month of dog roses in the hedges. Reed warblers chittering in the reeds, the grasshopper warbler, the 'reeler bird' of the old Fenman, reeling his thin, interminable song through the water-scented night. Shoals of fish moving in muted gold and silver in lucent green under the lily-pads, through the reeds, and the coarse fisher comes into his own. All beauty and all peace is his if he has but the luck and the sense to seek out the secret places and avoid the peg-down mob.

Half the charm of fishing is to get away from everyone else. That is why in this month of roses I shall go to the slow and reedy rivers of my native Fens or to those secret corners in Broadland where you can still escape the lout with the transistor.

The charm of fishing in Broadland is unmatched by that of any other district in England. It is the charm, not only of an infinite diversity of bird life, but of a wide and wild landscape of flat green marshes, cut up by shining dykes, sentinelled by windmills which, alas, no longer turn, bounded on far horizons by marching lines of shock-headed willows, that tread in leaning, wind-stricken files like tousle-headed soldiery—and, over all, the high wide skies of that sea country. There, indeed, is a country to exalt the heart and lighten the mind.

Whether one sees it under the incredibly blue sky of summer and autumn, or under the bleak, grey, racing clouds of winter, or in the whiteness of snow-squalls, it is a land of beauty.

Some of my most precious memories of fishing are set in that land of bright dawns and incredible sunsets. Memories precious not merely for the size of the bag, but because of rare birds seen, of skyscapes of fantastic beauty, with always the running sigh of wind in the reeds, the strong smell of the sea sharp on the wind, and the peace of slow rivers and glittering broads to enrich the mind. Nothing orthodox is likely to happen in that half-tamed country where the ancient wild treads close on the skirts of the tamed uplands, where the trees lean inland perpetually from their fierce buffeting by North Sea winds.

I know a little reed-bordered jewel of a private broad. It has everything in this month of June. Wild duck dibbling in the reeds.

Bitterns, tawny breasted, tiger-eyed, creeping through the hovers questing for eels. Once a rare bird the bittern is back and by no means uncommon. I have seen them on Norfolk Broads, on Cambridgeshire Fens, in the reed-beds of an Essex marsh fleet, on the water-meadows of the Hampshire Avon and the Dorsetshire Frome. The angler who sees one can count it among his most precious memories.

Did you know that a bittern carries its own powder-puffs. Two sacs hidden under the breast feathers. When the great bird has gorged himself on eels and his feathers glisten with slime, he squeezes the powder over himself and combs the slime out with his beak. After that he fluffs out his feathers in a cloud of powder.

If you put up a bittern by the riverside or from a reed-bed by the lake you will know him by his slow, flapping flight, his brownish colours and his size—almost as big as a heron. They are strictly protected. The man who shoots one will not only be heavily fined but have his gun confiscated.

You might well see one on Hornsea Mere in the East Riding of Yorkshire, on any of the Shropshire or Cheshire Meres, at Slapton Ley in Devon, or Fritton Lake in Suffolk, on a Home Counties reservoir or lake, or for that matter, almost anywhere where there is marsh, quiet reed-beds and peace. They are not the only rarities which the angler may see, particularly in Broadland.

This little broad, which I rented with the surrounding estate for enchanted years, has other birds which you will see in the lonely places. Black terns, graceful as swallows, gleaming bluish-black in the sun as they dip and sweep with slow grace over the water. Once they nested here. Now they come irregularly in summer and early autumn. They are part of the picture on that little broad with its snipe and springing redshank, its huge pike and lazy, golden-sided tench, its pretty Victorian echo of a thatched summer-house built upon an island called with a most charming sense of Victorian 'water frolic' gaity, 'The Pleasure Hill'.

There is another rare bird, tiny, confiding with a tinkling bell-like note who creeps among the reeds like winged mice. The natural history books call them bearded tits or bearded reedlings, the marshmen call them 'reed pheasants' because of their long tails. You may see them almost anywhere on the Broadland rivers in this month of June, but within living memory they were almost extinct. They are not a tit at all, but a separate family, a sort of finch called Panuridae. In the old days when collectors paid high prices for rare birds, the marsh gunners would wait until these tiny 'reed mice' huddled together in a ball at roosting time, clinging to each other among the reed stems for warmth. One shot would bag a dozen pathetic little mites. Hark to Arthur Benns of Reedham Ferry:

"We used to have a tidy lot of reed pheasants (bearded tits) in the rond across the river. Yu know what they are, sir, but a mort o' people don't. I went one mornin' by a rond arter snipes and there was fower or foive on 'em a-hoppin' through the reeds as quick as little hosses, a-keepin' time wi' me as I walked on the wall. They got woices like little bells. I couldn't no more shute them than shute meself."

You would know a bearded titmouse if you see one by his blue-grey head, long black 'moustache' drooping down from in front of and beneath his eyes, his white throat and brown back and body, with a streak or two of blue in the wing covers. The cock bird is about six and a half inches long. I have a stuffed specimen in my collection. On the back of the case are these words "Shot in 1794 on what is now the Edgeware Road, London."

The angler who fishes far from broads and marshes where Surrey heaths or Hampshire slopes of bracken come down to the edge of the water-meadows will hear in the dusk a churring noise, not unlike the purr of a far off motorcycle. The nightjar or goat-sucker, otherwise known as the churn owl or fern owl, is on the wing. He is no owl and he never sucks goats.

He flies by night catching moths, dorbeetles and insects on the wing. Here is a bird of mystery and of charm. One looks at me from a glass case as I write this. Its eyes large and limpid, the lower part of the beak has a tiny sort of beard, the overall colours are ashen grey on the back, flecked with dark brown and light brown. The hawklike pointed wings and long tail, are barred in dark and light brown.

During the day the nightjar lies low—on the ground where indeed she lays her two mottled white eggs. At night it swoops silently over woods and heaths and by streams where moths flutter and the late angler lingers. It is a witch-bird, the nighthawk of old legends, the bird of fear and phantasy, part of the old, immemorial wild magic of the woods and heaths of Saxon England. So if the jar owl—it has an infinity of local names—churrs its sudden note in your ear as you are reeling in and packing up, remember that

Alfred and his Saxons heard the same note when half England was the heath and the forest of wolf and deer, and salmon ran, sparkling like swords up the clean and lucent Thames. They have all gone—but the nighthawk still flies his witchlike, woodland way.

XI

THE PLACE OF RARE BIRDS

A Unique Sanctuary of Wild Life

No COMPARABLE area in England can show a wider variety of bird life than Norfolk and none, probably, has a longer record of rare birds. Broadland can claim a tremendous share of this distinction. That is because the blunt shoulder of Norfolk, which includes Winterton Ness, the most easterly point of England, juts boldly into the North Sea and thus receives the first inrush of spring and autumn migrants from Scandinavia, the Arctic Circle and the Low Countries. Norfolk offers these wing-weary travellers who voyage by the stars a welcome which suits almost every sort of bird.

Marshes, fens, lakes, broads, rivers, saltings and mud-flats greet wildfowl and waders. The high sandy heaths of Breckland welcome heathland birds which love wide miles of heather, gorse and ling, with the warm shelter of pine woods. Indeed, the 25,000 acres of Thetford Chase which cover much of the old, wild wastes of the original Brecks, are now a unique sanctuary, not only of woodland birds, including crossbills, the tiny gold-crested wren, hoopoes, redstarts, black redstarts, shrikes and many birds of prey, but they also hold a fantastic head of red deer, fallow deer, roe deer and such occasional oddities as barking deer and Japanese deer.

The rest of Norfolk, with its great estates, parks, deep woodlands, wide farmlands and lush river valleys, is a bird-lover's paradise.

Broadland, in this diverse picture, stands out unique. It is Holland in miniature—with improvements—for, since I have visited most of the Dutch meres and bird reserves, I think one can safely say from first-hand observation, that, although such places as the Naardemeer and the Island of Texel are unique, no part of

Holland can quite match the, shall one say, benevolent feudalism which still characterizes the layout and the running of many of the great and smaller estates of Broadland. This suits the birds since the factory farmer and the intensive horticulturalist are no friends of theirs.

In our grandfather's time there were no close seasons for wildfowl and many other birds. Shooting went on round the year. Rare birds were shot in breeding plumage, as young birds and in any state of growth to satisfy the insane craze for collection stuffed birds. Every country house, farmhouse and many cottages had their collections of stuffed birds. The Protected List was not dreamt of.

One recalls this fact with slight trepidation, since my own house contains a collection of some 400 British birds and animals, including many rarities from the Fens and Broads. Most of them have been given by friends and originally formed part of such large collections as that of the late Lord Walsingham at Merton Hall, Norfolk; Captain Robert Rising at Horsey Hall, Norfolk; the late J. C. M. Nichols who had the shooting on Buckenham Broads for many years; the late Count de la Chapelle, my first wildfowling partner on the east coast; the late Earl of Ashburnham Sir Vauncey Harper-Crewe, Bart., who collected extensively; and other collections which I have bought at country house and farmhouse sales. In most cases, the birds concerned would have been thrown on the rubbish heap or given away to museums or village institutes where too often after a brief moment of public glory, they are banished to the cellars or put in an outhouse. Thus, in a small way by gift and diligent collection, one has managed to save rare specimens which otherwise would have been lost. None have been shot personally for the sake of adding them to the collection. One can only hope that other lovers of birdlife will, whenever possible, rescue cases of stuffed birds which may come up at country auctions or in junk shops, providing that they are of outstanding local interest or fine specimens of the now rare and exceedingly expensive art of taxidermy.

I have mentioned this small collection of some 400 specimens because it includes such rare or uncommon East Anglian specimens as three great bustards, long since extinct as a breeding species; bitterns, avocets, ruffs and reeves, a Bonaparte sandpiper; spotted crakes and little crakes; marsh, Montagu's and hen harriers; merlins hobbys; long-tailed duck; garganey; gadwall;

hoopoe, bearded tit and a host of other small birds, wildfowl, waders and birds of prey, including golden eagle and osprey.

If any visitor to Norfolk wants to see a good private collection of wild geese and wildfowl shot on the Norfolk coast, I recommend him to pay a visit to that ultra-comfortable sporting hotel, The Manor House at Blakeney, where my good friend the late Roy Pope, one of the best wildfowlers of this century, got together a wonderful collection which his widow and son still preserve.

Now consider the bird reserves and nature reserves in general with which Norfolk is superlatively endowed. That far-sighted body, the Norfolk Naturalists' Trust, established in 1926 took the initiative in these matters, long before the Nature Conservancy and other recent bodies were thought of. The N.N.T. set the example for which every naturalist and country lover should be grateful. Their principal reserves, including some outside Broadland but in the Breckland and other areas are detailed in Appendix III.

The Trust also shares with the National Trust in the management of coastal reserves at Blakeney Point (1,335 acres), Scolt Head Island (1,821) acres and Arnold's Marsh, Cley (29 acres).

By agreement with Nature Conservancy, Scolt Head Island, Ranworth Broad, Hickling Broad and the Breckland Heaths have been declared National Nature Reserves.

Just as Norwich produced its individual school of painters, so Broadland has produced its own school of naturalists, of whom Sir Thomas Browne was perhaps the first, and its own rich range of literature dealing with its wild life.

Among the earliest writers were Sir James Paget and his brother C. J. Paget who, in 1834, produced that very readable little book, *A Sketch of the Natural History of Yarmouth and Its Neighbourhood*, which gives a remarkable picture of wild life on Breydon a century and a quarter ago, with many anecdotes of the unlettered brotherhood of wildfowlers and fishermen who with punt-gun, shoulder-gun, net and eel spear lived a primitive existence on that waste of water.

Later came the Rev. Richard Lubbock with his carefully documented and charmingly written *Observations on the Fauna of Norfolk*. The third volume was completed by another great naturalist, Thomas Southwell, F.Z.S. Another parson, the Rev. Churchill Babington, produced *A Catalogue of the Birds of Suffolk* with many references to the Broads. Then, over a period of years, my old friend, the late Arthur Patterson, produced a series of books dealing with broads wild life which are unique. No lover of the Broads should be without Patterson's *Notes of an East Coast Naturalist*, *Wild Life on a Norfolk Estuary*, *A Norfolk Naturalist*, *Man and Nature on Tidal Waters* or *Wildfowlers and Poachers*. His little monograph, *A Catalogue of the Birds of Great Yarmouth*, republished in 1901, of which he gave me one of the only two copies partly bound in red leather, is rare but good. Patterson began life running barefooted on the fish quays of Yarmouth, was more or less self-taught, became an attendant at a penny zoo, was the friend of every fisherman and wildfowler for miles around and, finally attaining some little financial security as a school attendance officer, he poured out book after book, article after article, all packed with racy descriptions of primitive Broadland characters, together with extraordinarily accurate records of bird, fish and animal life.

Before his death he not only received scientific honours, but was presented by the Lord Lieutenant with a purse of gold and an illuminated address in recognition of his work for the natural history of Broadland.

In more recent years Dr. B. B. Riviere has produced an exhaustive *History of the Birds of Norfolk* which, if read in conjunction with Mr. Claud B. Ticehurst's *History of the Birds of Suffolk*, will give one a good overall picture of the present-day bird life of this fascinating region. I suggest adding to it the scarce little *Notes on the Birds of Cley, Norfolk*, by the late H. N. Pashley, published in 1925. Cley is outside the Broads area, being some miles to the north, but the records collected by Pashley, who was the village naturalist and an accomplished taxidermist, are mainly of birds which belong naturally to the Broadland area.

Finally, there are the excellent chapters on bird life, fish life, entomology and botany in Dutt's charming book, *The Norfolk Broads*, published in 1903, and most beautifully illustrated in colour by the late Frank Southgate, one of the best marshland artists of bird life that England ever knew. His tradition is carried on today by Mr. Roland Green, the bird artist of Hickling. Now let me tell you a little about Roland Green, since he is a great artist, a first-rate naturalist, a man who shuns publicity yet produces pictures which adorn the houses of royalty. He is not like some of those TV 'birdie-boys' who smirk and prink at one from the gogglebox and always contrive to have the best photographers handy when they are about to embark on an expedition to some part of the earth which in any case has been visited by scores of naturalists before them. One knows the type so well. They are the band-wagon hoppers-on of the bird world.

Roland Green does not belong to this faintly nauseating breed. He is the hermit artist of the Broads. Son of a Kentish philosopher, who turned taxidermist because he loved recreating in death the beauty of wild ducks and the majesty of wild geese, he was brought up on the Rainham marshes on the Kentish foreshores of the Thames.

Forty years ago he went to Hickling Broad, the greatest fresh-water lake in the South of England, and there, first in a windmill and later in his thatched studio among the wild reeds, a studio built on piles driven into the floating marsh, he has lived alone, cooking, eating, and sleeping, without gas, electricity, or laid-on water, painting—always painting. Lord Desborough, that great sportsman and superb naturalist, 'adopted' him. Lord Desborough owned Hickling and its wild marsh. He protected its wild birds. He saved Hickling for the nation, and today it is the heart of that great marshland area which the nation will preserve for all time as a last echo of the wild untamed England of mere and fen, as untouched and as unspoiled today as it was when Elizabeth was on the throne.

Lord Desborough and others paid hundreds of guineas for Roland Green's pictures. Dukes and earls have welcomed him to their houses. Royalty has bought his pictures. But he, this shy, retiring hermit-artist, comes only to London once a year, when an exhibition is held of his work in a Bond Street gallery.

Roland Green is no drawing-room publicity-hunter. He paints no slick, mass-produced studies of wild life. He addresses no learned gatherings. He is neither photographed nor paragraphed.

He paints hundreds of pictures, and tears up half of them; no man is a more exacting self-critic. And for that reason, in my view and that of greater men, he is the supreme artist of birds today. For he lives among them from the green days of spring, through the heat and haze of summer, into the russet days of autumn when the reeds turn gold, until the winter wind brings frost and snow and the whooping music of the great wild swans from the Arctic North.

He paints wild geese on the slimy mud-flats and the sere saltings of the sea. He lies out in their punts on bitter eves of winter with the wildfowlers of Breydon Water, those rough fishermen-sailors who shoot and fish for the London markets and so earn their hard living.

They go creeping in their craft, these hardy gunners, with great muzzle-loading punt-guns like young cannon mounted in the slim bows of the grey punts. Guns nine feet long, an inch and a half in calibre; guns that weigh a hundred pounds or more; guns which shoot a pound of shot, and whose recoil is so terrific that they have to be mounted on springs and ropes to take the kick. For the kick of one of those great guns would break a man's shoulder or bash his face in. My small gun is nine feet six in length and weighs a hundred and ten pounds, and that is by no means the grandfather of them all. Such a gun will kill wild geese at a hundred yards.

Sometimes the gunners sit in reed-built hides on the water's edge with a dozen or more wooden decoy ducks bobbing in the waves to lure the wild birds down from the clouds and within range of their shoulder-guns.

At eventide they crouch low under the marsh wall to intercept the duck which fly in from the sea or up from the marsh to feed on the scattered corn of the stubble fields. Or they squat in sunken wooden tubs far out on the mud-flats, or on distant sandbanks, girdled by the creeping tide, to shoot geese and ducks as they scythe low over the sea. A hardy and desperate game, for if the gunner stays too long, until his retreat is cut off, he may be drowned. And with them, under bitter marsh wall or in slimy half-filled tub, crouches the artist, always watching, always sketching, sharing all the risks for the brief captured moments of wild winged beauty which he sets down in delicate colour.

He is a master of landscape. The pallid hues of winter reed, the bottle-green of cresting waves, the gold and glow of many-tinted marshes, and the high pastel blues and dove-greys of winter skies are all translated on to canvas in that lonely reed-thatched shack which crouches among the whispering reeds.

They say on those bleak Norfolk marshes that one day this hermit artist will be found drowned on the marshes or discovered dead, alone and unattended, in his lonely house. But at that he laughs. He intends to live till eighty, which is young as men go in eastern Norfolk, and he says, shyly, that perhaps in another ten years' time he may be painting pictures really worthwhile.

Hickling—home of wildfowl

Meanwhile he watches and sketches, paints and tears them up—watches the sweeping glide of the marsh harriers, the ragged flopping flight of the shy bitterns, the timid mouse-like creepings among the reeds of those tiny delicate rarities, the bearded tits, the swift, high flight of mallard and widgeon, the sudden electric spring of green-headed teal, jumping like sprites from reedy pools, the aerial acrobatics of snipe, the arrowy flight of redshank, and the tumbling, wailing stoop and quiver of plover.

That is his life; he lives, loves it, and paints it. And thereby England is the richer. One day Roland Green's works will hang high in the hall of fame where wild beauty is enshrined.

The outstanding fact of present-day wild life of Broadland, which must gratify every naturalist is that certain species, once extinct or nearly so, have now returned to breed and are comparatively common again.

Notable examples are the bittern and the bearded tit, that enchanting little reed bunting with the delicately pencilled moustaches and fascinating bell-like notes which the marshmen call 'reed pheasants'. Before long the avocet, the black tern, the ruff and reeve and the spoonbill may all re-establish themselves as breeding residents. Avocets have already returned to breed within the last few years on certain remote marshes in Suffolk, where they are strictly protected, and these colonies may extend to the Broads.

Wildfowl are, naturally, the largest and most interesting section of Broadland birds. Noblest are the wild swans. Both whoopers and Bewick turn up each winter on Hickling Broad, Horsey Mere and Breydon Water and occasionally on Barton Broad. I have seen thirty wild swans rise in a sheet of foam and a windy music of wings from the great reedy bay of Swim Coots on Hickling Broad on a day of steely, winter sky when between 400 and 500 mallard, widgeon, pochard and teal were crossing and re-crossing the wild sweep of sky in never-ending skeins and teams—a picture of unforgettable majesty. The Polish swan is said to have occurred on a number of occasions, but these should be treated with reserve. Riviere does not include it in his list.

Many mute swans breed on the Broads. In my view there are too many of them. These birds, lovely to look at, are the most unmitigated tyrants and inevitably drive wild duck away from any water which they regard as their kingdom. They will seize young ducklings, hold them under water and drown them. For this

The Norfolk wherry Albion *crossing Breydon* Water

reason, when I had the shooting on Martham Broad, I shot every mute swan which attempted to take up its residence. The result was that we had plenty of duck nesting in peace and roast swans by no means despicable for the flesh is close, darkish and a little sweet, almost like venison, was frequently on my table and those of many of the villagers.

The whooper swan, that magnificent wild trumpeter of the winter skies, who should never be shot may return one day to breed. Early in the spring of 1928, a friend, the late Lord Walsingham, who owned the Merton estate of some 12,000 acres in southwest Norfolk, which included two large meres, Stanford Water and Tomston Mere, and a number of smaller meres, wrote to tell me that a pair of whooper swans had started a nest at the foot of a willow tree on a tiny island in Westmere. One of the birds had an injured leg, which probably accounted for them remaining behind in England. They were strong on the wing and built a nest of dead rushes and water-weeds which, however, was deserted by 12th May. Dr. Sydney Long of the Norfolk and Norwich Naturalists' Trust, and Mr. Hugh Wormald, both saw these swans and identified them as genuine whoopers.

Almost every wild goose on the British list visits the Broads. The commoner varieties are the greylag and pinkfoot. The latter in thousands each winter on certain marshes. The white-fronted goose is not so common, whilst the brent turns up in varying numbers, according to the severity of the weather, on Breydon. The bernacle is an irregular winter visitor. The Canada goose, originally introduced as an ornament on the big lakes in Gunton Park and Holkham Park in north Norfolk, has now become common and is extending its range throughout the Broads. Several examples of the Egyptian goose, one of which is in my collection, have occurred, but these were almost certainly escapes from private waters.

Snow geese have been recorded from Cley and Holkham, but I have no record of them in the Broads area. The extremely rare red-breasted goose is said to have been shot on the Halvergate marshes in 1805. It was bought in Yarmouth market by an odd little bird-dealer named Lilly Wigg, one of a race of self-taught naturalists who earned a precarious living by selling rare specimens to wealthy collectors. He, little realizing what a rarity was in his hands, plucked it and ate it. It was afterwards identified by the feathers, to the eternal regret of the lamenting Mr. Wigg, who could easily have obtained £10 or £20 for his specimen.

Among the duck which frequent the Broads, mallard and teal breed in large quantities. Widgeon, locally called 'smee', are common in winter. Pochard, tufted duck, scaup, shoveller, and golden-eye are fairly common. Pintail are not uncommon in winter and are frequently taken in the decoy at Fritton Lake.

Among the real rarities are the ruddy shell-duck, four of which were seen by A. Nudd at Hickling in October 1916 and another at Breydon in 1918; the red-crested pochard, the first British example of which was shot on Breydon in 1818, since when a few others have been recorded from the district; the white-eyed pochard, which has occurred several times; the harlequin duck, said to have been killed near Yarmouth; the buffel-headed duck or morillon, the first of the only three British species of which was shot near Yarmouth about 1830; Steller's eider, the first of the only two British specimens of which was killed at Caister on 10th February, 1830; the surfscoter, three of which were identified by Miss Judith Ferrier, on 16th November, 1927, off Hemsby beach, the rare American hooded merganser, one of which was obtained near Yarmouth in 1829; whilst the gadwall and graceful little garganey teal, distinctly uncommon in other parts of England, are by no means uncommon on the Broads.

Sea-going ducks include that handsome fellow, the shell-duck, who can often be seen on Breydon in scores. Scaup, although a sea-duck, visit Hickling Broad fairly regularly, but are uncommon on the other broads. The graceful long-tailed duck, which I have shot off Holy Island, miles out at sea, arrives off the Norfolk coast in November and is seldom seen on the Broads, although one or two have been killed on Rockland. Another was shot on Hickling in 1856 and a third at Acle in 1885. The common eider occasionally turns up on Breydon, and one was found on Horsey Warren in 1918 after a gale. The common and velvet scoters are both frequently seen in winter, and the former occasionally visits some of the broads. I shot one on Martham Broad in the winter of 1947. The red-breasted merganser and goosander are both winter visitors, and the latter turns up on Hickling and Fritton, as does the smew. They generally leave in March.

Cormorants are common on Breydon and, according to Walter Mussett, the decoy-man at Fritton Lake, they still nest in a dead tree in the woods above the lake. In 1825, there were regularly fifty or sixty nests each year. Cormorants may often be seen flying up the Bure or the Yare. The shag is relatively uncommon. Gannets turn up off the coast in small numbers with the herring shoals.

Sir Thomas Browne stated that he had in his collection "a pellican shott upon Horsey Fenne 1663 May 22", and he guessed at the time that it was "one of the King's pellicans lost at St. James's". Since then, no pelican had been seen in Norfolk until 21st July, 1926, when one flew in from the sea and alighted on Breydon. There it spent the night and, according to Dr. Riviere, left again the next day at 9.30 a.m. in an easterly direction. A second pelican was recorded on Breydon on 24th September, 1915, and, when disturbed, "flew away to the north-east" and was never heard of again. It is a fascinating thought that both these birds may have been genuine wild specimens and not merely escapes.

The engaging little storm petrel turns up at sea most winters. The much rarer Leach's fork-tailed petrel has been recorded forty or fifty times, one of the specimens being in my collection. Two extremely rare shearwaters, the western Mediterranean and Madeiran varieties, have both been recorded from east Norfolk, one of the latter being picked up dead by a gamekeeper on the Earsham Hall estate on the Waveney in 1858. The Manx shearwater is an occasional autumn visitor, whilst the great shearwater has been recorded from Lowestoft, Gorleston beach and Caister beach. The fulmar petrel is fairly common on the herring-grounds in autumn and winter.

That handsome enemy of fish, the great-crested grebe, which, in the middle of last century, was on the verge of extinction, is now common enough on all broads, particularly the Trinity Broads. The Slavonian, red-necked and black-necked grebes are all winter visitors in small numbers, as is the great northern diver and black-throated diver. The little grebe is common on all broads and the red-throated diver is not uncommon on the coast. I have seen it in Meadow Duke and on Horsey Mere.

Pallas's sand-grouse occurred during the extraordinary immigration of these Asiatic birds which took place on various dates in the latter half of last century. Twenty were seen at Hickling in 1906 and ten at Somerton in the same year.

The stone curlew or Norfolk plover, common enough on the Breckland, has turned up once or twice near Norwich, notably at Honingham, Taverham and Drayton as recently as 1929. Several specimens of the rare pratincole have been recorded from Breydon and Yarmouth, where, incidentally, the first British specimen of the Caspian plover was shot in 1890. Oyster-catchers, dotterel and ordinary ringed plover are fairly common round about Breydon and elsewhere, whilst the very rare little ringed plover is said to have been picked up dead at Surlingham in 1938.

Kentish plover, golden plover and grey plover are all winter migrants in fair numbers, whilst the peewit or lapwing is common. The graceful little turnstone, with its fascinating changes of plumage, is not uncommon on Breydon, and I have seen them by the score on the beach at Waxham, Horsey and Somerton.

The ruff, once common as a breeding species, still turns up in spring and autumn in the Hickling and Horsey area, and before long they may breed again. Some reeves' eggs, brought from Holland, were put into redshanks' nests at Hickling in 1925 and seven hatched off.

Curlew and redshank are common everywhere, particularly on Breydon. The latter, ringing their million bells of song, are among the most fascinating springtime nesting birds on the marshes. Sanderling, knots, dunlin, curlew sandpiper, little stints and Temminck's occur more or less regularly on migration. Various rare sandpiper, including the buff-breasted, the broad-billed and the red-breasted, have been recorded. The purple sandpiper is common in autumn, as is the wood sandpiper and green sandpiper. That charming bird, the spotted redshank, of which I have six specimens in different plumage, has turned up on Breydon, Barton and elsewhere. The greenshank is a regular migrant and grey and red-necked phalaropes both occur in spring and autumn, and the latter may breed again before long. Whimbrel are common double-passage migrants. The great snipe has occurred whilst common and jack snipe are on every fen.

A bird which once bred in large numbers at Upton Broad and is now only seen as a migrant is the beautiful black tern. I have spent enchanted hours lying in a punt hidden among the reeds on Martham Broad, watching their lazy flight, their plumage gleaming blue-black in the sunlight. They are seldom seen before May and usually return in August and September.

Extraordinary 'falls' of woodcock sometimes occur on the coast in autumn under the 'Woodcock Moon'. When I had the shooting on the Burnley Hall estate, it was nothing uncommon to see thirty or more in a day. No less than 105 were shot in one day at Swanton Novers in 1872 and ninety-five at Holkham in December 1965.

Common and sandwich terns are reasonably common, the

former re-established as a breeding colony at Blakeney Point. The rare white-winged black tern has turned up at Breydon and Horsey Mere, whilst the even rarer whiskered tern has been twice recorded from Hickling, in 1847 and in 1906. The gull-billed tern, another rarity, has occurred several times on Breydon, where the Caspian tern was seen in 1910 and, again, at sea, off Yarmouth in 1918. The Arctic tern is a winter migrant. The last record I have was of one at Hickling in April 1936. The little tern, a regular summer visitor, breeds at Horsey, whilst the rare roseate tern is now becoming a more frequent visitor to the coast.

Black-headed gulls abound on all the broads, whilst herring gulls, common gulls, black-headed and lesser black-backed, are all birds of Breydon and the surrounding broads and marshes. Various rarer gulls, including the very rare Mediterranean black-headed gull, have been recorded from Breydon. The skuas are all occasional autumn and winter visitors to the coast, as are guillemots and razor-bills.

That remarkably interesting bird, the great bustard, as large almost as a turkey, which once bred on the heaths of the Breckland, has occasionally turned up in the Broads area. I believe the last recorded specimen was seen on Somerton Warren by my keeper, Pateman, in the autumn of 1945. He described it to me as "a great, big, brownish bird with whiskers on his face and long legs about a yard high, that kept on walkin' about on the marsh under the sandhills and only flew a few yards when I put him up. He came in from sea one morning, hung about here for several days and then cleared off." I have no doubt whatever from Pateman's careful description of the bird that this was a great bustard, of which, incidentally, I have a native Norfolk specimen, given me by the late Lord Walsingham and a native Cambridgeshire specimen, given me by J. C. M. Nichols, in my collection. Both are over a hundred years old.

A few years after Pateman's death in about 1962, that good Broadsman, naturalist, angler and wildfowler, Mr. Alan Savory, whose two books *Lazy Rivers* and *Norfolk Fowler* are 'musts' for any collector of books on the wild life of Norfolk, turned up at my house with a splendid stuffed hen great bustard in a glass case. He told me that Mrs. Pateman had given it to him to pass on to me, saying, in effect: "My husband saw one of them birds in the sandhills and Mister Wentworth said that if he shot it he'd get fined £20 or more and have his gun taken away. So I've had that bird in the backus ever since my man died. Do you give it to Mr. Wentworth and say I don't want to get into any trouble over it."

Now is this stuffed bustard which I still have the bird which Pateman saw and shot in 1945? Or, judging by the apparent age of the case, is it a specimen from the Rising Collection at Horsey Hall, dispersed many years ago? Stuffed birds from that collection still turn up in local farmhouses and cottages. I like to think that my specimen is the last great bustard shot in England.

The last great bustard recorded in Norfolk and, as far as I know, in England was the bird found dead at South Creake on 28th March, 1963. It had apparently been killed by hitting telephone wires. This bird had probably flown the North Sea from Belgium where a remarkable influx of thirteen to sixteen of them were seen at Biegen from 9th February to 7th March. Apart from one bird in November 1956, these were the first great bustards recorded in Belgium since 1940.

There is a magnificent case of these birds in the Norwich Castle Museum, where most of the other rarities I have mentioned can also be seen.

The late Captain Robert Rising saw a great bustard fly across Horsey Mere on 7th January, 1867, whilst a female was shot at Costessey, near Norwich, on 2nd February, 1894. A specimen of the eastern little bustard was shot at Hellesdon in 1835 and another on the Acle marshes in 1916. The crane is believed to have nested in the Broads district two or three hundred years ago. Odd specimens have turned up over the years.

Among the crakes, the very rare little crake, of which I possess two specimens, has been recorded about a dozen times in Norfolk, including specimens from Buckenham Ferry in August 1827; Neatishead, on Barton Broad, in 1828; near Yarmouth in 1833; Horsey in 1833; Heigham Sounds in 1847; Dilham Fen in 1852; Catfield, near Hickling, in 1855; the Bure Marshes in 1867; and Hickling in 1880. This tiny and secretive little bird may easily have occurred on other occasions without being recorded. Baillon's crake, which Gurney describes as "very rare but less so than the Little Crake", has been recorded from Barton Fen, Dilham, Buckenham Fen, Potter Heigham and Sutton Broad, where a nest with one egg was found in 1889. I have two specimens supposed to have been killed in Norfolk. The spotted crake, also rare, of which I have three specimens, is known to have nested at

Hickling, Brunstead and Potter Heigham. Within recent years a nest was discovered on the edge of Hickling Broad by my grand old friend, Henry Whittaker, who, at eighty-seven, bright-eyed and bearded like a bush was a splendid specimen of the old type of Broadsman.

Major Anthony Buxton, of Horsey Hall, tells me that the late Sir Samuel Hoare, later Lord Templewood, identified the very rare purple gallinule at Horsey in, I think, the 1930s, whilst the green-backed gallinule has turned up at Martham, Horning, Barton Broad and Hickling. The latter may have been escapes from the Duke of Bedford's remarkable zoo at Woburn Abbey, where sixty were turned down in 1897. The latest occurrence, of which I have a record, was at Barton Broad on 13th October, 1913. An example of the very rare Allen's gallinule was caught alive on a fishing-boat off Hopton, near Yarmouth, on 1st January, 1902, and passed into the collection of the late J. B. Nichols, father of my friend, J. C. M. Nichols, who presented the greater part of his remarkable collection to Charterhouse School, giving the remainder to myself.

Coots, moorhens and water-rails are the familiars of every broad, but the land-rail or corncrake is, alas, nowadays a comparative rarity. I shot one on a fen adjoining Calthorpe Broad in the autumn of 1945, whilst walking up snipe.

Among birds of prey the golden eagle passes up the coast on migration occasionally, the peregrine falcon is a regular winter migrant and the marsh harrier and Montagu's harrier, once on the verge of extinction, are now fairly common breeding species at Hickling and Horsey, where they are strictly protected. Goshawks have been recorded from Filby, Acle, Catfield and elsewhere. The kite, once common in the City of Norwich, is now a rarity. The last recorded one was killed at Winterton in October 1881. White-tailed eagles, or sea-eagles, once common on Horsey Warren, turn up at infrequent intervals in winter, but the osprey is a fairly frequent autumn and winter visitor. One was fishing for weeks on end on Hickling Broad and Horsey Mere in 1947. He roosted at night on an oak tree in the reed-girt plantation on Waggon Hill on the edge of the broad. At about the same time another one frequented Fritton Lake for some weeks. Lord Somerleyton gave strict instructions that it was not to be harmed.

Hen-harriers are comparatively scarce, but I have seen them on more than one occasion beating low over the fen like setters. The red-footed falcon has turned up on a number of occasions. One was at Hickling in June 1922. Three were shot by Mr. Heath of Ludham Hall at Horning in 1830. The merlin is a regular migrant, whilst the kestrel and sparrow-hawk are always with us. Honey buzzards are passage migrants, sometimes in fair numbers, whilst the common buzzard turns up in spring and autumn in small numbers.

The white stork is occasionally seen on Breydon, where the spoonbill is a regular visitor in April, May and June, sometimes as late as November. In Sir Thomas Browne's time spoonbills bred in the Reedham heronry, and the regularity with which they visit Breydon, Hickling and other places nowadays gives hope that they may re-establish themselves as a nesting species. Anyone who has seen these incredibly lovely birds nesting in scores on the Dutch fens can only pray that their ivory beauty will again add grace and charm to the marshland scene. A flight of spoonbills against the sunset is one of the loveliest sights on earth.

A hundred years ago that equally beautiful bird, the glossy ibis, was so common in Norfolk fens that it was known by the marsh-men as the 'black curlew' and was frequently shot. Nowadays, it arrives in small parties in spring and autumn. In 1936 four were seen and two were shot between 11th September and 3rd October. A much rarer bird, the black stork, has been recorded three times in eastern Norfolk, the last occasion in 1934. There is a good specimen in the Norwich Museum.

The heron is extremely common and heronries exist at Horning, Horstead, Hoveton and Mautby, where I have seen them recently nesting in the trees surrounding the decoy, at Reedham, Ranworth, Rollesby, Heigham Sound, Stokesby and in scattered trees around Wheatfen Broad. That charming bird, the purple heron, which gives so much grace to the fenland scene in Holland, is only a rare vagrant, whilst the great white heron is even scarcer. One was picked up near Yarmouth many years ago. A buff-backed heron was shot on Breydon Marshes on 23rd October, 1917, and, after being mounted by Saunders of Yarmouth, was bought by the late J. B. Nichols. The squacco heron has turned up at Ormesby, at Burlingham, at Surlingham Broad and at Horning, whilst about twenty specimens of the night heron have been recorded. The little bittern, seen at Hickling on 27th March, 1929, and at Wroxham on 10th May, 1938, probably occurs oftener than is suspected but, owing to its small size and skulking habits, it is a difficult bird to locate and identify. I have two specimens, believed to have been killed on the Broads in the '60s or '70s.

As for the common bittern, once rare and now no longer uncommon, these were such an everyday occurrence a hundred years ago that as many as half a dozen were sometimes shot in a day. At home, in the Cambridgeshire fens of Burwell and Wicken, my great-uncle often saw two or three in the course of a day's snipe-shooting. My father shot one there in 1905, after which none were seen for years. On the Broads they had decreased to such an extent that the last nest was said to have been found in 1868 at Upton Broad. After that, they appear to have completely died out as a nesting species, both at Wicken Fen and on the Broads, merely occurring as migrants from Holland.

Luckily, within recent years, this fascinating bird has re-established itself both at Wicken and on the Broads. On my own fen in Cambridgeshire, known as Adventurer's Fen, I always had two or three pairs breeding regularly each year until the place was drained in 1941. Today, an occasional pair still nests in Wicken Fen, but, fortunately, on the Broads they are becoming an everyday sight again. It seems that they began to re-establish themselves in Broadland in 1900.

Unfortunately there are still people who shoot anything on sight simply because they do not know what it is when it gets up. I have myself seen five bitterns shot 'by accident' in the following places: one on the Herringby Hall marshes, on the Bure, in the winter of 1935, when it was mistaken at night flight for a goose; two in 1938 on Adventurer's Fen, when one was mistaken for a pheasant; one on Martham Broad in 1946, when the shooter thought it was a duck; and the fifth on the Waxham Marshes in 1949, when the offender calmly informed me that "he thought it was an owl". The plain fact is that no man should raise his gun against any bird of whose identity he is uncertain. The average shooting man is a good sportsman, a good naturalist and a preserver of rare birds. Indeed, we owe it almost entirely to the efforts of such good sportsmen as the late Lord Lucas, one-time owner of most of the Hickling property; my old friend, Lord Desborough, who succeeded him; Major Anthony Buxton at Horsey Hall; Colonel Henry Cator at Ranworth and Captain Tom Blofield of Hoveton House, that the bittern has been given the protection which has resulted in its becoming once again an established breeding species.

Nothing is more enchanting than to hear that ghostly booming note, the essence of mystery in the silence of a marshland night, when stars glitter in the spring sky, oceans of reeds sigh in the wind and the silence can almost be felt. The bittern is the bird-spirit of these haunting solitudes.

Among smaller birds which are typical of the Broadland scene are the reed bunting, 'the reed sparrow' of the marshmen, that graceful and lively little spirit of the reed-beds; the grasshopper warbler, whose reeling song fills the midsummer night from dusk to dawn; the snow bunting, who usually arrives in October, goes in March and somehow typifies the white loneliness of the winter marshes; and the wagtails which flit with electric activity up the dykeside. The marsh titmouse is not uncommon and the rare willow titmouse has been recorded three times, once at Beccles, once at Hickling in 1927 and once on the coast. In winter the continental golden-crested wren arrives from the continent more or less at the same time as the herring shoals appear off the coast, which is why the marshmen call them 'herring spinks'. They arrive in October, sometimes in big 'rushes', and spread all over the Broads. The much rarer fire-crested wren has turned up about seven times.

Most charming of all is the bearded titmouse, that utterly delightful little bird with a call-note like the tinkling of tiny silver bells. This fairy bird, with its delicately pencilled dark moustaches, long graceful tail and endearing habit of flitting from reed to reed, whilst it follows the passage of a boat, was last century, on the verge of extinction. Gurney was told in 1889 that there were no more than two pairs in the whole area of Hickling and Heigham Sounds. This decrease was due almost entirely to the craze for collecting. Today, they have re-established themselves in reasonable numbers, despite the terribly hard winters of 1916–17, 1947–8 and 1962–3 which killed scores.

The day-to-day records of the passage of migrants and of breeding birds kept by the Norfolk Naturalists' Trust give a graphic picture of what one may expect to see on some of the Broads, provided you keep quiet, use your eyes and do not move about or wear startling clothing. Thus, in their report for 1963 the Trust gives these two revealing pictures of Hickling Broad and Horsey Mere during the bitter winter of 1962–3 when bird life suffered severely:

HICKLING. Hickling Broad became frozen in mid-December 1962 and remained ice-covered until March 6th. During this long period of severe weather there were many casualties among coot, bitterns, great crested grebes and water-rails. Large numbers of ducks, coot and mute swans were fed with corn daily by the Wardens.

Despite the severe winter a considerable number of bearded tits survived; they were often following the reed-cutters for food. Thirty-five to forty pairs are estimated to have nested at Hickling, Whiteslea and Heigham Sounds. Over thirty nests were found, the first on 3rd May. In September a gathering of 50 bearded tits was at Whiteslea.

The first bittern began booming 9th March at Heigham Corner, but there were only 2 pairs on the Reserve. Again no marsh harriers bred although single birds were seen on many occasions during the summer. A hen marsh harrier appeared on 28th February. No Montagu's harriers were recorded.

Swallows arrived 18th April, followed by cuckoos next day and sedge and grasshopper warblers on 22nd when an avocet was on Rush Hills. During the spring up to 3 drake garganey fed on the wader grounds with numerous shoveler and gadwall. A ruff complete with black ruff and ear-tufts passed through 25th April. Spotted redshank and greenshank appeared on several dates in May, whilst turnstone, spotted redshank and ruff, together with 3 wigeon, were all noted 7th June. A flight of 18 drake shoveler was noted 8th June. An osprey and 3 black terns passed through 5th June with another osprey on 24th. Two reeves appeared 1st July.

Five pairs of common terns nested including 3 pairs on Rush Hills. Other breeding birds included 8 pairs of great crested grebes, 6 pairs of herons, 2 pairs of feral grey-lag geese and a pair of Canada geese. Breeding lapwing and redshank were much reduced in numbers. Some 400 mute swans spent the summer at Hickling; 15 pairs nested. A pair of sheld-duck regularly visited Rush Hills in spring, but did not nest.

Many waders frequented Rush Hills during August. On 5th they included 3 spotted redshank; wood, green and common sandpipers and 5 greenshank. On 14th there were 4 spotted red-shank, 3 greenshank, 3 ruffs, dunlin and little stint. Single green-shank and spotted redshank with 2 little stints were noted 7th September. The first wigeon arrived 14th September with golden-eye 20th October.

A late greenshank was on Deary's marsh 17th December and a

hen harrier arrived on 29th. At this time some 5,000 duck had assembled on the Broad; the majority mallard with many teal, 200 wigeon, 400 tufted, 400 pochard and 50–70 golden-eye.

HORSEY. Horsey Mere remained frozen from the beginning of the year until 7th March. During this bitterly cold spell many birds died including redwing, woodcock and water-rails. Three half-starved bitterns were cared for in pens and fed mainly on sprats. They had become reasonably tame by the time they could be released. One dying mute swan was killed by a fox. Wrens suffered greatly and parties of 4–5 were found dead in out-buildings.

In George Crees' garden some 4 cwt. of apples were devoured by hungry blackbirds, song thrushes, fieldfares, redwings, bramblings, chaffinches and tits during this period. A pair of hen harriers appeared 6th January, a common scoter was found on the coast road on 20th, 3 barnacle geese were at Horsey Gap on 22nd when 8 Bewick's swans were noted with 4 hooded crows on 26th. Twenty-seven white-fronted geese passed through on 3rd March, with ten whoopers on 15th, 3 red-throated divers on the Mere on 17th, a black-tailed godwit on 23rd, great grey shrike on the Warren on 27th and well over 1,000 golden plover in early April when thirty gadwall were on the Mere.

Interesting migrants included ring ouzel 19th–20th April, female Montagu's harrier on 14th and 28th, short-eared owl on 19th, male pied flycatcher and grasshopper warbler on 21st, reed warbler, little tern and a pair of garganey all on 26th, turtle dove on 27th, 29 fieldfares on 30th, collared dove 3rd May, redstart on 5th, male ring ouzel on 9th, male red-spotted bluethroat on 24th and hawfinch next day.

The two surviving bitterns began booming 28th March and one pair bred successfully rearing 4 young. A few bearded tits remained throughout January and February and the first nest with 6 eggs was found 26th April; some 20 pairs nested round the Mere. An adult male marsh harrier headed north-east 21st February and wandering birds were seen from time to time including 3 on 16th May, but none nested. A water-rail's nest was found, but no stonechats, short-eared owls or sparrow-hawks bred. Little owls and kestrels have become scarce. A pair of red-backed shrikes and 3 pairs of bullfinches bred; the latter began breeding at Horsey in 1960. Two pairs of great crested grebes appeared in spring, but did not breed.

Autumn records include a passage of pied flycatchers and redstarts; grey phalarope 3rd October and great grey shrike on 31st for 3 days. 16th November was particularly interesting with 2 hen harriers, a merlin and a very late reed warbler.

In 1964 reports from various Broadland reserves included these:

ALDERFEN. The breeding colony of black-headed gulls increased and some 330 pairs nested.

BARTON. The heronry in Heron Carr showed a decline in numbers, only 4 pairs breeding compared with 10 in 1962. This decrease may have been a result of the severe winter of 1962–3. At least 15 pairs of great crested grebe and one pair of bitterns bred successfully. A firmer control of permanent moorings was exercised, authority for such facility being granted only to members, who are now required to pay an annual mooring fee.

HICKLING. Despite the aftermath of the severe winter of 1962–3, the year was a fair one for wild life on this Reserve. Although the effects of the ordeal on bitterns, great crested grebe and waterrails remained apparent for some months it was a very successful year for ducks, whilst the population of bearded tits was encouraging. Marsh harriers were seen occasionally but no Montagu's harriers were observed. Sparrow-hawks and an osprey were observed. Breeding waders were comparatively few, probably as a result of the severe weather early in the year.

Swallow-tail butterflies were first seen early in June, 50 being counted. The sharp weather seemed to have destroyed most of the remaining coypu. Otter tracks were observed on snow and ice near Sounds Wood.

During the latter part of the year a bittern in a weak condition was found near the broad. The Deputy Warden fed it by hand with live fish for some weeks. After partial recovery it died suddenly and the Nature Conservancy Laboratory diagnosed tuberculosis of the liver as the cause of death. A photograph of the bittern in the care of Warden George Bishop appears in this journal.

Further excavation was undertaken at Swim Coots to enlarge pools in front of the hides for waders. A new hide was erected at Derry's Marsh, near the Holkham Pit, and the Council is most grateful to Mr. Christopher Cadbury for meeting this expense.

Over 18,000 bunches of reed were harvested, although wet weather at the end of the cutting season was an impediment.

RANWORTH AND COCKSHOOT. The heronry population dropped
to 20 pairs compared with 39 pairs the previous year. Six pairs of
common terns nested on the rafts specially constructed for them
and about 12 pairs of great crested grebe bred on the broad. An
osprey was seen on 27th May whilst 16 cormorants lingered there
until the very end of May.

SURLINGHAM BROAD. With the virtual extinction of coypus in
this area during the severe winter of 1963 many plants formerly
kept down by these animals reappeared in the ensuing summer,
through the colonization of bared stretches of mud by seedlings.
New beds of greater reed-mace developed and there was an
exceptionally fine growth of angelica which became the dominant
species on many acres of the marshes. The reed also showed some
signs of recovery, although it proved unsafe to cut owing to the
treacherous nature of the swamps since coypus have destroyed the
reed rhizomes which used to form a firm mat over the liquid
ooze. No bitterns bred on the reserve this year, although one pair
nested successfully a little farther down the valley at Wheatfen.
Mallard bred much later than usual and enjoyed an exceptionally
good breeding season. Fewer black-headed gulls frequented the
flooded Outmeadows during the spring than in the preceding
three years and nesting proved abortive; 2 pairs of common terns
were present throughout the summer but did not appear to have
any breeding success. One pair of grasshopper warblers was seen.

The causeway cleared by the Nature Conservation Corps a few
years ago has been kept open and it is now of great interest for the
mosses flourishing on the old willow trunks.

Those who like to watch birds from boats or as a holiday
recreation, will be interested in the following list of birds, reported by one member of the Norfolk Naturalists' Trust as having
been seen or heard during a visit with his two young sons to the
Broads and north Norfolk from 22nd to 26th April, 1964.

Great Crested Grebe	Sheld-Duck	Ringed Plover
Little Grebe	Egyptian Goose	Grey Plover
Fulmar	Grey-Lag-Goose	Turnstone
Cormorant	Canada Goose	Common Snipe
Heron	Mute Swan	Curlew
Bittern	Sparrow-Hawk	Whimbrel
Mallard	Marsh-Harrier	Common Sandpiper
Teal	Hen-Harrier	Redshank
Garganey	Kestrel	Spotted Redshank

Gadwall
Wigeon
Pintail
Shoveler
Tufted Duck
Pochard
Eider-Duck
Common Gull
Black-headed Gull
Kittiwake
Black Tern
Common Tern
Little Tern
Sandwich Tern
Stock Dove
Wood-Pigeon
Turtle-Dove
Cuckoo
Barn-Owl
Little Owl
Tawny Owl
Short-eared Owl
Swift
Greater Spotted
    Woodpecker
Skylark
Swallow
Reed-Bunting

Red-legged Partridge
Partridge
Pheasant
Moorhen
Coot
Oystercatcher
Lapwing
House-Martin
Sand-Martin
Carrion-Crow
Hooded-Crow
Rook
Jackdaw
Magpie
Jay
Great Tit
Blue Tit
Coal-Tit
Marsh-Tit
Long-Tailed Tit
Bearded Tit
Wren
Mistle Thrush
Song Thrush
Blackbird
Wheatear
Nightingale
House-Sparrow

Greenshank
Dunlin
Sanderling
Ruff
Greater Black-backed
    Gull
Herring Gull
Lesser Black-backed
    Gull
Robin
Sedge-Warbler
Blackcap
Whitethroat
Lesser Whitethroat
Willow-Warbler
Chiffchaff
Dunnock
Meadow-Pipit
Pied Wagtail
Yellow Wagtail
Starling
Greenfinch
Goldfinch
Linnet
Bullfinch
Chaffinch
Yellow Hammer
Tree-Sparrow

SCROBY SANDS. The first landing was made 25th June, when 160
Sandwich terns' nests and 150 common terns' nests were counted;
the first young common terns were ringed. Some 250 kittiwakes
were present. Exceptionally high tides towards the end of June
washed away a number of common terns' eggs and caused the
death of several chicks, but a visit on 2nd July revealed scores of
newly hatched common terns and 110 were ringed, together with
the first 6 young Sandwich terns.

Another spring tide 12th July, caused further casualties among
the common terns and scores of eggs and drowned chicks littered
the tide-line. The Sandwich tern colony was on higher ground
and although it escaped high tides, it suffered from human
interference. Over 50 eggs were removed from the nest scrapes
and left in heaps.

Spinning for pike on the River Bure
A 20-pound pike caught in Broadland

On 4th August the kittiwakes had increased to between 600 and 700 and most of the surviving young terns were on the wing. Six late common terns' nests still held clutches of eggs. A week later the last 3 common tern chicks were ringed. A total of 206 young were ringed: 133 common and 73 Sandwich terns and a good proportion reached the free flying stage.

Many cormorants roost on Scroby and 116 were counted there 19th January. Twenty-five gannets were fishing off the sandbank 19th September with 9 there the following day.

BREYDON WATER. A hundred and forty-seven species were recorded in the area, highlights being 160 Bewick's swans in March and a unique concentration of short-eared owls towards the end of the year:

January: Up to 280 white-fronted geese remained in the Halvergate area throughout the month; a remarkable passage movement occurred on 25th when skein after skein crossed the estuary from the east. Over 4,000 white-fronts were involved. Noteworthy was an adult lesser white-front at Halvergate on 15th and an immature on the estuary on 5th. Pink-feet were again scarce and no gaggle exceeded 13. The bean geese normally wintering higher up the Yare valley, visited the adjoining marshes and on several occasions roosted on the estuary. At least one was shot.

Wildfowl counts included 509 shelduck, 1,450 wigeon and 52 pintail; also 13 scaup, 14 golden eye on the lower Bure and a scoter on 19th. Five brents were noted 3rd–5th and up to 17 Bewick's swans. Other visitors included peregrines, short-eared owls (11 in one locality), 44 Lapland buntings, 130 snow buntings and 65 twites.

February: 5 pink-feet remained till the 5th and by 22nd, white-fronts were down to 150. Wildfowl included 456 wigeon, 28 pintail, 355 shelduck, 6 scaup and 31 pochard. Surprises on 2nd were long-tailed duck and goosander. Waders included 1,500 knot and 26 grey plover. Fifty-two cormorants were present, also male hen harrier and single peregrines. On 9th, over 50 Lapland buntings were on a single marsh with 120 snow buntings.

March: 40 white-fronts headed east on 12th, with 21 on 15th and 3 remained until 22nd. Bewick's swans were the highlight and on 1st 2 herds totalled 61 birds. A large herd of 164 stayed from 5th to 7th. On 8th, 154 were in the area in several groups and at 4.30 p.m. 50 headed due east; 32 passed east over Yarmouth next day. Twenty-two present on 22nd.

12

Wild swans over Hickling Broad

Other wildfowl counts included 319 wigeon, 16 pintail, 27 shoveler, 42 teal, 6 scaup, 5 goosanders (22nd) and a brent (21st). Single black-tailed godwits were noted on 15th and 27th with an early avocet on 18th. Fourteen Lapland buntings remained on 1st with 2 till 7th. Fifty twites were still present on 30th when 37 whimbrel arrived.

June: Spoonbills were a feature with 4 present from 4th till the 10th when one departed eastwards; only one remained by 14th. This was joined by another on 21st and they both stayed till 28th. An avocet appeared on 4th–5th and one (perhaps the same) was on a Bure salting at this time. Late Northern waders included common, wood and curlew-sandpipers, knot, both godwits, greenshank and little stint. Spotted redshanks passed on four dates. Whimbrel had returned by 23rd and green sandpiper and little ringed plover were both new on 27th. Eight black terns passed east on 2nd with 4 on 14th and one on 27th. Two barnacle geese on 27th were undoubted 'escapes'.

Among breeding birds, redshank showed an increase with a small number of lapwing. Three pairs of oystercatchers bred with a fourth pair on arable at Runham. Mallard had a good season, 4 nests being found on one salting and 3 pairs of shoveler nested. Gadwall summered. First broods of shelduck appeared 24th May and 186 young were counted 19th July. Short-eared owls nested at Halvergate, Tunstall and Berney. Four pairs of kestrels are known to have bred and stonechats nested unsuccessfully.

July: 2 drake scaup stayed from 19th to 23rd; 2 spoonbills arrived on 9th with 2 more over Berney on 27th. A probable 'escape' was a white pelican which arrived on 15th (it was at Scroby on 9th–10th) remaining here, apart from visits to the beaches at Caister and Yarmouth and to Scroby, till 31st January, 1965, when it departed westwards at a great height. It was found dead on the Thet at East Harling 20th February, 1965.

Bar-tailed godwits, greenshank, knot and golden plover all arrived on 5th followed by black-tails, ruff and common sandpiper. Little terns peaked at 45.

November: Surprises included merlin on 15th and red-necked grebe on 29th. Greenshank appeared on 1st with spotted redshank till 17th. Sharp frost on 29th resulted in 181 mute swans collecting on the estuary with others on the frozen marshes. A hundred and fifty wigeon, 217 shelduck and 19 pintail were present. Ten pink-feet came on 8th with 15 on 15th. Two day-time short-eared owl roosts contained a total of 45 birds by 30th. Black redstart was new on 8th with 3 bearded tits at Berney on 29th.

December: Wildfowl counts remained low: only 200 wigeon, 303 shelduck and 44 pintail with small numbers of teal and shoveler. The first 12 white-fronted geese arrived on 5th soon increasing to 112. Five pink-feet were seen on 19th and 8 next day. Three brents joined the wigeon. Small herds of up to 12 Bewick's swans were present from 6th and a green sandpiper on 24th.

Exceptional numbers of short-eared owls were on Breydon marshes. On 27th, the larger roost in a ruined cotttage and its garden had a maximum of 52 owls; the other roost, in a derelict marsh garden, held 25. It is likely as many as 100 short-eared owls were in the Breydon area by the year end.

CLEY AND SALTHOUSE. Spring migration was spectacular at Cley and Salthouse when the unusual visitors included green-winged teal, crane, osprey, Kentish plover, Temminck's stint, buff-breasted sandpiper, Mediterranean gull, white-winged black tern, a shy-headed and grey headed wagtails, and woodchat shrike. The year's highlights appear in the following summary:

January: New Year's Day brought a ruff (which stayed until early March), red-necked grebe, 10 Lapland buntings, 8 great Northern divers and 2 hen harriers. A rough-legged buzzard appeared on 3rd and 14th; 7 wax-wings headed east on 18th when a Scandinavian chiffchaff arrived (staying till 1st March); 2 black-tailed godwits were new on 23rd and water pipit on 24th.

April: Six ruffs arrived on 2nd soon increasing to 18 and over 30 were present for a short time; during the last week of this month almost continuous display. Spotted redshank appeared on 4th with a little gull next day (and again on 6th), rough-legged buzzard on 6th and 2 little gulls and a drake green-winged teal on 7th (staying till 11th). Highlight on 8th was a crane heading west; also first yellow wagtail followed by swallows and a very early swift next day.

Another Montagu's harrier appeared on 23rd (and 26th); reed warblers arrived and on 24th an adult male and a first summer female little gull were displaying and feeding over Round Pond. Four greenshank and a spotted redshank passed on 25th and redstart on 26th. An osprey passed high over the Heath on 27th with a pair of marsh harriers, black tern and wood sandpiper on 28th. A red curlew-sandpiper came on 30th and the Sandwich tern assembly totalled 400.

May: 2 marsh harriers appeared on 1st with grey plovers, spotted redshank, 5–6 greenshank and 2 wood sandpipers. Next day came male blue-headed wagtail and 4 white wagtails and on 7th a wood sandpiper was singing and 2 little gulls and 500 Sandwich terns were noted. Another marsh harrier (the seventh this year) appeared on 5th, also male merlin. Buzzard and sparrowhawk were new on 6th also 2 curlew-sandpipers and 7 greenshank with 23 turnstones and little stint, also 25 turtle doves and a collared dove west. Among new arrivals on 7th was a wood warbler in hawthorn beside the coast road. Enormous numbers of swifts, many sand martins and swallows and a few house martins passed through on 8th and another male blue-headed wagtail and nightjar arrived. Five drake garganey were chasing a duck. An osprey headed west on 9th, also a Montagu's harrier and a Temminck's stint were new. The first spotted flycatcher was at Blakeney. A buff-breasted sandpiper was an exciting visitor on 11th–12th feeding at Salthouse with greenshank, ruff, spotted redshank and wood sandpipers.

A three-hour early morning watch produced 287 turtle doves flying west in 25 parties (maximum 35 in a party). An osprey headed west on 13th and waders included 9 wood sandpipers; 90 turtle doves passed west, the first red-backed shrikes appeared on the Heath and a dead roseate tern was at Salthouse. A curlew-sandpiper was new on 14th, a spoonbill next day and a Kentish plover on 16th when a wood warbler was on the Heath and 130 turtle doves passed west. An influx of wood sandpipers (some singing) took place on 17th and little stint and Temminck's stint arrived.

The animals of Broadland, are naturally, far fewer in species than the vast variety of birds, but they are none the less highly interesting. Foxes which are increasing all over Norfolk are not as yet particularly common in the Broads area. Just as well. For the fox is the deadly enemy of the sleeping duck.

Badgers are distinctly uncommon throughout Norfolk and almost unknown in the Broadland, although one was reported from Acle, and another from Surlingham in 1963, possibly both the same animal. They like dry sandy soil and if you want to see a badger look for them at Weybourne, Kelling, Sheringham and in the Breckland.

Otters on the other hand were relatively common up to a dozen years ago. Now they seem to have become much less common, partly owing to the severe winter of 1963 and partly, as the Norfolk Naturalists' Trust report says "the pollution of rivers could make their survival problematical". None the less, the visitor has a very fair chance of seeing one or hearing their distinctive whistle at night. Barton Broad and the shallow reedy wastes of Rockland are strongholds of otters. At Hickling you may see their slides on muddy banks and, when ice has covered the water and snow has fallen on the ice, you may see also where otters at play have pulled another along on his back over the frozen mere. They are kittenish, playful, easily tamed, creatures of infinite grace, more English than the English race itself, but, alas, they eat not only fish, of which heaven knows there are plenty enough, but they kill full-grown wild ducks and even, in sharp winters, go up into the woods and kill pheasants. Otters have been killed on the Broads up to thirty pounds or more in weight. They will always endure so long as reed and water last.

Two years ago in 1964 a big dog otter, three feet nine inches long, weighing thirty pounds was found dead on the Acle New Road. They will run to greater weights than this. The most remarkable report in recent years came from King's Lynn also in 1964 where an otter suddenly appeared from a small stream near the centre of the town with a fish in its mouth which it proceeded to eat by the light of a street lamp.

Personally I never kill an otter unless as happened during a severe winter at Burnley Hall, when they started killing pheasants in the wood because the dykes and broad were frozen. Pheasant feathers and remains of corpses were everywhere. The otter also used one of my duck shooting hides as a dining room and left the wooden floor littered with the mangled remains of wild duck. I tracked him down in the snow and shot him.

The most controversial animal in Broadland today is the coypu or Great South American Marsh Rat which has become acclimatized in recent years. They look like enormous rats with the difference that the females have their teats on their back whilst their mouths are decorated with ferociously curved orange teeth. They run up to twenty-eight pounds in weight and breed two or three times a year. They established themselves as wild animals during the last war when many of them escaped from local fur farms where they were bred commercially for their fur, known as nutria.

Coypu have the remarkable faculty of being able to submerge

completely under water for twenty minutes or so. I have timed them on a small lake in the park surrounding a friend's house on the edge of Broadland. One could watch them squatting on the bottom of the lake in water no more than three feet deep. They peered upwards at us occasionally letting a bubble escape. After twenty minutes or so they came up for a breath of air and went down again.

Coypu do a lot of good on grown up broads and marshes because they chop down and eat a vast amount of the vegetation which has overgrown so many vanished broads and hidden waterways. They will clear a quarter of an acre of marsh growth in a night. Unfortunately they will also clear root crops on farms and can do an immense amount of damage.

Because of their rapid rate of breeding and the speed with which they spread practically all over England as far west as Somerset and as far south as Hampshire, the Ministry of Agriculture declared war on them and all the ponderous bureaucratic artillery in which it delights was let loose on them. The coypu became not only a menace to the farmer, but a little godsend to the chair-bound 'rural experts' of Whitehall, who never by any chance get mud on their boots. The coypu was a wonderful excuse for orders, instructions and memos in quadruplicate. The Ministry promptly extended the 50 per cent grant to rabbit clearance societies to the cost of 'approved work' on coypu. The societies and the internal drainage boards destroyed thousands of them. Despite the officials and the 'pest officers'—the bureaucratic term for official rat catchers—the coypu beat them every time. He bred, increased and travelled! So the Ministry mounted a tremendous three-year campaign to wipe out the coypu, outside Broadland, and reduce the numbers within the Broads area itself. This campaign as the report on Broadland says "included the employment by the Ministry of staff and operators and the provision of traps, other necessary equipment, and transport facilities. The campaign is proceeding satisfactorily with the help of the agricultural executive committees, the National Farmers' societies, river authorities, drainage boards, individual landowners and occupiers, the Nature Conservancy and other organizations.

"The hard winter of 1962–3 helped to reduce the overall numbers but it also caused the remainder, in their search for food, to spread into new areas. This hindered the campaign temporarily, but steady progress has been made since then.

"Coypu are rodents within the terms of Section 98 of the Agriculture Act, 1947, and under this Act any person having the right to do so may be required by a written notice to take steps to kill, take or destroy coypu for the purpose of preventing damage.

"The Coypu (Importation and Keeping) Order, 1962, prohibits the keeping of coypu within Great Britain except under licence. It also makes the provisions of the Destructive Imported Animals Act applicable to coypu, one of which requires occupiers of land, who know that coypu not being kept under licence are to be found there, to give notice of the fact to the Minister of Agriculture Fisheries and Food. The manner in which coypu are to be kept in Great Britain and the precautions to be taken to prevent their escape are prescribed in the Coypu (Keeping Regulations), 1962."

The result of all this was that more than 100,000 coypu were killed and about 90 per cent of the remainder were wiped out by the hard winter of 1963 when all dykes and most of the broads were frozen solid from the end of December until the beginning of March. The Norfolk Naturalists' Trust reported that on their marshes at Cley "the Warden had killed over 2,600 since these animals made their first appearance there. Of these 800 were killed in the latter months of 1962 and the early months of 1963. The Ministry of Agriculture officials set traps in April and caught only seven more. The last live coypu in Breydon marshes was seen 20th February, but a few are known to have escaped the control of the marshmen. One was shot in September, four in October and two in November.

"The campaign is gradually extending the areas of clearance towards the Broads. The western half of the county and south up to a line parallel with Harleston is stated to be clear."

However, since this was written I have seen coypu taken in traps in the winter of 1965–6 on a certain marsh and sent privily in wooden travelling boxes, well ventilated and full of food, to zoo proprietors and others in the Midlands—at £5 a time! So, one way or another, one has a feeling that despite the Ministry and its minions, the coypu will survive. He is probably here for good. He is harmless to man and will only attack you if you attack him. Incidentally he is good to eat and, when roasted, very much like roast pork. If you attempt to skin one, cut the skin down the backbone, not on the belly. Thus you will obtain the best fur.

Meanwhile the acreages of open water which have been increased by the activities of coypu eating down the vegetation are given in the *Report of Broadland* thus:

		Acreages of open water	
	1946	1952	% increase
Decoy Broad	15·6	17·8	14
Ranworth Broad	48·6	59·2	22
Cockshoot Broad	5·6	7·8	40
South Walsham Broads			
(Inner and Outer)	28·8	37·6	31

Polecats are extremely rare, but a few may exist, and it is doubtful if they will ever be utterly exterminated. As I pointed out in *Norwich and the Broads*, they manage to hold their own, sparsely but doggedly, in the treeless and almost reedless cultivated fens in west Suffolk and Cambridgeshire, near Mildenhall, Littleport, Magdalen Fen and the Isle of Ely, where odd specimens have turned up during the last few years, so there is every reason to expect a few scattered pairs to recur among the Broads.

Stoats, known to every marshman as 'lobsters' or 'minifers', are common enough, as are weasels, locally called 'mouse-hunters'.

Hares swarm on the marshes and rabbits abound in the sand-hills. Moles are abundant on every marsh and hedgehogs pursue their spiny, midnight ways on the higher and drier land.

Rats, like the plagues of Egypt, are universal and incorrigible, but that loathsome tribe provides the almost unique distinction that, in Yarmouth, you might still find the old English black rat and the even rarer Alexandrine rat, an exotic escapee from visiting ships which has somehow established itself with tenuous persistence.

The water-rat, or vole, that charming little miniature beaver, is the beady-eyed brown and harmless little friend of every holiday-maker who moors his boat by the river bank, or pitches his tent beneath a waterside willow. As for field voles, which the marshmen call 'rannys', they swarm on every marsh and upland, and when, as periodically happens, there is a plague of them, the short-eared owls who breed on the marshes and wheel by day like buzzards above the spreading levels are reinforced by hordes of their cousins, who flock in across the North Sea from Holland, drawn by the same strange, wild telepathy which causes the snowy owls and eagle owls at Baltic forests to attend in deadly trains upon the periodic plagues of lemmings.

Seals, porpoises, whales, grampuses and dolphins, are creatures of the sea, all of which have been recorded from Yarmouth and the coast. A seal has been up-river nearly as far as Norwich, and I know a man who hooked one, to his nightmare fright, on a pike-line in the Yare.

The seal colony on the Scroby Sands off Great Yarmouth is one of the most notable on the east coast. The Scroby Sands themselves are well worth a visit by motor-boat from Yarmouth. At low tide this enormous sandbank which seems to be rapidly becoming a permanent island, is a wonderful place for a picnic and a natural history wonder. Hundreds of terns and small waders nest on it— and frequently lose their eggs owing to high tides but the main interest of the place, apart from the sad bones of wrecked ships, are the seals. The Norfolk Mammal Report for 1963 reported the populations as remaining more or less static. Approximately 400 were counted at the end of 1962.

The report goes on to say that "numbers of the Common Seal (*Phoca vitulina*) fluctuated during the summer, the peak number being approximately 200 on 30th June. The first pup, a dead one, was found 9th June. The first week in July was again the peak pupping period and seventeen were found, with ages ranging from a few hours to a few days on 14th July. The mortality rate was again very high and six dead ones were found on 30th July. This probably helps to maintain a steady population and the avoidance of a fisheries problem. Along the east coast from Lincolnshire to Caister the total population is estimated at 5,000. The majority live in the Wash where some control has to occur. Any stranded pups are, however, cared for. More than twenty were picked up during the season, fed on a mixture of whale oil, cow's milk and cod liver oil for three weeks, and then returned to the sea. Others were similarly catered for at Yarmouth.

Small groups of between ten and twenty Grey Atlantic Seals (*Halichoerus grypus*) were seen at Scroby during the summer; they were usually separated from the Common Seals. Several attempts were made during early December to visit Scroby, but unfortunately they were prevented by bad weather. A visit on 27th December, however, showed that there were seven live pups and two dead ones. Some of these were already in moult. A pup was found stranded on the shore at Waxham 19th January."

A few porpoises are stranded on the coast annually and the hind part of a small white-beaked dolphin was washed ashore at Runton during a gale in 1963.

Indeed a walk along the beach at, say, Horsey, Waxham, Winterton—most easterly part of England—Scratby or Yarmouth, all points easily reached from those living aboard a boat, may yield almost anything in the way of highly interesting flotsam and jetsam, including prehistoric relics from the buried forests and vast marshes which once covered most of the bed of the North Sea.

In fine, Broadland is a place of infinite enchantment and variety to the naturalist, botanist, entomologist, archaeologist, marine biologist or the ordinary man who delights in the flight of a bird.

It will always, one may pray, remain a unique place of bird life and the home of rare birds. Even if the boats and the visitors increase beyond their present horrifying proportions and the din, vulgarity and pollution of high summer touch a new nadir of horror, there will always be quaking swamps, impenetrable weed beds and hidden waterways where birds and animals will be safe from humanity in its least attractive form, The total acreage of Nature Reserves in Broadland at the moment is 3,468 acres, with a further 3,960 acres of reserves on the nearby coast. These acreages are likely to be increased. They must never be allowed to become the stamping grounds of herds of so-called bird-watchers, too many of whom were aptly summed up by my old marsh keeper at Salthouse, when I rented the Salthouse Broads, as 'weekend gull-worriers'. The true ornithologist is a solitary person. Like the birds he watches he loves peace and quiet. He does not wish to be one of the mob.

Bird-watching, however, like hiking, club fishing and pop 'music' has become a cult—a cult which too often attracts people of sheep-like mentality, with little real interest in the subject to which they are attracted.

One remembers the sad scene of a bittern's nest on a Dutch fen which had been so tramped round and round by camera carrying, sandwich munching, queues of bird-watchers that the clump of reeds in which it was situated stood up like an island. No wonder the birds deserted the nest.

Then there was the horn-rimmed self-important youth who turned up in the middle of my own fen in Cambridgeshire where two pairs of bitterns were nesting and proceeded to march all over the place. When stopped and asked what he was doing he replied importantly: "I'm a bird-watcher. I'm looking for the bittern's nest."

At that moment a snipe, circling high above, darted suddenly earthward, tail wing feathers spread stiffly out whilst the slip-stream from its extended wings vibrated them and produced that odd 'drumming' which with its goat-like bleating, is the spring love song of the snipe.

"What on earth's that queer thing?" The bird 'expert' de-manded. I told him that if he could not recognize a snipe he would certainly never know a bittern and that if he was not off the place in double quick time he would end up in the dyke.

Such bird-watchers are as much a menace to bird life as the bogus 'wildfowlers' who in winter patrol the tide line and shoot anything and everything which flies.

The moral of all this is that the would-be bird-watcher should never trespass; avoid disturbing birds on the nest; ask permission if he wishes to visit private land and above all familiarize himself with the birds he wants to watch. A good bird book will lay the foundations of elementary knowledge, plus a visit to the magni-ficent museum of Natural History housed in Norwich Castle, which, incidentally, includes what is probably the finest Diorama of bird life in any museum in Britain, London not excepted. A useful pocket book for the bird-watcher is Roland Green's ex-quisite little handbook *Wingtips* which enables one to identify birds in flight by the contours of their wings. Finally birds come to those who sit tight and keep quiet. They flec from the man who walks, talks and splashes about.

XII

PROBLEMS OF TODAY

Pollution, Litter, Hooliganism and Squalid Development

TODAY the Broads face problems which, unless they are curbed, may well develop to such an extent that they will ruin much of the area, as a holiday resort for people of discrimination. These problems are the result of too many people, both visitors and the newer sort of resident, using the Broads without consideration for their amenities, their water purity or their beauty.

Pollution; litter; wanton damage to property; squalid and unsightly development; trespass; speed boats; hydroplanes and water skiing; erosion of river banks and, finally, too many boats, are the main problems.

I will deal with pollution last since it has been the subject of a recent inquiry, the findings of which are worth giving in some detail.

Litter is a minor but increasing nuisance. Consider the evidence of one man, an entirely unbiased visitor whose experience could be matched by that of thousands of other visitors. Dr. Charles Houlder of Hutton, Essex, an eminent medical man and a police surgeon, took his family for a week's cruise on the Broads in the late spring of 1966. At the end of it he reported to me:

"At almost every spot where we landed, away from boatyards or public staithes, we found litter. Broken bottles were a constant hazard. Jagged tins lurked in the most unexpected places. Plastic containers and polythene bags floated in the reeds or had been thrown ashore on grazing marshes where they could be eaten or swallowed by cattle to which they are a real danger. Old newspapers, cardboard boxes and general debris had been dumped in the most out of the way corners, such as the trodden down riverside stances of anglers, where the reeds had been beaten down in order to allow them to make their casts. Dykesides where boats had tied up for the night were equally untidy. In several places we found pretty little spots sheltering under trees which would have been ideal for a picnic but for the fact that someone had been there before and left jagged tins and broken bottles half hidden in the grass—absolute accident traps for children. As for bathing I wouldn't have dreamt of doing it. The water looked too filthy."

This is the disillusioned plaint of a man who went in the off-season hoping to avoid the peak holiday crowd and find peace and unspoiled beauty. In case it should seem an overdrawn picture this is what the *Report on Broadland* for 1965 says on the matter: "The rise in holiday and recreational use of Broadland has been accompanied by increasing trespass and vandalism. Litter is also a difficult problem to solve because road access to allow easy collection is lacking in many places. Irresponsible behaviour by a small section of the public has created difficulties with neighbouring landowners and farming tenants and does nothing to encourage their support in extending facilities for the visitors."

Trespass is particularly infuriating to farmers. Their cattle are stampeded, sheep chased by dogs, gates left open and in-calf heifers slip their calves because they have been terrified by hooligans from boats. I have heard of cattle being shot at with airguns and air pistols.

"I've got my remedy in the stock yard," one marsh farmer said. "My young bull. He's five years old and he can go like a race hoss —and jump a gate. I'm letting him out on the river pasture and God help anybody he catches. If one or two of 'em get tossed in the river they'll begin to think twice about chasing my cattle and upsetting the sheep. As for campers, I won't have one on the farm. They can go back to the Midlands and stop there."

This declaration of war by one man voices the seething indignation of many. Well behaved holiday-makers and campers will suffer because of the lunatic behaviour of a relatively few louts. In this age of high wages and short working hours which some starry-eyed idealist has christened the Age of Leisure, it is all too obvious that far too many people do not know how to enjoy leisure without being a nuisance to others.

Before the war, the Broads boat owners compiled a Black List of boat hirers who had been reported to the boat owners for causing damage, riotous behaviour and generally making a nuisance of themselves. The word went round quietly from boatyard to boatyard. Quite a lot of people were barred from ever hiring a boat again. That Black List needs expanding and tightening up today.

Wanton damage to property includes not only damage to boats but to boathouses, empty riverside bungalows and chalets, farm premises and even drainage mills. It is difficult for the police to be in all places at once, but a thumping fine or, better still, six months in jail for a few offenders would work wonders.

When we come to the problem of squalid and unsightly development, Broadland faces one of its most insidious dangers. The jerry builder is the enemy of mankind. He produces shoddy houses at high prices, which begin to deteriorate before the mortgage on them is half paid, and he has a demoniac flair for putting the most appalling housing designs in the worst possible places.

The average chalet is an architectural abomination, bad enough in a third-rate suburb, whence it emanates, but utterly inexcusable and an affront to the eye when it is dumped down against a background of reeds, water, green pastures and immemorial beauty. Broadland is being smothered by eruptions of this disease. Their design is, almost invariably, cheap, common and nasty and, alas, too often indicative of the people who live in them. Thus Englishmen destroy the beauty of England.

In 1949 I wrote in *Marshland Adventure* these few paragraphs—applicable then, but infinitely more applicable to far worse conditions today:

"It is a pity that the urban English, in their search for simplicity, almost inevitably burden the countryside with neat little lawns, flagged paths, crazy-paving, bird baths, masts which never conceivably fly a flag, and other decorations amid which they plant themselves in their Moorings or Broadsides or Castle Braes.

"Irstead Shoals has suffered less than, say Horning from this form of Tottenham-Court-Road-gone-rural, but, although it is a hundred miles better than the dreadful waterside rabbit-runs—or should I say water-rat-runs—of Potter Heigham, places originally erected by holiday-makers and now inhabited willy-nilly by unfortunate people who cannot find a home elsewhere, yet the type of residence which clusters about Irstead Shoals is equally to blame. It does not fit in. Apart from its roof, it does not try to fit in. It would be equally happy, and in place, on the edge of Putney Common. Why come to Norfolk, the county of flint, of reed-thatch, of wattle and daub, of calm, collected, traditional architecture, and plant down, as has been done on the outskirts of Norwich and elsewhere, little standardized boxes of mock Tudoresque which are as much out of place in the countryside as a woman with fox furs and high red heels in a muddy lane?"

Far worse than the mock Tudor villa and the thatched bungalow which, after all, make an attempt to fit into the traditional scene, are the endless shacks, constructed of breeze blocks, glass and formica, each in its plat of concrete, which have sprung up as dreary conurbations to many of the villages. I once liked Potter Heigham. Today I avoid it like the plague. Wroxham is little better and a bad copy of a cheapjack London suburb, tattered at the edges.

Miles of the coastline have been utterly prostituted by the jerry builder.

Must more of Norfolk beauty be squandered on the altar of opportunism? The people of that bleakly attractive village of Sea Palling have apparently voted by a majority in favour of the construction of a 'holiday chalet town' to accommodate 8,000 visitors. At present Sea Palling has 350 inhabitants. It stands with its face to the sea and its back to flat farmlands and the encompassing marshes of Hickling Broad and Horsey Mere. It is a place of great natural beauty of that austere sort which is the essential soul and beauty of the north Norfolk coast.

In the past Sea Palling bred an heroic breed of fishermen and lifeboatmen. It will need all its heroism to face the future unless its inhabitants are resigned to the squalid attractions of bingo halls, ice-cream kiosks, beat 'music', dance halls, long-haired louts and the rest of the embellishments of this Age of the Common Man (and how common can he be). This may enrich a few people who propose to sell building plots, concrete garden gnomes, plastic storks, candyfloss, transistors and steel guitars. Their market should be limitless.

What, however, will happen to that superbly beautiful range of sandhills which sweep southward by the towered walls of that unique house, Waxham Hall? The coast runs on, lonely and unspoiled, by Horsey—which fortunately the National Trust controls—to the Smugglers' Gap at Somerton and so south to Winterton where there are plenty of holiday camp facilities already. These few miles of coast are unique not only for the wind-tossed beauty of the sandhills and the lonely splendour of the marshes but because they are one of the few remaining unspoiled stretches of Norfolk coastline. Bird-watchers, artists, those who walk because they love walking and holiday-makers who seek the peace and beauty of an unspoiled shore are the people who will suffer. Why should they?

Too much of the East Anglian coastline is already ruined by squalid holiday development—huts, shacks, bungalows and caravans. Many of them stand empty and unkempt for months on end. Why add to the mess? Blakeney has stood up to this menace —and defeated it. Let Palling do the same.

I sincerely hope that Norfolk County Council and Enterprise Neptune will put a stop to this plan. A Sea Palling farmer puts it pithily in a letter to me: "God knows what will happen! I dread to think of swarms of holiday-makers from the Midlands breaking loose all over the farm, leaving the gates open, lighting fires and picnicking where it suits them. The answer is to put up a few barbed wire entanglements and let the bull out! I think I'll get a couple of Alsatians too. As for our roads, they will be full of amateur Donald Campbells on motor-bikes and Dads towing caravans. I only hope the day never comes when we have to swallow our principles, sell the farm at an inflated price for more development and get out. We are supposed to grow food—not holiday shacks. Anyway I hate to think what will happen to the sandhills down the coast."

I think I can tell him what will happen there. Broken bottles. Jagged, stinking tins. Discarded ice-cream cartons. Sodden newspapers. Polythene bags blown on to the marshes for grazing cattle to swallow—but not to digest. There will be picnic fires in the 'hills' and, sooner or later, prairie fires sweeping through the miles of marram grass whose roots help to hold the sandhills together. These hills are the fragile barrier which hold the savage winter tides at bay.

Need one remind Norfolk people of what happened when the sea broke through in 1938 at Horsey and flooded thousands of acres from Somerton to Hickling, from Martham Holms to Wax-ham? Horsey, its church, hall and village, became an island again. The damage done to farmland and food production was incredible. Cattle stampeded for the high lands. Hares made for the islets and the upland fields. Rabbits were drowned by the thousand. Moles, voles, rats, field-mice, and worms were slaughtered in thousands. For a year or more there was no worm in the soil.

A bittern at bay with a beak like a sword

Between 10,000 and 15,000 acres were all either one great lake or poisoned by salt.

I do not say that a chalet camp at the new Sea Appalling will cause the sea to break in again but a marram fire could conceivably weaken parts of the sandhills to a dangerous degree. In any case why squander money, materials and labour on temporary buildings when so many people require permanent homes? Sea Palling could be a gross misdirection and waste of our housing resources.

I have emphasized the danger of more cheapjack coastal development for the reason that the coastline of Broadland is a physical and spiritual part of the whole picture. Less than a thousand acres of the whole British coastline are 'undeveloped' today. Heaven forbid that what remains of the unique beauty of the north and east Norfolk coasts should be squandered to make fortunes for jerry builders.

Vulgarity, whether exemplified by building development, bad manners, vandalism or 'water hogs', can be the ultimate death of Broadland. Its unique function is to remain as a place of peace where the angler, the small-boat sailor, the quiet cruiser, the artist, the naturalist and the lover of peace and beauty can find a refuge from the noise and vulgarity of the urban world. If urban visitors bring urbanized vulgarity and mechanized din with them, they will ruin the place. This is a very real threat. It is on the doorstep.

Speed-boats, hydroplaning and water-skiing should be banned absolutely except from Oulton Broad where there is special provision for them. They are a nuisance and positive danger in all other parts of Broadland.

I have in the past had the privilege of piloting what was in its day one of the fastest speed-boats in the world, so I do not speak without practical experience. The proper place for speed-boats is either on salt water or on the great reservoirs of the Midlands or elsewhere and on the waters to be developed in the Lea Valley Scheme. They are not wanted on the Broads. They should not *be* on the Broads.

The Broadland Report has something to say about shoddy development and about speed-boats. Cautiously it observes "A further impact on the Broadland environment has come from changes in the pattern of the resident population and the demands of the holiday and recreation users. These have led to a growth in shore-based facilities in the form of boatyards, servicing stations, mooring berths, shops, caravans and camp sites, car parks, chalets and

13

Suburbia at Oulton Broad

riverside dwellings. There is controversy about many of these developments in view of the widespread repercussions which they are having on the environment. There are also doubts about the standards (for example, of design) which have been adopted." A magnificent under-statement.

It is more outspoken on the subject of speed-boats and power-driven craft: "Speed boating and water-skiing on the relatively confined areas of the waterways are a hazard to other users and create an undesirable amount of noise and disturbance which detracts from the peaceful character of the Broadland scene. Owing to their relatively shallow draught, speed-boats are able to penetrate into areas which cannot be reached by the larger tourist craft. Because their propellers can damage aquatic life and their noise and pace cause disturbance to nesting wildfowl in these situations, they are discouraged on nature reserves such as Barton and Hickling Broads. At Oulton Broad, on the other hand, a special time is set aside each week during the holiday season for speed-boating and hydroplane racing."

The Report goes on to say: "The great increase in the numbers of holiday craft using the waterways has resulted in a shortage of mooring places and in temporary overnight congestion at the more popular centres, mainly Yarmouth, Lowestoft and Norwich, where boats are often tied up two or three deep. This, in turn, aggravates the problems of noise, litter, vandalism and pollution.

"The increasing number of power-driven craft has led to oil pollution on the waterways. This is particularly serious when due care is not exercised during refuelling and during the cleaning down of the craft between bookings and at the end of the season. At such times a film of oil can be seen on the water surface which threatens the general amenity of the area as well as the aquatic and wild life interests of the waterways.

"The East Anglian Water Company is concerned by pollution of the kinds mentioned above, and also because the movement of craft contaminates water supplies by stirring up bottom deposits. This has led the Company to be selective in the kind and amount of use which they allow on the stand-by reservoir formed by Ormesby, Rollesby and Filby Broads." All this brings us to the vexed question of pollution. At the moment it is only a threat. Before long it may become a real danger.

When Christopher Davies wrote of the Broads at the end of last century he referred frequently to "their clear and crystal waters".

He would have to look a long way for them today. When I rented Martham Broad in the 1940s we used to bathe in the little South Broad. Its waters were clear and crystal. They still are. That is because it is one of the remotest of all broads and, as a private water, access to it is barred by a chain. I would still bathe in it with infinite pleasure.

Nothing, however, would induce me to bathe in Wroxham Broad, in the River Yare, or in many other Broads. The "clear and crystal waters", during the holiday season are a dirty, turgid brown.

This is caused partly by the bottom mud being stirred up by the churning screws of motor craft; partly by effluent and sewage and partly by the discharge from the lavatories of hundreds of boats. Detergents from innumerable bungalows and craft add their particular form of poisoning to the brew. The wonder is that the fish survive in some of the waters.

This state of affairs, which has been getting progressively worse for years, caused so much fear of disease that in 1960 my friend Mr. H. F. Brooker, Managing Director of Blake's (Norfolk Broads) Holidays Limited, who is also Secretary of the Norfolk and Suffolk Broads Yacht Owners Association, and Mr. James Hoseason of Hoseasons Norfolk Holidays, who is Secretary of the Broadland Owners Association, instituted on behalf of their two associations, a thorough scientific investigation into the state of affairs. Dr. Roy C. Hoather of The Counties Public Health Laboratories was given the task to analyse and report on the purity of Broads water. The results of his inquiry confirmed without a doubt that in most places the quality of the water was surprisingly good. Its purity, though fighting a losing battle, has maintained itself—so far.

It is the most comprehensive survey ever conducted to ascertain the state of purity of Broads water. Hundreds of water samples were taken at strategic points regularly once a month throughout the twelve-month period ending in February 1965.

They were followed by nearly a thousand laboratory tests to establish the degree of water purity.

Why was the investigation made? "In view of the attention rightly focused in recent seasons on the purity of water at seaside and river resorts, not to mention the purity of the air itself in smokeless zones in cities," said H. F. Brooker and James Hoseason in a joint statement, "we felt it right to keep abreast of modern trends, as we consistently do, by taking a careful scientific look at the Broads water quality.

"On the Norfolk Broads we are deeply conscious of the rapidly growing need in Britain for first-class leisure and holiday amenities. We are delighted, therefore, that the results of our investigations are, as we anticipated, gratifyingly satisfactory.

"Broads water was judged after severe tests as being as pure as that regularly taken from the River Thames to supply London's drinking water."

Dr. Hoather's laboratory findings are set out in a 6,000 word 'Water Quality Report' with statistics and tables, prepared by The Counties Public Health Laboratories. They were circulated to the East Suffolk and Norfolk River Authority, the Press, and various national and local authorities, including the Ministry of Housing and the Ministry of Health. The reports show conclusively that the body or volume of water in the Broads and rivers is more than sufficient to meet the work load currently put upon it.

Dr. Hoather was asked early in 1964 by the Broadland Owners' Association and the Norfolk and Suffolk Broads Yacht Owners' Association to "investigate the condition and state of the Broadland Waterways in their areas of extensive navigation and use, and to compare this with the adjacent waterways that have little or no navigation."

The unusually dry and warm 1964 season meant that the presence of any invalidating factor in water purity would have been more noticeable than in a year of more rainfall. In fact, after a week's cruising on the Broads during 18th July to 25th Dr. Hoather reported:

"The almost complete absence of any sign of nuisance even in places congested with boats seemed to me very noteworthy."

Monthly sampling began on 3rd March, 1964 at midstream waterway points at Wroxham, Horning, South Walsham, Thurnemouth, Acle Bridge, Potter Heigham, Martham Ferry, Martham Broad, Ludham Bridge, Wayford Marina and Filby Broad.

These points (with the exception of Filby Broad) were carefully and deliberately selected because they represented the section of the Broads most densely used by river traffic.

Dr. Hoather's laboratory tests of the monthly samplings dealt mainly with Bacteriological Count, Detergent Residue, Turbidity, Sodium Chloride (salt), Ammonia, Nitrogen and Oxygen.

In brief, Dr. Hoather's results (as detailed in the 'Water Quality Report') showed:

Bacteriological Count. "Relatively and surprisingly slight" and about as good as for the River Thames at the intakes for public water supplies.

Detergents. Nearly all the analyses showed virtually none—"less than the lower limit for detection." Further proof was the absence of foam in spite of agitation of the waterways by the wash of boats.

Turbidity. Water mostly appeared brownish, due to stirring by power craft. The cause according to the tests . . . "about 70 per cent mineral (earth) with a strong admixture of harmless 'peaty' vegetable matter from the banks and the river bottom".

Chloride. Unusually high tides very occasionally brought the sea-water content at Acle, Potter Heigham and Martham Broad up towards a maximum of less than one part in twenty.

Ammonia. Increased slightly during the holiday season. Figures were higher in winter when freezing prevented the self-purification process.

Nitrogen. Peaty material in suspension contributed substantially to albuminoid nitrogen. "On several occasions one of the highest results was for Filby Broad (an enclosed water) where there were practically no boats."

Oxygen. High content of dissolved oxygen is very desirable for cleanliness, sweet odour, and the health of fish and waterplant life. "On the whole," says Dr. Hoather, "I consider results for Biochemical Oxygen Demand and Dissolved Oxygen to be very good." Summing up, Dr. Hoather's report concludes: "Results might be regarded as surprisingly good if we consider that the floating population on the waterways is fairly large."

His full conclusions are worth giving verbatim:

"In many places the water had a turbid brown appearance due largely to the stirring up of mud and peaty organic matter; otherwise conditions in the waterways and on the banks appeared pleasant and reasonably clean and tidy. Careful observations were made for any odour from the water. A slight earthy odour was found in a few places. In only two places was an objectionable 'sewage' odour found very locally; in one of these places the main cause was the sewage discharge from a large hotel and in the other place it appeared that the main cause was similar."

With regard to sewage discharge "from a large hotel and one other place" Dr. Hoather says elsewhere in his report:

"There are only two localized places in which I (or my wife/ or daughter) were able to find an objectionable 'sewage' odour from the water. One was at Horning Ferry and there can be no doubt that the highly polluted dyke passing behind the hotel and receiving its sewage effluent was the main cause. The other place was immediately upstream of Potter Heigham bridge where there are hotels and similar establishments on both sides of the river. The nearby 'Haven' just below the bridge held roughly thirty boats at the time and if cruisers were to cause an objectionable odour or other nuisance in the water this is one of a number of places where I should expect to have observed such nuisance. In fact we were unable to detect any odour or other noticeable signs of sewage (the fact that the best public conveniences I saw anywhere on the Broads were within this 'Haven' did not appear very relevant to this comment).

"We saw only two persons swimming in the waterways or Broads, and that was in Barton Broad.

His remarks concerning the effect on fish are highly interesting:

"It is obvious that fish are numerous in the waters in very many places, although the turbidity of the water already mentioned prevents them being seen very much until they are caught. In view of the large numbers of fish, the fact that many are caught and kept in nets before being returned to the water and the possibility of damage by craft, it is probably not surprising that single floating dead fish are a fairly common sight. However, I was surprised by the number of dead fish we saw when cruising up the Ant on the morning of Friday, 22nd July. We counted altogether roughly thirty on one side from the confluence with the Bure up to Irstead Church. We did not observe nearly as many going down the Ant on the previous Monday, and nor could I find any near Ludham Bridge on 23rd September. Anticipating subsequent discussion on dissolved oxygen concentrations, it is convenient to state here that it seems to me very doubtful if the death of these fish can be attributed to lack of oxygen. It seems that a few fish, in closely restricted places could die from this cause. However, the Water Pollution Research Laboratory have published work on the effect of suspended solid mineral matter on fish. It can cause deterioration of the gills and death and I am inclined to think that this could be a major cause in the River Ant. The turbid appearance of water in that river has been mentioned on a previous page.

"However, the question of fish is a very wide one, involving biological factors and requiring expert knowledge of the fish and their breeding, feeding and habits in general, whereas I cannot do more than attempt to assess the main chemical and physical factors in the water.

"The almost complete absence of any visible nuisance (sewage, etc.) from discharges from boats, even in congested places, seemed to me very noteworthy. The results of the analyses show signs of sewage or other similar pollution only in a highly diluted or largely oxidized form. The concentration of dissolved oxygen in the water has, on the whole, been found very satisfactory although somewhat lower figures have been found at two sampling points in the River Ant.

"I consider it important and very fortunate, that these analyses and observations have been made during an exceptionally dry summer. I have concluded that the state of the water has been reasonably satisfactory in most places, and it is therefore possible to say that pollution from boats has not been excessive and has not had a very significant effect on amenities in general, even in this exceptionally dry summer. In a normal season there would be a greater volume of water available for dilution of all impurities.

"These results might be regarded as surprisingly good if we consider that the floating population on the waterways is fairly large and that theoretically its contribution to pollution of the water should probably be greater than sewage works on land. One of the favourable factors is doubtless the wide distribution of craft over very extensive areas of water. On the whole, impurities added to the water are being very effectively oxidized and removed by the combination of physical, chemical and biochemical processes known as 'self-purification'.

"Finally, although it may be just outside my terms of reference to water quality, I feel that it may not be out of place to observe that the closet accommodation in the boats is an obvious asset to private health and avoids the well-known public health dangers of intestinal diseases via public lavatories unless kept scrupulously clean and provided with facilities for washing hands."

This report submitted by the independent authority acknowledged as Britain's most expert, is felt by the boat industry "clearly and soberly to destroy the ill-informed, irresponsible statements that have been made in the past about the quality of Broadland's waters."

A damper is cast on these optimistic findings by the report of the Nature Conservancy. They state that oil pollution is causing; "damage to amenity and scientific interest, especially invertebrate fauna. Makes purification of domestic water supply difficult." Commenting on its incidence in Broadlands it says "frequent, especially at main holiday centres and near waterside filling stations. Increasing as number of motor craft rises". In quoting actual examples in Broadland it sites the River Bure at Wroxham, River Thurne at Potter Heigham, Stalham Dyke, etc.

With regard to sewage effluents from rivercraft, houseboats and riverside dwellings, the Report lists the effects as "widespread but most noticeable in crowded waterways. Damage to amenity. Risk to public health if contaminated water is used for domestic consumption. Water rendered unfit for swimming. B.O.D. of water may rise to abnormal levels, especially in confined waterways in hot weather".

It cites as particularly bad examples, Malthouse and Oulton Broads, the River Bure between Wroxham and Horning and it points out that sewage from Great Yarmouth penetrates up the Bure on a rising tide.

The Report says that the remedy is to "Prohibit disposal of crude sewage from river craft, houseboats etc. Fit 'slipper' tanks to all new craft and provide shore-based unloading facilities. Use of chemical closets of 'Elsan' type not possible as phenols give very unpleasant taint to chlorinated drinking water. Also very toxic to fish and wild life."

The effluents from sewage disposal plants are a serious problem in Broadland and in other parts of the country. The Report particularly criticizes the outfall from Norwich Sewage Works at Whitlingham on the Yare and other smaller sewage works which release effluents in upper reaches or tributaries of main Broadland rivers, particularly at North Walsham and Beccles. It urges stricter standards of inspection, regular maintenance of the works, replacement of out of date equipment and, very properly, urges "more research on effects of detergents on fauna and flora".

It naturally condemns the wholesale tipping of rubbish "often tipped overboard or thrown on to banks" which it says is "widespread and increasing during the holiday season". It emphasizes the danger to livestock caused by broken glass etc. and says that more rubbish bins and disposal facilities should be provided. This is an obvious need.

With regard to housing estates and individual houses, the Report praises the good planning of the Avenues Estate at Wroxham, points out that other estates cause "pollution and litter". Good planning is the answer.

It is scathing about holiday chalets developments, particularly at Potter Heigham, blames the boat and chalet hire agencies, points out that occupancy is usually only seasonal and says bluntly that the solution is to "demolish and redevelop in accordance with site characteristics". This is plain common sense. All proposed and future chalet development should be subject to the most stringent control. Broadland cannot afford further vulgarization of the natural beauty which is its capital. If that capital is squandered, the income which it now produces from holiday-makers and visitors will vanish. "Man destroys the thing he loves." The idiot always will—given uneducated freedom.

XIII

THE NEED FOR MORE WATERWAYS

The Cost of Re-opening Old and Creating New Broads

WITH less than a thousand acres of open broads available for cruising and general holiday-making, it is absolutely essential that new broads be created. The cost need not be astronomic. Some of it could be recovered by creating new peat-diggings. Peat at present is imported from Scotland, Somerset and I believe Lancashire to London and south-eastern England. It is an expensive luxury for which many people pay gladly. Norfolk peat would have the same high-class market that Norfolk reeds have today. Thus a revival of peat digging would help to create new broads exactly as the existing broads were created by medieval peat diggers four to six centuries ago.

The new broads could be created on large areas of low-quality reclaimed marshes much of which is of poor grazing value and should not be too expensive to buy.

A second method of creating new open waters would be to re-instate existing broads which have either silted up so that their open waters are un-navigable or, like Sutton Broad, have become completely overgrown with reeds and bulrushes.

The suggestion that unreclaimed Fenland should also be excavated, is not a sound one. Unreclaimed fen is usually several feet higher than the surrounding drained marshes. It is frequently overgrown with dense thickets of buckthorn, sallows, willows, birch and even oak. The cost of clearing the timber and brushwood and then of digging six or eight feet down through the more or less high and dry peat would be considerable.

The Yarmouth Port and Haven Commissioners have already pioneered the reinstatement of existing broads with outstanding success on South Walsham Broad and Malthouse Broad. They used an ordinary dredger to bring up the mud from the bottom and load it on to barges. The mud was taken to a dump where it was off-loaded by a second dredger.

The *Report on Broadland* went very carefully into the cost of creating new broads. It says definitely that: "The cost of removing and dumping the material in this way at present amounts to 7s. 8d. a cubic yard; therefore, the cost of reinstating the broad by dredging, say three feet of detritus from its bottom amounts to about £1,900 an acre. Thus, at present prices, a fifty-acre broad could be reinstated for about £95,000, or one the size of Oulton Broad for approximately £152,000. It is important not to put too much reliance on such figures since operating conditions and cost of working in other areas might differ substantially from those encountered by the Port and Haven Commissioners at Malthouse and South Walsham Broads.

"The most practicable way of creating a new Broad in an area where the marshes are drained and reclaimed would probably be to embank and flood an area and then use a floating dredger to remove the mud to give a sufficient depth of water. The mud would have to be removed on barges and off-loaded on one side of the excavation, as at Malthouse Broad. The cost of excavation by this method would amount to about 9s. a cubic yard. If a suction dredger could be used, the cost would be reduced to about 6s. a cubic yard, but such a machine would require a settlement pond to trap and retain the mud before the water was returned to the excavation.

"The entrance of each new broad would require a lock, which would be costly to build and maintain and which would form a considerable obstacle to the free movement of boat traffic. Each broad will, therefore, have to be dug out to a depth at least forty inches below the level of Low Water Spring Tides in the adjacent river. Unfortunately, no accurate figures of the relationship between the levels of L.W.S.T. and the surface of the grazing marshes are available, but it is believed that the level of the marsh surface is about the same as the level of low-water mark of ordinary tides. Assuming that spring tides fall a foot below the level of ordinary tides, it would be necessary only to dig about five feet of mud to create a broad with a water depth of about four feet at all states of the tide.

"Such a broad would cost £3,630 an acre to excavate, or, say, £3,700 an acre, allowing for contingencies. A new fifty-acre broad could, therefore, be created for an outlay of £185,000 and one the size of Oulton Broad for about £300,000. This figure does not, of course, take into account the cost of acquiring the necessary land.

"Although it would be practicable to excavate new broads on areas of unreclaimed fenland, it seems likely that the cost of creating open water in such areas would be considerably greater than the cost of creating new broads on reclaimed grazing marshland. Most of the unreclaimed fen in Broadland is now thickly covered by bushes and trees, and these would have to be cut down and burned before the work of excavating could be started. The cost of clearance would depend very greatly on the density of the trees and bushes, but experience with comparable areas at Woodwalton Fen National Nature Reserve suggests that it would cost between £50 and £75 to clear an acre of fen which was moderately thickly covered by carr.

"As the surface of the unreclaimed fen is sometimes eighteen to twenty-four inches above the level of the adjacent river, some six feet of material would have to be excavated in order to ensure that there was a depth of four feet of water in the Broad under all conditions. Although a bulldozer could be used to remove the surface layers of peat, the high-water table would soon render the use of such a machine impracticable, and the same technique as described above would have to be used. The probable cost per acre of excavating a new broad in unreclaimed fen can therefore, be summarized as follows:

Tree and bush clearance at say	£75
Excavation of 6ft. of peat at 9s. a cu. yd. dredged	£4,350
TOTAL	£4,425 per acre or say £5,000 allowing for contingencies.

"Thus a new fifty-acre broad could be created in an area of unreclaimed fen for about £250,000, and one the size of Oulton Broad for about £400,000.

"The provision of a new broad on that part of the island bounded by the Yare, Waveney and Haddiscoe Cut appears to offer good prospects because of the excellent access to it by road and river (especially if the Bure–Yare Cut were created) and the proximity of an existing centre of development at St. Olaves. Tidal factors as well as the reactions of agriculturalists to this suggestion merit careful study. The extension of Oulton Broad in a westerly direction towards the Waveney, or the creation of a new broad between Oulton Dyke and the Waveney is another possibility; so is the creation of a new broad and mooring haven in the Beccles area. It would be an advantage to shipping if some of the bends on the River Yare were straightened; this would also create extra open water for general use. In addition, there is scope for creating a new broad or broads in the Strumpshaw-Postwick-Brundall area.

"Although a main aim in suggesting these new cuts and broads is the relief of the pressure on the northern rivers, there are, nevertheless, a number of areas near that system which seem to offer opportunities for similar development. These include Womack Water and the marshes in the Upton area.

"It has also been suggested that some variants of the proposal for a barrage at Breydon—the confluence of the northern and southern river systems—could lead to the creation of a large permanent area of open water. The implications of this proposal are far-reaching and would require detailed study before any decision could be made."

The foregoing estimates of the cost of creating new broads are taken from a summary prepared by Messrs. May, Gurney and Co. Ltd., of Trowse, Norwich, for the *Report on Broadland*.

They go on to give other estimates and costs of the first importance. They begin with the proposed cut between the River Bure and the River Yare. This might run from near Tunstall Bridge on the Bure to a point near the Reedham end of the New Cut on the Yare. It would not be straight but would follow a line separating the reclaimed grazing marshes from the upland area. Much of this land is of low agricultural productivity.

Locks would probably not be needed at the ends of the channel because the levels in the lower reaches of the two rivers do not differ sufficiently. A full report on the scheme would be required from the Hydraulics Research Station, who would be able to advise whether the creation of a channel would lead to silting problems in either of the two rivers.

The new channel would be some five miles long and would have to be excavated to a depth of about six feet and would be sixty-six feet wide at the top and thirty-six feet wide at the bottom in order to give plenty of room for boat traffic and to provide the necessary embankment materials.

The excavation would probably cost about 3s. 6d. a cubic yard or a total of about £85,000. If it were necessary to pile the whole length of the channel to stop bank erosion, this would cost some £4 a foot, or over £210,000. Initially, piling would probably be necessary only at bends and on stretches where boats were to be allowed to moor by the bank.

The course of this proposed channel is crossed by two railway lines, a minor road connecting Halvergate village with the Acle-Yarmouth road, and four rough tracks from Halvergate marshes to the adjoining upland farmland. Bridges required to cross the minor road and the four tracks would each cost about £15,000, and the cost of each railway bridge, with approach ramps for the railway lines, would be about £100,000. (The major road bridge would probably cost about £125,000.)

The cost of the channel can be summarized as follows:

	£
Excavation of channel	85,000
Piling	42,000
Four small bridges at £15,000 each	60,000
Two railway bridges and one major road bridge	325,000
Isolators	40,000
	£552,000

The cost of acquiring the necessary land would be additional to this figure.

Re-opening the River Waveney between Geldeston Lock and Bungay is a definite possibility.

Accurate measurements of the depth of this stretch of river are not available, but it is known to be relatively deep in places. Elsewhere a certain amount of dredging would be needed to obtain a sufficient depth of water to allow navigation by holiday craft. The work could be done by a floating dredger or by a dragline excavator working from the bank. The cost of dredging by either method would be about 3s. 6d. a cubic yard. Tree clearance would cost an additional 4d. a cubic yard in places.

Assuming that the river is forty-five feet wide and that it is necessary to dredge two feet throughout its whole length, of say, four miles, this would cost £12,320. Add, say, £680 for tree clearance and contingencies and the total cost of dredging and clearance work would amount to about £13,000. This is probably an over-estimate because it is most unlikely that two feet would have to be dredged throughout the whole four miles.

There are three locks on this stretch of river and, although their condition varies, all three would need considerable repairs at an estimate of between £5,000 and £10,000 each to make them serviceable. Assuming that all three would cost £10,000 to repair, the total cost of making this stretch of river navigable would be £43,000. Again this is probably an over-estimate because only one of the locks is in really bad condition and the best of the three could probably be repaired for about £5,000. It is obviously unlikely that it would cost more than £50,000 to make this stretch of river navigable to holiday craft.

Re-opening the North Walsham and Dilham Canal is another obvious move. They estimate the cost of dredging this canal would be the same as the cost of dredging the River Waveney, i.e. 3s. 6d. a cubic yard for dredging, plus an extra 4d. a cubic yard to cover the cost of cutting back any overhanging trees.

Although this canal is a good deal narrower than the River Waveney, it is more heavily silted up. Assuming that three feet would have to be dredged out of the canal for a distance of four and a half miles between Honing Lock and Swafield Bridge and that the canal is thirty feet wide throughout its length, the cost of dredging would amount to £13,860. Tree clearance would, perhaps, increase this figure to about £14,500. There are four locks on this stretch of canal between Honing and Swafield Bridge, and although these are in poor condition, especially that at Bacton Wood, it would not cost more than about £40,000 to put all four locks back into commission, and it might cost considerably less. The total cost of making the North Walsham and Dilham Canal navigable between Honing Lock and Swafield Bridge would, therefore, be about £54,000 or allowing for contingencies, £60,000.

My own view is that much of these various costs could be recovered from lock fees payable on entrance to any new or re-opened water and by mooring fees; apart from any income from peat and reed harvests.

To sum up, the future of Broadland is in the melting pot. There must not only be more restrictions on piecemeal development and on shoddy building design, but pollution must be watched; vandalism must be punished ruthlessly, hooligans and nuisance makers must be black-listed by all boat hirers, camp site owners and those who let chalets; the dumping of dangerous litter such as broken bottles, tins and plastic and polythene goods should also be punished by heavy fines. I have known a cow swallow a plastic mackintosh and pass it entire out of her system. Had that valuable animal not passed it it could have meant a loss of some hundreds of pounds to the farmer.

I have already referred to the need to create new broads on derelict marshes and to re-create old broads which have been silted up. A new waterway to link the North River or Bure with the Yare is also a necessity. It would give more sailing water and cut out congestion at Yarmouth and Breydon Water.

Furthermore, a sharp watch must be kept on the design of motor-cruisers and other craft intended for Broadland use. Eight knots should be the top speed for any motor craft and half that speed is preferable. High speed causes heavy washes which erode the banks, are a danger to small boats and children, and an infernal nuisance to anglers. The 'water hog' should have no place on the Broads. If he wishes to be a nuisance and a show-off let him go to sea where he can cause little damage to others and may, with luck, drown himself.

So far as moorings are concerned, the boatyard proprietors cater very well for their own craft. There is a case, however, for extra moorings that would be available to all boat users. These need not have boat-building yards attached to them. Dance halls and cinemas are already available in most villages. There is no need for more. Broadland's unique character should not be cheapened by this type of development or by the 'sea front' type.

Any new bungalow or chalet development should be designed to harmonize with the surroundings. If it is screened by trees, so much the better.

Road traffic at peak holiday periods is a positive headache, particularly for the police and people of Norwich, since much of it is funnelled through that city. The result is a traffic problem of the worst sort.

Car parks near waterways must be carefully sited and most definitely screened by trees. Nothing ruins the quality and beauty

Ormesby Broad—its like could be created

of this flat countryside more than the distant glitter and flash of acres of shining car roofs, caravans or garish bungalows. Above all the standard of public behaviour must be improved—even if it means more prosecution by the police. The report on Broadland says: "Many of the difficulties in Broadland could be remedied if visitors behaved more responsibly. A Code of Behaviour for Broadland, based on the Country Code but extended to take account of the special needs of Broadland, should be prepared as a matter of urgency by the interests concerned as a guide, and measures put in hand to ensure its implementation. The need for such codes is recognized in other recreational areas of Britain and similar proposals have been put forward recently in the Report on 'Inland Waters and Recreation'. The effectiveness of a code in Broadland will depend on the provision of adequate facilities for visitors, for example, litter bins and mooring places."

This is a pious hope. The Country Code may have worked in some districts, but it does not stop motorists dumping old bedsteads on the roadside, thoughtless people pulling up bluebells, or starting heath fires and it certainly does not prevent 'ton-up kids' making country lanes hideous with din and loaded with death on Saturdays and Sundays. There is a type of visitor to the Broads who will only understand one 'Code of Behaviour' the code imposed by a magistrate. The word would soon reverberate throughout the Midlands, London and even the towns of East Anglia which provide some of the worst of the two-legged nuisances.

The expansion programme for the Broads proposed by the Nature Conservancy, will cost money, but as the Conservancy rightly points out, it will only "cost roughly the same as the Greater London Council's scheme for tree-planting in the next ten years". And it adds "the expenditure will only be a fraction of that on rehabilitating an environment degraded by neglect and misuse". The proposed Lea Valley scheme and the lower Swansea Valley scheme are cases in point which justify this claim. The final warning, lest I may seem personally pessimistic is sounded by the Nature Conservancy in one terse, telling phrase: "Time is not on the side of Broadland. To do nothing is to abandon the region to erosion, conflict and decay. To take refuge in piecemeal palliatives will only delay the ruin of the Broadland environment as it is known and valued today."

14

No motor craft on Filby Broad

APPENDICES

LIST OF BROADS, THEIR ACREAGES, DEPTHS, ACCESSIBILITY AND SPECIAL USES

(By courtesy of the Nature Conservancy)

Abbreviations: N.N.R.—National Nature Reserve
N.N.T.—Norfolk Naturalists' Trust
P.N.N.R.—Proposed National Nature Reserve

Name of Broad	Approx. acreage of open water shown on Tithe awards c. 1840	Acreage of open water shown on 25 in. O.S. maps 1881–1938	Approx. acreage of open water in 1946. Aerial photographs	Approx. acreage of open water in 1962. Aerial photographs	Approx. depth of water in 1964	Accessibility from main river system for public navigation	Special uses e.g. zonation in space
1. Alderfen Broad	27	20	13	—	2–3 ft.	None—landlocked	N.N.T. Nature Reserve
2. Barnby Broad	27	9.5	7	—	2–3 ft.	None—landlocked	—
3. Barton Broad	284	259	162	—	3–5 ft.	Yes—channels across Broad to staithes	N.N.T. Nature Reserve
4. Belaugh Broad	12	10	3	—	6 in.	Private and too	—

Name of Broad	acreage of open water shown on Tithe awards c. 1840	Acreage of open water shown on 25 in. O.S. maps 1881–1938	Approx. acreage of open water in 1946. Aerial photographs	Approx. acreage of open water in 1962. Aerial photographs	Approx. depth of water in 1964	Accessibility from main river system for public navigation	Special uses e.g. zonation in space
5. Blackfleet	12	9.5	5	—	2–3ft.	Private and too shallow	—
6. Bridge Broad	12	12	10	—	2–4ft.	Yes, but western part private	Yacht moorings in eastern part
7. Broad Fen, Dilham	27	Nil	1	—	2–3ft.	None—landlocked	—
8. Buckenham and Hassingham Broad	26	16.5	6	—	6in.–2ft.	None—sluice	—
9. Burntfen Broad	16	14.5	15	—	3–4ft.	None—landlocked	—
10. Calthorpe Broad	16	5	3	—	2–3ft.	None—landlocked	—
11. Crome's Broad	15	13	12	—	3–4ft.	None—sluice	—
12. Norton's (Cockle) Broad	6	2	Nil	—	—	Broad now extinct	—
13. Cockshoot Broad	29	12.5	6	8	2–3ft.	None—private and too shallow	Pt. of N.N.R.
14. Decoy Broad	23	23	16	18	3–7ft.	None—private	Scouting; Angling Pt. of N.N.R.

Name of Broad	Approx. acreage of open water shown on Tithe awards c. 1840	Acreage of open water shown on 25 in. O.S. maps 1881–1938	Approx. acreage of open water in 1946. Aerial photographs	Approx. acreage of open water in 1962. Aerial photographs	Approx. depth of water in 1964	Accessibility from main river system for public navigation	Special uses e.g. zonation in space
15. Dilham Lake	16	14	Nil	—	—	Broad now extinct	—
16. Filby Broad	116	116	83	—	11–12ft.	None—Muckfleet Sluice	Used by Norfolk School Sailing Assoc.; Angling; Stand-by reservoir
17. Flixton Decoy	18	17	15	—	6–9ft.	None—landlocked	—
18. Fritton Lake	163	153	150	—	11–14ft.	None—sluice	Angling; Reservoir
19. Heigham Sound	111	107	65	—	4ft. 6in. in channel	Yes	Pt. of N.N.R.
20. Hickling Broad	485	426.5	302	—	4ft.	Yes	Pt. of N.N.R.
21. Horsey Mere	109	120	65	—	4ft.	Yes	—
22. Hoveton Great Broad	103	88.5	16	47	2–4ft.	None—private	Pt. of N.N.R.

Name of Broad	Approx. acreage of open water shown on Tithe awards c. 1840	Acreage of open water shown on 25 in. O.S. maps 1881–1938	Approx. acreage of open water in 1946. Aerial photographs	Approx. acreage of open water in 1962. Aerial photographs	Approx. depth of water in 1964	Accessibility from main river system for public navigation	Special uses e.g. zonation in space
23. Hoveton Little Broad	51	51	47	—	2–4ft.	Outer part open between Easter and September. Inner part private and too shallow	—
24. Hudson's Bay	15	12	3	—	2ft.	Private and too shallow	Pt. of N.N.R.
25. Little Broad	Not known	6	1	—	2–3ft.	None—Muckfleet Sluice	—
26. Malthouse Broad	27	27	22	—	4–6ft.	Yes	—
27. Marsham Broad	115	63	37	—	4ft. in channel, 2–3ft. elsewhere	Channel only—remainder private	—
28. Ormesby Broad (north)	189	189	139	—	7–8ft.	None—Muckfleet Sluice	Stand-by reservoir; Angling

Name of Broad	Approx. acreage of open water shown on Tithe awards c. 1840	Acreage of open water shown on 25 in. O.S. maps 1881–1938	Approx. acreage of open water in 1946. Aerial photographs	Approx. acreage of open water in 1962. Aerial photographs	Approx. depth of water in 1964	Accessibility from main river system for public navigation	Special uses e.g. zonation in space
29. Ormesby	121	121	88	—	8–10ft.	None—Muckfleet Sluice	Angling
30. Oulton Broad	86	84.5	84	—	4–6ft.	Yes	Hydroplane racing
31. Ranworth Broad	141	81	49	59	3–4ft.	None—private	Pt. of N.N.R.; Angling
32. Rockland Broad	87	53	27	—	3–4ft. in channel 2–3ft. elsewhere	Yes	Pt. of P.N.N.R.
33. Rollesby Broad (inc. Lily Broad)	97	97	61	—	8–10ft. (4–5ft. Lily Broad)	None—Muckfleet Sluice	Stand-by reservoir; Angling
34. Salhouse Broad	27	17.5	21	—	4–5ft.	Yes	—
35. Snape's Water	7	7	2	—	2–3ft.	None—private and too shallow	—
36. South Walsham Broad (Inner and Outer)	69	51	29	38	5–6ft. outer 3–4ft. Inner	Yes	—

No.	Name of Broad	Acreage of open water shown on Tithe awards c. 1840	Acreage of open water shown on 25 in. O.S. maps 1881–1938	Approx. acreage of open water in 1946. Aerial photographs	Approx. acreage of open water in 1962. Aerial photographs	Approx. depth of water in 1964	Accessibility from main river system for public navigation	Special uses e.g. zonation in space
37.	Strumpshaw Broad	22	6	2	—	2–3ft.	None—private and too shallow	Pt. of N.N.R.
38.	Surlingham and Bargate Broads	72	17	8	—	5ft. in channel, 2–3ft. elsewhere	Yes—via channel through Bargate Broad. Remainder private and too shallow	Pt. of N.N.T. Nature Reserve P.N.N.R.
39.	Sutton Broad	115	194	Channels only	—	4ft. in channels Nil elsewhere	Channels only Rest of Broad extinct	—
40.	Upton Broad	29	13.9	4	—	3–4ft.	None—landlocked	—
41.	Womack Water	8	6	Channels only	—	5ft.	Yes	—
42.	Wroxham Broad	80	80	69	—	3–5ft.	Yes	Sailing by members of the Norfolk Broads' Yacht Club

Appendix II

ANGLING: PRACTICAL INFORMATION

The Rivers Bure, Waveney and Yare, their tributaries and the broads connected with them are among the most notable coarse-fishing waters in England. They contain pike, perch, roach, rudd, tench, gudgeon and bream, but are particularly noted for rudd and bream. In many of the broads, low-lying lakes and meres, rudd provide good sport on fly, though it is necessary to cast a long line. The former Norfolk Fishery Board did much restocking and trout were introduced. The rivers are mostly free to R.B. licence-holders, but some broads are preserved and can be fished on payment. Rivers very busy in summer, when early morning and late evening give best results. Autumn and winter fishing best. Fishing permitted in close season at Easter and Whitsun.

Bure

A notable coarse-fishing river of the Broads district, mostly free to licence-holders. Strong current from Yarmouth to a little above Acle; upper reaches gentle and ideal for float-fishing. Well stocked for entire length with coarse fish and restocked with trout above Buxton. Excellent roach, bream, perch, etc., at Thurne Mouth, St. Benet's, Horning, Wroxham, and beyond. Several broads are connected and can be fished, as well as its tributaries, Thurne and Ant.

Stokesby (Norfolk).—Bream, roach, pike, perch. Strong tides and sometimes brackish; legering best, especially for big bream early in season; free.

Acle (Norfolk).—Bream, roach, pike, perch. Tides often strong, legering recommended, or float carrying plenty of shot. River traffic heavy in summer. Lakes: Upton Broad, 4 m. N.W. Inns: Queens' Head and King's Head, both 1 m. from river; Bridge Inn (close to river); Hermitage and the Thurne Lion at Thurne Mouth.

Horning (Norfolk); n.s. Wroxham, 3½ m. Good coarse fishing; free to licence-holders; boat almost essential; roach, rudd, bream, perch, pike, tench; river very busy in summer and early morning and late evening fishing gives best results. Broads: Ranworth (preserved) and Malthouse downstream; Hoveton Great and Black Horse (preserved), Decoy (small charge; inquire Swan), Salhouse (d.t. 1s.) and Wroxham (small charge—see Wroxham) upstream. Tackle, licences and bait at post office. Several boatyards. Hotels: Swan (boats), New Inn, and Petersfield House Hotel.

Wroxham (Norfolk).—Roach, rudd, bream, pike, perch, tench; good pike and bream in winter; fishing free; boats only. Much river traffic, summer. Broads: Bridge Broad, right bank; permission and boats from C. R. Chamberlain, Hoveton. Wroxham Broad, right bank; fishing, 2s. 6d. per boat, collected by keeper. Hoveton Great Broad, left bank, 2 m. S.E. private. Salhouse Broad, right bank 2 m. S.E. (fishing on payment); private. Little Hoveton or Black Horse Broad, 2 m. N.E.; private. Burntfen Broad, 3 m. E. King's water, 3 m. E. Beeston Hall lake, 4 m. N.E. Oliver Broad, 6 m. N.E.; private. Club: Wroxham and Dist. A.C. Hotels: King's Head, Broads, Bure Court, Horse Shoes, Tackleists S. J. Sacret; Messrs. Roy's.

Coltishall (Norfolk).—Roach, bream, perch, pike; free. Boats: Allen's Hotels: King's Head, Rising Sun.

Buxton Lamas (Norfolk).—Pike, good bream and roach, perch; leave freely given, but Fakenham A.A. has water also. Lake: Scottow pond, 2 m. N.E. Inns: Anchor, Black Lion, Crown.

Aylsham (Norfolk).—Trout, roach, rudd, dace and pike. Heavily weeded in summer; best Oct. onwards. Some water free on permission of farmers. Other water preserved by Aylsham and Dist. A.S.; members of other clubs may fish free; apply hon. sec. Licences and tackle from J. B. Postle, Market Place. Hotels: Dog, Ship, Black Boys.

Blickling (Norfolk).—The Upper Bure holds trout; fishing controlled by Blickling Fishing Club; permits for members' friends only. Blickling lake is National Trust water; coarse fish; d.t. 7s. 6d.; excellent bream and plenty of tench; tickets and R.B. licences from Mr. C. J. Crisp, 4 Park Gates, or N.T. office. Hotel: Buckinghamshire Arms.

TRIBUTARIES OF THE BURE

Thurne
Thurne Mouth (Norfolk).—Good roach, bream, perch. Hotel: Thurne Lion.

Potter Heigham (Norfolk).—Coarse fish; free; bank fishing. Bure, 3 m. S.; mostly bank fishing. Lakes: Womack Broad, $1\frac{1}{2}$ m. (now dredged and cleared of weeds); Hickling, Somerton (private) and Heigham Sounds. Hotels: Bridge and Broads-Haven. Boats from Herbert Woods, Ltd., and Applegates Ltd., Licences, tackle, etc. at Bridge Stores.

Martham (Norfolk).—Rudd, tench, bream, roach, perch, pike; good bank fishing; free. Heigham Sounds and Hickling Broad reached by boat; rights held by Norfolk Naturalist Trust, Whiteslea Lodge; d.t.

1s. (pike 2s. 6d.) from keepers. Top Sounds and Duck Broad closed 1st
Oct. to 1st Feb. Horsey Mere private, but d.t. 1s. (pike 2s. 6d.; spinning
only) from millman; closed 1st Oct. to 31st. Jan. Boats and licences;
Martham Boat Co. Inn: King's Arms (see also Hickling).

Ant

Catfield (Norfolk).—Barton Broad, 1 m. W.; free fishing. Womack
Broad, 2 m. S. by Ludham; now cleared. Catfield Broad, 2 m.; over-
grown. Hickling Broad, 2 m.; d.t. 1s. Irstead and Neatishead (Norfolk).
—Ant and Barton Broad. Good bream, perch, rudd, pike; also tench
and small roach. Fishing free. Hotel: Barton Angler (tackle, bait, boats);
Boats also from Cox, Barton Turf.

Stalham (Norfolk).—Free fishing; river clear, slow-running and
weedy in summer; roach, rudd, bream, perch, pike and a few tench.
Broads: Barton, 1 m.; rudd, bream and big pike; free fishing. Hickling,
3 m. by road; good fishing; small charge made. Sutton Broad is overgrown. Tackle, bait, R.B. licences and information from Stalham
Radio Ltd. Inns: Swan, Grebe and Maid's Head.

Wayford Bridge (Norfolk).—Upper Ant; head of navigation; fishing
free to licence-holders; roach, rudd, perch, pike, tench, bream; boat
advisable; river is narrow and fairly busy at times in summer; weedy
and clear. Fishing boats and houseboats from Wayford Bridge Yacht
Station and H. A. Simpson. Bait and tackle from Stalham. Good fishing
also above the head of Ant navigation in Dilham and North Walsham
Canal, navigable to rowing boats as far as Honing Lock. Accommodation at Fairview Café (also licences); Wayford Wood Farm (also
licences); The White House; and Wayford Bridge Inn.

North Walsham (Norfolk).—Ant, 1 m. E. Gunton beck, 4 m. W.
Lakes: Perch pond, Mill pond, Heath Plantation (2 m. S.). Antingham
ponds, 2 m. N.W. Licences and tackle at Webb's and F. Randell Ltd.,
North Walsham. Accommodation at Cross Keys, Dilham, and most
local inns. See Wayford Bridge for canal fishing. Local club; Dilham
and D.A.C.

Gunton Lake: Fishing Station: Gunton (Norfolk).—Saw Mill lake
(16 acres) in Gunton Park, 3 m.; coarse fish; s.t. £4 4s., d.t. 5s., from
estate office.

BROADS CONNECTED WITH THE BURE
(*Arranged under 'fishing stations'*)

Horning; n.s. Wroxham.—Salhouse Broad; d.t. 1s.; rather too much
traffic in summer, but good fishing in early mornings and from Oct.
to March. Ranworth Broad; preserved. Malthouse Broad; free. Black
Horse Broad; preserved. Woodbastwick or Decoy Broad; preserved,

but open for fishing on payment of small fee; apply Swan Hotel, where boats may be had. Tackle, licences, bait at post office (see also Bure).

Ormesby and Petersfield.—Ormesby Broad; free. Rollesby Broad, free. Filby Broad; free. These broads are connected and undisturbed by motor-cruisers and yachts; fishing is good everywhere. Pike fishing good in winter. Inn: Eel's Foot (boats and accommodation), Ormesby. Boats also from W. Tennant (Filby) and G. Skoyles (Ormesby).

Salhouse.—Salhouse Broad, 1 m. N.E.; a few pike in winter. Wroxham Broad, 1 m. N.; fishing on payment; good fishing for bream in summer, fair pike fishing in winter. Decoy or Woodbastwick Broad, 2 m. N.E.; fishing on payment. Little Ranworth Broad, 3 m. E.; good for bream. Ranworth Broad, 4 m. E.; preserved. Pedham Mill dam, 4 m. S.E.; private. South Walsham Broad, 5 m. E.; private; good bream and pike fishing; leave from owner.

Wroxham.—Wroxham Broad, right bank; fishing 2s. 6d. per boat, collected by keeper. Bridge Broad, boats and permission from C. R. Chamberlain, Hoveton, Snapes water, left bank; private. Hoveton Great Broad, left bank, 2 m. S.E.; private; fine pike water. Salhouse Broad, right bank, 2 m. S.E.; fishing by payment. Little Hoveton Broad, 2 m. N.E.; private. Burntfen Broad, 3 m. E.; private. Alderfen Broad, 6 m. N.E.; private. Hotels: King's Head, Bure Court, Broads, Horse Shoes.

BROADS CONNECTED WITH THE THURNE AND ANT
(*Arranged under 'fishing stations'*)

Broads connected with the Thurne.

Potter Heigham.—Hickling Broad (see Hickling). Somerton Broad; private. Heigham Sounds; fine rudd fishing in summer; pike fishing excellent in winter for a small fee. Womack Broad has been dredged and cleared of weed. Hotels: Bridge, Broads-Haven and Thurne-Haven, and the Homestead in village. Boats from Herbert Woods, Ltd., and Applegates, Ltd. Licences, bait, tackle from Bridge Stores.

Hickling.—Heigham Sounds, Horsey, Barton and Hickling Broads. Rudd, tench, bream, roach, pike, perch, Barton free. Other waters d.t. 1s. (pike 2s. 6d.) from keepers. Licences from Post Office and stores; boats available. Accommodation: Pleasure Boat Inn; guest houses.

Martham.—See Martham on River Thurne.

Broads connected with the Ant.

Catfield.—Barton Broad, 1 m.W.; excellent rudd and bream fishing and noted for its big pike. Calthorpe Broad; private; fish killed by 1953 sea flood. Hickling Broad, 2 m. Catfield Broad; overgrown.

WAVENEY

Flows along the Norfolk-Suffolk border. Beccles is a noted centre for roach fishing, and the reach between Geldeston Lock and St. Olaves gives some wonderful sport with bream in most seasons.

Lowestoft (Suffolk).—Oulton Broad and Waveney, which connects with the broad; bream, perch, roach, pike, etc.; one station by rail or short walk. Boats at broad. Flounders and smelts in harbour. Railway and Claremont Piers. Good sea-fishing in Oct., Nov. and Dec. from boats, piers and beach for whiting, cod and flat-fish. Flixton Decoy. 3 m. W. Lake at The Villa, 4 m. N.W. Fritton Decoy, 6 m. N.W. Hotels: Royal, Harbour and Suffolk. Licences and size limit as in Norfolk. Fishing stations within short railway journey; Beccles, Geldeston, Bungay, Somerleyton, Haddiscoe, Reedham, Cantley, Buckenham, Brundall. Motor omnibuses now help.

Oulton Broad (Suffolk).—Waveney (near). Free fishing (East Suffolk and Norfolk R.B. licence required) best from boat. Perch (some good fish); pike (good, best Oct., Nov.); roach (good all season, best Jan., Feb., Mar.), bream (moderate, best Sept., Oct.); dace. Oulton Dyke; bream (excellent Aug., Sept., Oct.); perch; roach. Club; Oulton Broad Piscatorial Society. Lakes; Oulton Broad; same fish; boats at the Broad side. Fritton Decoy, 2½ m. N. (see Haddiscoe). Lake at The Villa, 2½ m. N. Fishing free to licence-holders. Map of best fishing areas on Oulton from Publicity Manager, 7 Esplanade Lowestoft. Hotel: Wherry.

Carlton Colville (Suffolk).—Lake: Oulton Broad; pike, perch, bream, roach, etc.; free. Hotel: Flying Dutchman.

Belton (Suffolk).—Waveney, 1 m. Yare, 2 m. Lake: Fritton Decoy, 2 m. S.; boats at Fritton Hall (see Haddiscoe).

Haddiscoe (Norfolk).—New Cut. Lakes: Fritton Decoy, 1 m.; bream, carp, perch, pike, roach, rudd, tench, d.t. 2s. for bank fishing; accommodation and boats at Fritton Hall. Hotels: Crown, Queen's Head. The River Club at St. Olaves is a good centre.

Burgh St. Peter (Norfolk).—Lakes: Fritton Decoy (see Haddiscoe). Hotel: Waveney House; licences, boats.

Beccles (Suffolk).—Good roach, bream, pike, etc.; best Oct. onwards, when river traffic eases off. Boats can be hired at several places; fishing free, but controlled for parties of six and over from mouth of cut to old Swing Bridge. Suffolk bank. The local club is the Beccles A.C.; hon. sec. will be glad to supply information. Hotels: King's Head, Waveney House. Tackleists: L. Tilney (who will advise on pike fishing), R. Cuddon and A. G. Brand, who will also be pleased to give information and supply licences and bait.

Geldeston (Norfolk).—Good pike, roach, perch, bream, etc.; free;

R.B. licences at post office. Inns: Wherry, Garden House and Geldeston Lock. Tackle in Beccles (3 m.) Bungay (Suffolk)—Good roach, chub, bream, perch, pike and tench; fishes best at back end. Cherry Tree A.C. has water upstream to Homersfield and around Bungay Common; members only; subs. 5s. p.a. Lakes: Ditchingham Pit; restocked with good tench and carp. Cherry Tree no longer an inn but still caters for fishermen (club H.Q.).

Homersfield (Suffolk).—Pike, perch, roach (large), dace, tench. Licences from landlord, Black Swan Hotel.

Harleston (Norfolk).—Waveney, 1 m. S.; coarse fish. Harleston, Wortwell and D.A.C. has private pits stocked with tench, carp, perch, roach; visitors' tickets 2s. 6d. p.d. from Weybread Heath House adjoining pits. Hotel: Magpie.

Eye (Suffolk).—Dove brook; large dace. Fishing in Waveney at Hoxne, 3 m.

Diss (Norfolk).—Good sport in river, especially with roach. Diss mere; fishing indifferent. Tackle dealer; E. Nunn, Mere Street. Hotel: King's Head.

BROADS CONNECTED WITH THE WAVENEY
(*Arranged under 'fishing stations'*)

Lowestoft (Suffolk).—Flixton Decoy, 3 m. W. Hotels: Royal, Harbour, Suffolk. Oulton Broad. Hotel: Wherry.

Belton (Suffolk.)—Brendon water; salt estuary; no fishing. Fritton Decoy, 2 m. S.; (see Haddiscoe).

YARE

Rises a few miles from East Dereham and flows through Norwich to Yarmouth. Suffers from pollution in Norwich area, but is still one of the best rivers for roach and bream. The best roach fishing is in the middle reaches; bream in the lower. Great Yarmouth (Norfolk)—Broads and rivers. Rivers Yare, Bure and Waveney fall into Breydon water (Bure is joined in upper reaches by Rivers Thurne and Ant). In all, some 200 miles of rivers well suited to both boat and bank angling are within reach; some of the broads are landlocked, strictly reserved for angling and free from any river traffic, others are connected to the rivers, but all in the main are best fished from a boat. The broads are abundantly stocked with coarse fish; bream, roach, rudd, perch, tench and pike. Yarmouth is excellent centre. All broads well served by bus and rail. Within 6 m. are Filby, Rollesby and the Ormesby broads (136,240 and 207 acres, respectively) forming part of the Ormesby group; also Fritton lake (163 acres). Other broads scattered around are Hickling (464 acres), Heigham Sounds (127 acres), Barton (207 acres), Wroxham (102 acres), Salhouse (53 acres) and South Walsham (57 acres). There are several other broads such as Ranworth and Decoy Broads. A few of the popular and easily accessible bank angling spots on the river are—River Bure: Acle, St. Benet's Abbey, Horning and Wroxham. River Thurne: Thurne, Potter Heigham and Martham. River Ant: Several miles either side of Ludham Bridge. River Waveney: Beccles area. River Chet. All waters have been re-stocked (including trout in Bure). The close season is from 15th March to 15th June; it is, however, permissible to fish this district at Easter and Whitsun. There is also good sea-fishing. Tackle, baits and further information from Pownall and Sons Ltd., Anglers' Depot, 74 Regent Road, Great Yarmouth. Numerous hotels: details from Town Guide.

Reedham (Norfolk).—Strong tidal; leger tackle best; (bream sometimes good), roach, pike, perch, eels, free. Chet near, upstream. Hotel: Ship.

Cantley (Norfolk).—Pike, roach, bream, perch; bream and roach plentiful; fishing free; poor fishing during beet processing (Oct.-Jan.). Inn: Red House.

Buckenham (Norfolk).—Bream, roach, perch, pike; boats at Beauchamp Arms; fishing free. The mouth of Hassingham Dyke is a good spot. Lakes: Stumpshaw Broad, 1 m. N.W. Buckenham Broad and Hassingham Broad, 1 m. S.E.; preserved. Rockland Broad, 1½ m. S.W. on other bank of river; free.

Brundall (Norfolk).—Roach, some bream, perch in Yare; fishing mostly by leger; d.t. 1s., from Riverside Estate gives access to river and new dyke; fish plentiful. Several reaches between Coldham Hall and Surlingham Ferry can be fished by boat. Surlingham Broad belongs to National Trust; fishing little good in summer; water shallow and weedy; pike in winter. Plumstead Hall lakes, 2 m. N.; private.

Norwich (Norfolk).—Good centre for Broads fishing, though Yare suffers from pollution in vicinity of town; elsewhere sport with roach, bream, etc. Wensum above town holds fine roach, perch, dace and pike. Good roach and bream fishing at Rockland Broad; 7 m. from Norwich; boats from Mr. Taylor, Broad Cottage, Rockland St. Mary's. Bait, licences and tackle from Bill Cooper, Bridgewell Alley, and C. F. Browne, Timberhill, both in Norwich. Hotels: Royal, Maid's Head, Bell and many others. C. F. Wickham, hon. sec. Lakenham A. C. will give further information.

TRIBUTARIES OF THE YARE

Chet

Loddon (Norfolk).—n.s. Beccles, 7 m. Free coarse fishing in Chet from Loddon down to Reedham on Yare; roach, dace, bream, perch, occasional trout; this water now navigable and fishes best in autumn and winter when traffic finishes; licences, river and sea bait and tackle from W. H. Ragar Ltd., Post Office, Loddon. Hotels: Swan, and Angle Inn, Loddon; White Horse, Chedgrave.

Wensum

Honingham (Norfolk).—Tud brook; private. Trout.

Hellesdon (Norfolk).—Fishing free at Green Lane; preserved above. Tud brook; private.

Drayton (Norfolk).—On Wensum; free on permission of landowners; otherwise strictly preserved. Spixworth beck, 2½ m. N.E.; free adjoining Crostwick Common; there is also free fishing in Bure. Hotel: Red Lion.

Attlebridge (Norfolk).—There is good trout fishing here, some miles of water being preserved. Tud, 4 m. S.; private. Lakes; Haveringland, 3½ m. N.; private. Hopground lake, Honingham, 4 m. S.; private.

Lenwade (Norfolk).—Trout fishing by ticket at Lenwade Mill; tickets from cafe. Accommodation at Bridge House Inn. Norwich Kingfisher A.C. has pits; carp, tench, pike; d.t. from bailiff. Blackwater brook; private.

Lyng (Norfolk).—Dereham and D.A.C. has water; excellent roach fishing; also Wensum Pit; good tench, pike, perch; d.t. from Fanthorpe's Tackle Shop, Norwich Street, Dereham. Dereham and D.A.C. also have a lake.

APPENDIX III

NORFOLK NATURALISTS' TRUST: PRINCIPAL RESERVES

FIRS MARSH (2½ acres)
Hon. Warden: C. E. Collier,
The Firs, Burgh St. Peter,
Beccles, Suffolk.

HOCKHAM FEN (20 acres)
Hon. Warden: E. J. Campbell,
Hilldrift, Gt. Hockham,
Thetford.

RANWORTH BROAD (124 acres)
Hon. Warden: F. Cator,
Ranworth Old Hall,
Norwich, NOR 55Z
Telephone: S. Walsham 300.

SCARNING FEN (10½ acres)
Hon. Warden: K. C. Durrant,
F.R.E.S.
31 Sandy Lane, Dereham.
Telephone: Dereham 282.

SURLINGHAM BROAD (253 acres)
Hon. Warden: E. A. Ellis, F.L.S.,
Wheatfen Broad,
Surlingham, Norwich, NOR07W
Telephone: Surlingham 239.

THURSFORD WOODS (25 acres)
Hon. Warden: G. T. Cushing,
Laurel Farm,
Thursford, Fakenham.
Telephone: Thursford 238.

ALDERFEN BROAD (72 acres)
Hon. Warden Major A. C.
Holden,
Beech Grove Farm,
Neatishead, Norwich, NOR 372
Telephone: Horning 305.

Deputy Hon. Warden: B. E.
Chaplin,
Broad Cottage,
Irstead, Neatishead, Norwich,
NOR 372.

BREYDON WATER
Warden: R. W. Coleman
(Marshes)
6 North Parade, Lowestoft.
Warden: R. Harrison (Water),
52 King Street, Gt. Yarmouth.

COCKSHOOT BROAD (12 acres)
Hon. Warden: F. Cator,
Ranworth Old Hall, Norwich,
NOR 55Z
Telephone S. Walsham 300.

HICKLING BROAD (1,215 acres)
Warden: G. Bishop,
Heathcote,
Staithe Road, Hickling, NOR 31Z
Telephone: Hickling 349.

ROYDON COMMON (140 acres)
Hon. Warden: E. L. Swann,
282 Wootton Road,
King's Lynn.

STARCH GRASS, MARTHAM (26
    acres)
Hon. Warden: G. Crees,
Swiss Cottage,
Horsey, Gt. Yarmouth.

THETFORD HEATH (225 acres)
Hon. Warden: J. Pallant,
25 Albemarle Cottages,
Elveden, Thetford.

WEETING HEATH (343 acres)
Hon. Warden: N. Parrott,
Fengate Farm,
Weeting, Brandon.
Telephone: Brandon 317.

BARTON BROAD (Herons Carr)
Hon. Warden: Col. D. Scott,
    C.B.E., M.C.,
Irstead Manor,
Neatishead, Norwich, NOR 38Z.
Telephone: Horning 274.

BARTON BROAD (347 acres)
Hon. Warden: Dr. B. Blaxill,
White Lodge,
Barton Turf, Norwich, NOR
    36Z
Telephone: Horning 278.

CLEY AND SALTHOUSE (476 acres)
(including Arnold's Marsh)
Warden: W. F. Bishop,
Watcher's Cottage, Cley, Holt.
Telephone: Cley 380.

EAST WRETHAM HEATH (362 acres)
Hon. Warden: R. Codling,
Park Cottage,
Brettenham Road,
Kilverstone, Thetford.

GLOSSARY OF BROADLAND WORDS AND PHRASES

Broadland, like every other out of the way corner of England has its own language. Many of the local terms still in use are of Norse origin. They should be preserved, since they are an integral and a unique part of the English language. The tripper, complete with transistor and bogus American phrases, who sneers at the 'Broad Norfolk' of the marshmen, might stop to consider that their English is of infinitely older, and possibly purer, root than his own.

The list of words and phrases here given is taken largely from Dutt, but I have added a good many which I have come across in the course of many years shooting and fishing and mixing with local farmers, farm-workers and marshmen—the salt of the earth.

Babbing or *Bobbing*—eel-catching with a bunch of worsted-threaded worms.

Blade—the leaves of the reeds or sedges.

Blood-ulph—a bullfinch.

Bolder—the real bulrush, *Scirpus lacustris*.

Bor—a form of address; probably an abbreviation of 'neighbour'. "Hallo, bor; how are you?"

Bottom-fye—to clean out, applied to dykes.

Buskin-net—a net formerly used along the borders of reed-beds, from which the fish were driven into it by beating the reeds with long poles.

Buttles—bitterns—also *Budley-bumps*.

Camping—a brutal game somewhat resembling football, formerly very popular in East Anglia.

Carr—a marshland copse or plantation, usually of alders or sallows.

Cob—a black-headed gull. Hence Cobholm at Yarmouth.

Colts—young reeds.

Crome—a kind of rake used for cleaning out dykes.

Crome-stick—a stick with a curved or hooked handle, generally used for carrying a 'frail'.

Dag—A ground frost. Also in the Fens.

Dart—A fish-spear. Also in the Fens.

Deek—dyke.

Denes—dunes. Sandy tracts near or among the coast sandhills.

Ding—a blow; 'full ding'—with full force.

Dodman—a snail. Also *Hodney-dod*.

Dow—a wood-pigeon.

Drawing, dyke-drawing—cleaning out dykes.

Drey—nest; usually applied to a squirrels'.

Drift, driftway—a marsh or drove road along which cattle are driven to the marshes.

Drifter—a boat used for herring or mackerel netting.

Dutch Owl—short-eared owl. Also 'Woodcock Owl'.

Dydle or *Dydall*—a kind of spade used in dyke-cleaning.

Eel-box—a box in which eels are kept alive in the water.

Eel-picking or *eel-trunk*—eel-spearing; *eel-pick*—an eel-spear.

Eel-sett—a large fixed net used for taking eels.

Elvers—young eels.

Enow—enough.

Fare—appears, seems, 'He fare to know'.

Fared—seemed, appeared.

Fathom—five or six sheaves of reeds.

Flappers—young wild ducks.

Flats—mudbanks, oozy tracts left uncovered by the ebb tide.

Flee—to skin, e.g. a rabbit.

Fleet—sometimes a marsh dyke, sometimes a shallow pool.

Frail—a basket made of plaited rushes.

Frawn—to freeze.

Fitten—feet, e.g. "That were that cowd that frawned my fitten."

Ganzy—a fisherman's guernsey.

Gin—give.

Gladen—yellow iris or water-flag. Really *Iris foetidissima*, but in Broadland usually applied to *Iris pseudacorus*.

Glaive—a broad tined eel-spear.

Groundsels—foundations.

Gun-boat or *gun-punt*—a boat used by marshmen and Broadsmen for gunning, eel-spearing etc.

Haar—a sea mist; from the Danish.

Ham—a small bay or inlet of a Broad.

Hard—'on the hard'—on the shore, on the bank of a broad or river.

Haysel—Haymaking time.

Hinder or *hinderway*—*this* way as opposed to 'Yinway'—*that* way or the opposite way.

Holls—upland ditches.

Holm—an upland amid marshland, e.g. Martham Holm.

Howlet or *Hullet*—an owl.

Hornpies—lapwings.

Hovers—boggy ground or floating vegetation by the riverside; peat.

Hull—to throw.

Hulver—ivy.

Hyst—hoist.

Keeler—a wash tub.

Kentishmen—hooded crows. Also *Deuchmen*, e.g. Danish men.

Laid (with ice)—covered with a thin coating or layer of ice.

Lantern-men—will o' the wisps, *Ignes fatui*. An escape of marsh gas which ignites in hot weather.

Ligger—(1) a kind of trimmer, buoyed by a bunch of rushes, used for catching pike; (2) a plank footbridge over a dyke.

Mash—marsh.

Meak or *meag*—an implement used by reed-cutters.

Merrimills—maram hills, sandhills.

Mind—remember.

Minifer—a stoat. Weasels are 'Mouse-Hunters'.

Nigh—nearly.

Oily—a fisherman's waterproof coat.

Olive—an oystercatcher, favourite bird of the Saxon Saint Olave. Also in Essex.

Orters—otters.

Pattens—skates. Also 'mud pattens', e.g. boards lashed to water boots for walking or rather sliding on tidal mud-flats such as on Breydon Water.

Picking—spearing.

Pightle—a meadow.

Pokers—pochards. Also *dunbird*.

Pot or *pod*—a kind of bow-net forming part of an eel-sett.

Puit—black-headed gull. Also *cob* or *cob-gull*.

Pulk—a small pool or marsh pond.

Quant—a pole used for propelling yachts and wherries.

Quanter—punter.

Red-heads or *pokers*—pochards.

Reed pheasant—the bearded titmouse.

Rodger's blast—a sudden wind-gust of whirlwind.

Roke—fog.

Rokey—foggy.

Rond or *rand*—the swampy margin of a river or broad. Usually applied to the boggy ground between the water and the river wall.

Roudding—spawning.

Saddle-backs—black-backed gulls.

Saltings—salt or meil marshes.

Salts—salt tides.

Scissor-grinder—grasshopper warbler. Also *Reeler-bird*.

Scoulton cobs—black-headed gulls, e.g. from the gullery on Scoulton Mere in West Norfolk.

Sea-smoke—sea fog. Also *haar*.

Sele of the day—greeting or 'Good Day', e.g. 'I give him the sele o' the day'.

Sets—willow wands or boughs.

Sharming—making a noise, crying.

Shooves—sheaves.

Shutting-in time—sunset.

Sight—good deal. 'A sight more'—a good deal more.

Skep—a kind of basket. Also a bee-hive, e.g. bee-skep.

Slads—oozy grounds from which water has receded, or pools of flood-water on the marshes.

Slud—mud.

Slugging—cleaning mud, etc., out of the dykes.

Smee—wigeon.

Smelters—smelt-fishers.

Staithe—a wharf or landing stage.

Stint—dunlin, a small wading shore-bird. *Oxbird* in Essex.

Stuff, marsh stuff—marsh vegetation.

Tewkie or *tewk*—a redshank.

Thowt—thought.

Tru—through.

Turf—peat.

Wakes—holes or unfrozen places amid ice on a broad.

Walls or *river walls*—artificial banks constructed for the protection of the marshes from floods.

Wor—was.

Worams—worms.

Wuth—worth.

Yarwhelp or *awl-bird*—an avocet, the first name from its cry, the second from the upturned shape of its beak.

INDEX